FOREWORD

The ACS SYMPOSIUM SERIES was founded in 1974 to provide
a medium for publishing symposia quickly in book form. The
format of the SERIES parallels that of the continuing ADVANCES
IN CHEMISTRY SERIES except that in order to save time the
papers are not typeset but are reproduced as they are sub-
mitted by the authors in camera-ready form. As a further
means of saving time, the papers are not edited or reviewed
except by the symposium chairman, who becomes editor of
the book. Papers published in the ACS SYMPOSIUM SERIES
are original contributions not published elsewhere in whole or
major part and include reports of research as well as reviews
since symposia may embrace both types of presentation.

ACS Symposium Series

Robert F. Gould, *Editor*

scarborough

public library

Library of Congress CIP Data

Textile and paper chemistry and technology.
  (ACS symposium series; 49 ISSN 0097-6156)

  Includes bibliographical references and index.

  1. Paper making and trade—Congresses. 2. Textile industry—Congresses.
  I. Arthur, Jett C. II. American Chemical Society.
Cellulose, Paper, and Textile Division. III. Series: American Chemical Society. ACS symposium series; 49.

TS1080.T43   677'.0283   77-7938
ISBN 0-8412-0377-6   ACSMC8   49 1-304

Textile and Paper Chemistry and Technology

Jett C. Arthur, Jr., Editor

Southern Regional Research Center,
USDA

A symposium sponsored by

the Cellulose, Paper and

Textile Division at the

171st Meeting of the

American Chemical Society

New York, N.Y.,

April 5–9, 1976

ACS SYMPOSIUM SERIES 49

AMERICAN CHEMICAL SOCIETY

WASHINGTON, D. C.   1977

CONTENTS

ENERGY AND ENVIRONMENT

PREFACE

The Centennial Meeting of the American Chemical Society gave the Cellulose, Paper and Textile Division the opportunity to hold a timely symposium on International Developments in Cellulose, Paper, and Textiles. Research scientists from academia, industry, and government, representing more than sixteen countries, presented significant research accomplishments in paper, wood, and cellulose chemistry and in cotton, wool, and textile fiber chemistry.

In this volume, research achievements in textile and paper chemistry and technology are discussed in four areas—chemistry, dyeing and finishing, pulp and paper, and energy and environment. Two additional volumes, "Cellulose Chemistry and Technology" and "Cellulose and Fiber Science Developments: A World View," will include other contributed manuscripts.

I would like to thank the participants, presiding chairmen, and particularly P. Albersheim, D. F. Durso, C. T. Handy, B. Leopold, A. Sarko, L. Segal, and A. M. Sookne whose leadership made the twenty-two sessions of the symposium truly international in scope. Herman Mark kindly made significant remarks to open the Symposium.

Southern Regional   JETT C. ARTHUR, JR.
Research Center, USDA
New Orleans, La.
March 14, 1977

Chemistry

New Methods for Studying Particles in Viscose and Their Effects on Viscose Rayon Production

JOHN DYER
ITT Rayonier Inc., ERD, Whippany, NJ

FREDERICK R. SMITH
Avtex Fibers Inc., Front Royal, VA

Cellulose is made into rayon through the viscose process outlined in Table I. In this process, wood pulp is steeped in aqueous sodium hydroxide to convert the cellulose to the more reactive sodium celluloseate. After steeping, the pulp is pressed to remove excess steeping liquor and then shredded into alkali cellulose crumbs. The crumbs are aged to reduce the cellulose DP before reacting with carbon disulfide to form sodium cellulose xanthate. The derivative is dissolved in dilute aqueous sodium hydroxide, yielding a viscous orange colored solution called viscose. The viscose is aged, during which time air is removed, and chemical and physical changes occur. Then, the solution is filtered before extruding through very small holes of a jet into an acid spin bath. There regeneration of the cellulose as filaments of rayon occurs.

A normal jet for regular staple manufacture can contain more than 20,000 holes. Typical hole sizes are 1–3.5 mil or 25–90 microns. Particles or other discontinuities, even having size appreciably less than a jet hole, will interfere with viscose flow through the hole, changing the flow from laminar to plug over an area equal to the profile the particle presents to the hole.

It is well established that many particles exist in viscose solutions. These originate from the raw materials used in the process – the pulp, caustic and water and from contaminants introduced with the raw materials or from line deposits.

The normal practice to avoid interruption in fiber formation at the jet is to remove the particles by filtration. But it has been conclusively shown in several independent studies (1,2) that viscose cannot be completely freed of particles, even with repeated filtration. Rather, there is a distribution of particle sizes meeting some critical parameters of the filter media, filtration pressure and particle nature that will pass through the filters and reach the jet.

The potential problems these particles can cause are jet hole plugging, either completely or partially, leading to high spinning

pressure and denier non-uniformity. If the particles pass
through the jet holes, and most do, they would be expected to
influence fiber structure formation. Adverse effects of viscose particles on fiber properties have been documented in work
by Philipp, Schleicher and Arnold (3) and by Zubakhina, Serkov
and Virezub (4).

Based on particle count measurements by conductometric,
microscopy and light scattering methods, Trieber (5) has suggested a size distribution for viscose particles which begins
with molecules of cellulose xanthate and extends to masses
larger than 30 microns diameter. The majority of particle
count studies on viscose have been made by measuring the change
in conductivity as the particles flow between electrodes. Viscose conductivity is primarily dependent on the concentration
of free NaOH and cellulose. Conduction in a gel particle is
accomplished by movement of Na^+ and OH^- ions. An increasing
concentration of cellulose in a gel decreases the local concentration of NaOH and the ease with which ions move through it.
The Coulter counter is usually calibrated using some uniformly
sized non-conducting particles. It is then assumed that any
particle in viscose, which has the same effect on conductivity,
has the same dimensions. This is obviously erroneous since
cellulose gels may have conductivity near that of the suspend-
ing fluid. If the specific conductivity is four times that of
the non-conducting calibrating particle, the measured size will
be 1/4 the actual size. If a significant portion of particles
classified 4-8μ are in reality gels 16-64μ in diameter, then
the difficulties in relating particle count to the effect on
filters and spinning becomes more intelligible. It has been
pointed out that it is very important to dilute viscose for
conductometric counting so that the concentration of free NaOH
is not changed. The effect of diluting, which can cause changes
in the extent of solvation and mechanical degradation due to
mixing on the particle size and distribution, had not been
established.

In recent years, equipment for particle count measurement,
based on changes in light transmission, has been developed (6).
This equipment can be used with undiluted viscose, the measurements thus being more representative of the viscose solution at
the various process stages from which samples may be taken.

The equipment is illustrated in Figure 1. It consists of
two basic units, the sensor and the counter. A constant volume
pump was used to feed viscose through the sensor. For less
viscous liquids, constant flow rates were obtained with a bottle
sampling device using pressurized air or nitrogen.

The basic operation of this equipment is straightforward
(Figure 2) examination of a sample taking two minutes once the
sensor has been flushed with the sample. The sample flows
through a small rectangular fluid passage past a window.

TABLE I

AN OUTLINE OF THE VISCOSE PROCESS

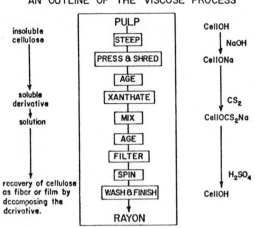

Pacific Scientific Co.

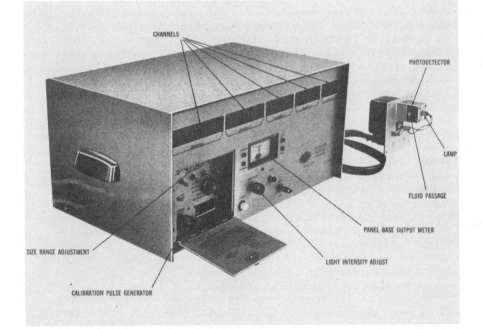

Figure 1. The HIAC automatic particle counter (11)

Particles in the fluid pass by the window one by one as long as
specified limits of particle concentration are not exceeded.
Light from a tungsten lamp is formed by the window to a parallel
beam of exact size and directed onto a photodetector. Using the
light intensity adjust, the operator establishes the proper base
voltage from the photodetector as indicated on the panel base
output meter. Each particle, as it passes the window, inter-
rupts a portion of the light beam according to its size. This
causes a specific reduction (or pulse) in the voltage which is
proportional to the size of the particle. Five counting circuits (channels) with preset thresholds tally the particles by
size. A size range adjustment is provided for each channel to
permit the operator to select any desired size ranges. A built-
in calibration pulse generator provides the operator with reference pulses to simulate any particle size for adjusting and
verifying the size ranges. The particle count is registered in
each channel as either total - the total number larger than the
size for which the channel is set or Delta - the number larger
than the setting of that channel but smaller than the setting of
the next higher channel. For the studies described in this
paper, the Delta mode was used.

Various sized sensors are available. One convenient for
use with viscose is a 5-150D sensor. Sensor dimensions for the
constricted passage through the light beam shown in Figure 2
are 150μ square by 2450μ deep. Particles are sized according
to the extent to which they interrupt the light beam. The different orientations of an irregular particle passing through the
sensor produces an output more closely related to the actual
size of the particle than would a microscopic examination in a
static field.

All particles in the light beam at any one time are counted
as one particle of size proportional to the excluded light beam.
A large number of small particles will appear as a single large
particle. This phenomena of "coincidence" is avoided by speci-
fying that there should be no more than one particle in ten sensor volumes. For the 5-150D sensor, there are 17000 sensor
volumes per c.c., establishing a limit of 1700 particles per
c.c. of sample.

The 5-150D sensor is suitable for use with viscoses having
viscosity of up to about 300 poises. Higher viscosity solutions can be examined - the sensor will withstand pressures of
2000 psi but problems with blockage and cleaning of the sensor
increase substantially at high viscosity.

The flow rate used for viscose was 36.5 g/m; the particle
counts have been reported on a per gram basis calculated from
the counts determined over a total time period of two minutes.
The reproducibility of the count data is good; results for ten
consecutive counts each of twelve seconds on a single viscose
are given with averages and standard deviations of the measure-

ment in Table II. Since particles should not be removed from
the sample during the counting, samples can be recycled or used
in further experiments but care must be taken to avoid contamination with air.

Results given in Table III were for a filtered viscose with
and without air and with two recycles on each sample. The inclusion of only a small quantity of air (about 0.5 cc/100 g) in
the viscose had a pronounced effect on the particle count. The
change in the particle count on recycling indicates that small
amounts of air were trapped in the viscose with each cycle; the
number of large particles apparently increased and the number of
small particles decreased. When there was an appreciable amount
of air in the viscose, some deaeration occurred during the particle count measurement and the count on the recycled sample
shows a decrease in large particles with an increase in the
number of small particles.

In the early stages of evaluating the HIAC particle counter,
attention was directed toward resolving the question of what
changes occur on diluting viscose. A comparison was made of particle counts on viscoses using the Coulter counter and HIAC
counter. Both diluted and undiluted viscoses were examined with
the latter equipment.

The number of particles counted in viscose by the Coulter
counter and HIAC counter was very different, being much greater
for the HIAC as seen in Table IV. This was predicted because
one method counts changes in an electric field while the other
counts changes in light transmission. For the Coulter count
the viscose was diluted 1:6 using 6% NaOH. The sample is changed
by dilution. The HIAC shows the number of small particles is
greatly increased in the diluted samples.

A closer examination of the effect of diluting viscose was
made. A standard viscose was mixed in various proportions with
6.45% NaOH. HIAC particle counts per gram of sample measured
on the viscose, the diluted samples and the diluent are given
in Table V. The particle distribution was also calculated from
the measured distribution in the undiluted viscose and caustic.
Generally, the number of large particles decreased in proportion
to the dilution but the small particle count was relatively un-
affected. Similar calculated and measured particle distributions
have been observed for other viscose diluted 1:10 with caustic
or water.

To a certain extent, this observation is the result of coincidence. But, at 1:4 and 1:10 dilution, the total number of
particles calculated is appreciably less than the 1:10 coincidence limit of 1700 particles per c.c. or one particle in every
10 sensor volumes. As will be shown later, there have been real
changes in the nature and number of particles on diluting viscose, many more of the particles can be removed by filtering the
diluted viscose than when the undiluted viscose is filtered.

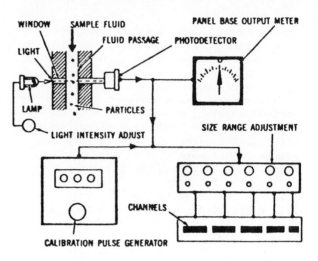

Pacific Scientific Co.

Figure 2. The HIAC automatic particle counter (11)

TABLE II

Reproducibility of HIAC Particle Count

12 Second Count # at 36.5 g/m	Particles/g Viscose				
	5	10	15	30	60μ
1	1789	975	734	128	8.6
2	1717	954	731	137	11.8
3	1680	928	728	132	12.8
4	1770	978	749	126	7.6
5	1767	953	727	137	9.2
6	1746	934	735	124	9.9
7	1693	944	717	133	8.3
8	1818	972	734	126	8.9
9	1720	955	737	126	12.2
10	1706	925	740	141	12.2
Average	1741	952	734	131	10.1
Standard Deviation	45	19	8.5	5.9	1.9

TABLE III

Effect of Air and Recycling Sample

Sample	# Times Recycled	Particles/g 5	10	15	30	60μ
Viscose	0	3559	233	24	6	2.6
	1	3402	225	27	9	3.6
	2	3142	203	34	15	6.4
Viscose + Air	0	41	57	200	383	453
	1	64	67	223	408	368
	2	90	83	255	443	266

TABLE IV

Comparison of HIAC and Coulter Counts

Viscose Sample	Particle Count/g. Coulter (8–32μ)	HIAC (7–30μ) d	u	Ratio HIAC/Coulter d	u
Filtered A	452	3771	2000	8.3	4.4
B	78	1867	2297	23.9	29.5
C	262	3639	1978	13.9	7.6
Unfiltered					
D	969	11911	2534	12.3	2.6
E	4333	5334	6609	1.2	1.5

d: diluted

u: undiluted

This is shown by the results given in Table VI. The filter
medium was glass fiber paper. Particle counts before and after
filtration of the undiluted viscose, the viscose diluted 1:10
with 6.2% NaOH and 1:10 with water and for the mixer charge and
diluents, show that only a few of the larger particles were removed from undiluted viscose. Particle removal from the diluted
viscose was much more effective, the particle counts on the filtrate being similar to those measured for the filtered diluents.

Two filterability tests have been widely used for evaluating viscose quality. One is the K_w test based on viscose flow
through a standard filter medium at constant pressure. The
other test uses a constant flow and the filtration "T" value is
calculated from the pressure build-up. Particle counts measured
on viscose, after filtering or passing through a jet with 1500
x 63.5 micron diameter holes under constant pressure and at constant flow rate, are compared in Table VII. The filter element
was that normally used in filtration "T" test – a candle filter
wound with four layers of cotton yarn. Constant flow, 29 g/m,
was obtained from a volumetric pump and constant pressure, 39
psi, was obtained using compressed nitrogen.

At constant flow rate, the pressure build-up was insignificant when about 500 g viscose was filtered through the candle
filter or passed through the jet. The candle filter removed the
large particles, causing an apparent increase in the number of
small particles from 2200 to 3200 due to coincidence. Particulate material sized at greater than the hole dimension (63.5μ)
was not removed by the jet under similar conditions of flow.
This observation suggests that the large particles are not
spherical. All particles in the sensor at any one time are
counted as one particle of size proportional to the excluded
light beam. It is possible that elongated particles (fibers)
will pass through the sensor in several sensor volumes. The
small particles in these volumes will not be counted unless the
large particles are removed.

At constant pressure, 39 psi, the candle filter again removed the larger particles and increased the small particle
count. The same viscose filtered through the jet at this pressure appeared to have an increased number of large particles
with no change in the number of small particles. There is some
indication that particle size is increased by agglomeration
possibly occurring during a transient holdup of the larger gel
particles in the jet holes. It is expected that, if this does
occur, the mechanism could be analogous to silting and channel-
ing phenomena and will be influenced by particle deformability,
the pressure in the system and defects in the jet holes. There
is evidence that, at constant flow rate, particles plugging jet
holes break away and are extruded as pressure increases.

Making certain assumptions on the average particle size,
the total particulate volume in one c.c. of the viscose sample

TABLE V
Effect of Diluting Viscose

Sample	Particles/g Sample				
	5	10	15	30	60μ
Undiluted Viscose m.	2849	1059	346	28	5.3
Diluted Viscose 2:3 c.	2055	715	237	22	3.8
m.	2999	866	266	22	3.2
1:2 c.	1659	543	182	19	3.1
m.	3162	828	234	19	2.2
1:4 c.	1063	285	100	14	2
m.	2316	390	133	19	1.9
1:10 c.	706	130	51	11	1.3
m.	2300	397	129	11	.5
6.45% NaOH m.	468	27	18	9	.9

m. measured   c. calculated

TABLE VI
Effect of Diluting Viscose

Sample		Particles/g Sample				
		5	10	15	30	60μ
Viscose	U	1944	855	507	84	6.7
	F	1945	792	463	72	5.6
Viscose Dil.	U	1781	250	94	15	1.5
1:10 w̄ 6.2% NaOH	F	661	51	15	1	.2
Viscose Dil.	U	2476	302	101	10	.8
1:10 w̄ H_2O	F	266	46	21	1	.3
6.2% NaOH	F	250	46	23	2	.1
H_2O	F	410	37	23	2	0

U: unfiltered,   F: filtered

was calculated. The results are shown in Table VIII. In this
case, coincidence has much less impact on the distribution
since, although a much larger number of small particles are
counted after the large particles have been removed, the increase in particulate volume due to the small particles is a
relatively small fraction of the total particulate volume.

These results show that particulate material was removed by
the candle filter but not by the jet. This is not unexpected
since the larger particles are not spherical and will be able
to pass through the 63.5 micron diameter holes.

In the next experiment viscose was passed through a 325
mesh, stainless steel screen in which the openings were approximately 50 microns square. The particle counts and filterability
measurements shown in Table IX were made before and after. Although the screen was not an efficient filter, it did remove
half of the particles in the 30 and 60µ counts and the filterability improved (a low "T" value corresponds to improved filterability). A portion of the residue was removed from the screen -
there was insufficient for particle count - and mixed with the
unfiltered viscose. As expected, the number of large particles
increased and the filterability was adversely affected. The
effect of coincidence on the small particle count is evident.

Much effort has been expended to show correlation between
filterability measurements and some function of a particle count
or distribution. The very limited success of those efforts has
led to arguments of explanation.

The statements of particle size distribution say little, if
anything, about the nature of the particles or their shape.
Treiber (7) has recently studied the shapes of particles re-
movable by filtration; a similar study was also suggested by
Meskat (8). Both have recognized the possibility that many of
the particles are deformable gels. The elaborate viscose gel
fractionation procedure used by Durso and Parks (9) involves
dilution and consequently cannot avoid changes in particle
number and size.

It is suggested that the existing data is sufficient to
conclude that within a body of viscose (e.g. 1 g) there exists
thousands of particles having a wide distribution of sizes,
shapes and viscosities or deformabilities. The range of viscosities at the micro level is probably from that of the solvent
to the extremely high values of poorly substituted alkali cellulose fibers. Alkali cellulose does not flow at 40,000 psi but,
as seen on the macro scale, even poorly xanthated alkali cellulose flows at 1000 psi.

The problem of filtration may then be interpreted as a
function of the behavior of many different small volumes or
masses of various viscosities. Those particles having dimensions smaller than the filter openings will probably pass
through readily. As the size of the particle approaches that of

TABLE VII

Effect of Filtering

Sample Condition	Particles/g Viscose				
	5	10	15	30	60μ
Unfiltered	2197	1785	1518	34	2.6
Constant Flow					
Filter	3262	1549	296	2.4	0.4
Jet	2152	1753	1484	34	2.5
Constant Pressure					
Filter	3009	1761	610	7.2	1.4
Jet	2193	1755	1529	60	5.4

TABLE VIII

Effect of Filtering

Sample Condition	Particulate Volume cm^3 x 10^6					
	5	10	15	30	60μ	Σ
Unfiltered	.40	1.61	6.33	1.21	.78	10.33
Constant Flow						
Filter	.59	1.39	1.22	.08	.11	3.39
Jet	.39	1.58	6.19	1.21	.75	10.12
Constant Pressure						
Filter	.54	1.58	2.55	.26	.40	5.34
Jet	.39	1.58	6.38	2.18	1.56	12.09

the filter opening, it will pass through at some speed determined by its viscosity and the pressure gradient or it may
block the passage if it is not deformable by the forces around
it. Particles larger than the passage, if not deformable at the
relatively low pressure differential across their dimensions,
will simply bridge across the filter openings and become part
of the filter. The larger particles, which are deformable, will,
of course, pass through or block passages inside the filter as
determined by viscosity and pressure.

Hermans and Bredee (10) have shown that filtration of viscous liquids follows one of four filtration laws. These are,
in order of increasing severity; sludge, intermediate, standard
and pure choking. Most viscoses follow the intermediate law
when the blockage rate $= K_w$

$$2.303 \log P/P_o = Kt$$

where P = pressure drop across the filter at any time

P_o = initial pressure drop

t = time

K = filtration constant

w = resistance of filter at time t.

Some viscoses obey the standard law:

$$\frac{1}{\sqrt{P}} - \frac{1}{\sqrt{P_o}} = Kt$$

In this case, the blockage rate is $K_w^{3/2}$. The particles
in the viscose form a layer around the inside of the pores of the
filter media, gradually plugging them. A problem in evaluating
viscose is that not only can the particles deform but the filter
media is not rigid and there is a broad spectrum of rates for
the plugging of individual pores.

In the manufacture of rayon, there will still be many particles in the viscose when it is extruded through the jet, even
though it has been filtered several times. The jet contains
relatively few large holes compared to the very numerous small
pores of the filter media.

The passage of particles through jet holes is a random
event. It was speculated, assuming uniform dimensions for the
holes, that jet hole plugging also would occur randomly. At
constant flow rate, the plugging of some holes will cause increased flow through the other holes. To study this effect, two

jets, one with large holes (980 x 3.5 mil diameter) and one with
1500 small holes (2 mil diameter) were connected to a common viscose supply from a volumetric pump or a pressurized container.
The setup is outlined in Figure 3. The test was made at constant flow rate or constant pressure, recording at convenient
time intervals the amount of viscose delivered from each jet.
Large particles, >3.5 mil, block both jets randomly and, generally, to similar extents. Particles 2-3.5 mil will not pass
freely through jet A but are expected to pass through the holes
of jet B though, perhaps, not without some effect. Small particles, >2 mil, will pass through the holes in both jets until
their passage is restricted as the holes plug. This occurs
first in the small hole jet as particles are deposited by a filtration mechanism. The overall effect is to reduce the flow
through the small hole jet and increase it through the other.
Examples of measurements made at constant flow and at constant
pressure are given in Table X. The change in flow distribution
is measured as the ratio of the flow through the two jets.
Accompanying the change at constant total flow, pressure builds
up and will eventually cause particles to break loose and be extruded and the flow pattern will become erratic. This is not
seen in this example. The pressure at which this occurs appears
to be related to the deformability of the particles plugging the
holes. At constant pressure, the total flow is decreased as the
jet holes plug. Both streams are affected in the same way with
the flow from the small hole jet being reduced to 25% and from
the large hole jet to 87% of their original values over a 60
minute period. At constant pressure, the flow will eventually
stop when all the holes are completely plugged.

The results in this table (Table X) were obtained using an
unfiltered viscose. They show the method - Differential Flow -
appears to have significant potential for use in evaluating viscose filtering quality, perhaps even spinning quality. In
practice, viscose is filtered before spinning. The jet hole
plugging characteristic of the filtered viscose, although it
contains numerous particles that have passed through the filters
for reasons of size, shape or deformability properties, is expected to be quite different to that for an unfiltered viscose.

A comparison of results from the differential flow test on
filtered and unfiltered viscose at constant total flow is given
in Table XI. Substantial pressure build-up was observed with
the unfiltered viscose to the point where particulate material
was extruded from plugged holes and the flow ratio became
erratic. With the filtered viscose, there was no pressure build-
up and no significant change in the flow ratio. Filtering had
removed the particles causing jet hole plugging.

In conclusion, the HIAC particle counter is used with undiluted viscose, avoiding changes caused when the sample is

TABLE IX

Effect of Filtering

Sample	Particles/g Viscose					Filter-ability "T"
	5	10	15	30	60μ	
Unfiltered	3258	1394	440	37	9	14.8
Filtered	3278	1472	433	20	4	10.0
Unfiltered + Residue	2610	1201	572	91	19	20.4

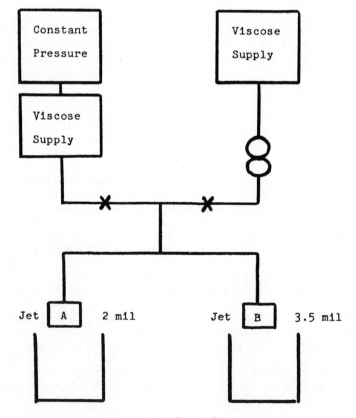

Figure 3.   Differential flow test

TABLE X

Differential Flow Test at Constant
Flow Rate and Constant Pressure

Viscose Flow g/m

	Constant Flow 27 g/m				Constant Pressure 20 psi			
Time (min.)	Jet A 1500 Holes (2 mil)	Jet B 980 Holes (3.5 mil)	psi	B/A	Jet A 1500 Holes (2 mil)	Jet B 980 Holes (3.5 mil)	Flow	B/A
0	8.66	17.79	18	2.05	7.83	15.05	22.88	1.92
15	7.17	20.35	20	2.84	5.02	14.43	19.45	2.87
30	5.04	21.89	24	4.34	3.49	13.82	17.31	3.96
45	3.70	23.67	25	6.40	2.42	13.53	15.95	5.59
60	2.98	24.04	28	8.07	1.92	13.13	15.05	6.84

TABLE XI

Differential Flow Test for Filtered and Unfiltered Viscose

Time (min.)	Viscose Flow g/m							
	Unfiltered				Filtered			
	Jet A 980 Holes (2 mil)	Jet B 350 Holes (3.5 mil)	psi	B/A	Jet A 980 Holes (2 mil)	Jet B 350 Holes (3.5 mil)	psi	B/A
10	9.45	17.45	23	1.85	11.7	15.9	24	1.36
20	7.65	19.1	35	2.50	11.75	16.1	24	1.37
30	5.55	21.5	45	3.87	11.75	16.25	24	1.38
40	4.1	22.55	55	5.50	11.5	16.25	24	1.41
50	4.25	21.9	72	5.15	11.7	16.05	24	1.37
60	4.5	21.4	95	4.76	11.75	16.25	24	1.38

diluted for conductometric counting. The measurements were
thus more representative of the viscose solution at the various
process stages from which the samples were taken. It is probable that a test to evaluate the deformability of viscose particles can be developed using the particle count before and
after filtering under different applied pressures. To detect
the effect of particles in filtered viscose, the pore dimensions
must be much smaller than normal jet holes.

As described in this paper, the differential flow method
was insensitive to particles in filtered viscose because the jet
hole sizes used were too large. It is suggested that useful information about viscose particles could be obtained by using
filter media of controlled pore size rather than the jets.

Literature Cited

1. Samuelson, O., Svensk Papperstidn. 52 465 (1949).
2. Treiber, E., J. Poly. Sci., 51, 297 (1961).
3. Arnold, A., Philipp, B., and Schleicher, H., Faserforsch u. Textiltech. 21 361 (1970).
4. Zubakhina, N. L., Serkov, A. T., and Virezub, A. I.,
   Khim. Volokna, 14 33 (1972).
5. Treiber, E., and Nadziakiewicz, H. C., J. Poly. Sci.
   Part C (2) 357 (1963).
6. Krueger, E. O., Bull. Parenteral Drug Assoc., 26 2
   (1972).
7. Treiber, E., Lensinger Berichte, 18 5, 12 (1965).
8. Treiber, E., Faserforsch u Textiltech. 15 618 (1964).
9. Durso, D. F., and Parks, L. R., Svensk Papperstidn.
   64 853 (1961).
10. Hermans, P. H., and Bredee, H. L., Rec. Trav. Chim.
    Pays-Bas 54 680 (1935).
11. Figures 1 and 2 reproduced by kind permission of HIAC
    Instruments Division, Pacific Scientific Company, P.O.
    Box 3007, Montclair, California 91763.

2

Cellulose: Pores, Internal Surfaces, and the Water Interface

STANLEY P. ROWLAND

Southern Regional Research Center, Agricultural Research Service,
U.S. Department of Agriculture, New Orleans, LA 70179

The microstructure of fibers is important to textile performance properties, but it is the pore structure and surfaces of pores that are critical to moisture regain, imbibed water, and the modification of fibers with finishes that must enter fibers in order to perform their function. In the case of cellulosic fibers, most specifically cotton fibers, pores allow penetration of dyes, polymerizable monomers, and cellulose-reactive reagents. Additionally, pores provide space for polymer deposition and hydroxyl-rich surfaces for sorption and reaction. Flame-retarding finishes for cotton generally operate by deposition of insoluble phosphorus- and nitrogen-containing polymers, for which pore volume is important. Conventional shape-retentive finishes, on the other hand, operate by formation of covalent linkages from reagent to cellulosic hydroxyl groups, for which pore surfaces are important. In both cases, the finishes are generally more effective or more durable, or the products exhibit better balances of textile properties when the degree of penetration is greater. Considering the practical importance of chemical finishing of cellulosic fibers and the increasingly sophisticated requirements for performance qualities of textile fabrics, the current state of our knowledge concerning penetration of water-soluble solutes into cotton fibers and interactions of the solutes with pore surfaces is less than adequate.

The purpose of this review is to examine evidence from several approaches and methods concerning the nature of water in pores of cellulosic fibers and to examine the nature of interactions of solutes in aqueous solution with pore walls of cellulose. Pore formation, bound water, nonsolvent water, inaccessible water, solute-pore wall interaction, and the structure of water near cellulose surfaces are considered in sequence in order to develop an overall perspective and a conceptual model for the manner in which water is held and behaves in cellulosic fibers. A chronological approach is taken within each section for orientation, and a summarizing

paragraph is appended in appropriate sections for brief
evaluation of the results in that area of research. Overall,
the primary objective of the exercise is to better understand
certain aspects of interactions of chemical finishing agents
with cotton cellulose (and other cellulosic substrates), since
therein would appear to lie the key to achievement of new and
optimum balances in performance properties.

Pore Formation

Pores arise from discontinuities of molecular packing in
polymeric substrates. More specifically, in the case of
fibers, pores develop from submicroscopic and subelectron-
microscopic imperfections in lateral packing of microstructural elements. Networks of interconnecting channels do not
exist in substantial amounts in typical dry fibers (1a), but
channels and pores are opened up on exposure to suitable
agents. The pore model of penetration of fibers is tenable
insofar as the major portion of the network of channels and
pores is created by inter- and intrafibrillar swelling agents.
Relative penetrating abilities are illustrated in sorption of
water vapor and organic vapors by cotton and rayon fibers at a
specific relative vapor pressure. Sorption is proportional to
hydrogen bonding capacity of the agent: i.e., water > acetic
acid > methanol > ethanol > less polar organic agents (1b).
Swelling of cotton measured by yarn untwisting and by increase
in fiber width, which are in qualitative agreement (2), shows
a similar sequence with decreasing hydrogen-bonding capacity.
Agents that are slightly stronger than water in hydrogen
bonding (e.g., formic acid, dilute salt solutions, and dilute
base solutions) appear to reach limits of interfibrillar
penetration and swelling, whereas agents that are substantially
stronger than water in disrupting hydrogen bonds and that
associate strongly with the cellulosic hydroxyl groups (e.g.,
liquid ammonia, ethylenediamine, and mercerizing alkalis) act
as intrafibrillar swelling and decrystallizing agents. For
both inter- and intrafibrillar swelling, the opening up of a
network of channels and pores in the fiber depends upon
penetration of the agent; that, in turn, depends upon the
ability of the agent to disrupt less-ordered hydroxylic
hydrogen bonds between fibrils, between microfibrils, and
between elementary fibrils, or to disrupt highly ordered
hydrogen bonds within elementary fibrils.
The significance of pores and internal surfaces is quite
evident in measurements of surface areas by adsorption of
nitrogen, a nonswelling agent, and application of the BET
equation. Results for dry fibers are 0.6-0.7 m^2/g (3,4),
values which agree closely with estimates of the area of the
external microscopic fiber surface. Areas measured with

vapors of water, acetic acid, methanol, and ethanol are,
respectively, 137, 18.3, 20.1, and 7.3, m^2/g (5), indicative
of the relatively large internal surfaces that are readily
developed in the cotton fiber. That the situation is dynamic
is shown by the fact that pore structure opened up by water is
retained only to the extent of about 15% after solvent exchange
through organic solvents to nitrogen for surface area measurements (6,7).

There are few pieces of data that provide reasonable
basis for assessment of the effect of pore size upon penetration
of typical reagents into cotton. One set of data (8) deserves
mention because it illustrates interesting differences in
degrees of penetration. For purified native cotton, about 49%
of the hydroxyl groups are accessible to water ($H_2^{18}O$), about
37% are readily accessible to water (D_2O), about 20% are
readily accessible to N,N-diethylaziridinium chloride (mol wt
136, representative of common finishing agents) in dilute
aqueous solution, and an estimated 2.5% of hydroxylic surfaces
are accessible to Diphenyl Fast Red 5BL(mol wt 676) in dilute
aqueous solution.

Two concepts are called upon to explain the vast differences
of accessibility noted in the preceding paragraph. (1)
Strong interactions between water and cellulose may form
"bound water" or "nonsolvent water" that substantially reduces
the swelling action of the water or the pore volume available
to solutes, and (2) channels and pores are available in a
range of sizes, some being too small to accommodate ingress or
passage of solutes. The two concepts may be complementary,
although they were not necessarily considered that way in
early research. Bound water on cellulosic surfaces is the
conceptual description for reduction in thermodynamic activity
or in partition coefficient of small molecules between the
aqueous phase and the cellulose polymer phase. Exclusion of
larger molecules is conceived to occur on the basis of a
sieving action. These concepts are discussed in subsequent
sections.

Bound Water

Considerable accumulated evidence indicates that part of
the water within a moist cellulosic substrate exhibits properties
that are markedly different from those of the rest of the
water. Only the most pertinent publications on this subject
(and subjects of other sections) are referenced in this
report. Filby and Maass (9), from measurements of density of
moist cellulose in moist helium, found that the apparent
density of adsorbed water was nearly constant at a value of
about 2.5 times that of ordinary water, up to 0.06 g water/g
cellulose. With further increases in moisture content, the

apparent density of water decreased, becoming normal at about
0.08 g/g. Their conclusion, published in 1932, was that
initial water in cellulose is combined strongly and chemically,
that further addition of water increases the amount of available
cellulosic surface, and finally that normal liquid water fills
the capillaries.

Stamm and Loughborough (10) in 1935 measured differential
heat of water sorption by cellulose and wood and showed that
part of the water adsorbed by cellulose involved evolution of
more heat than later portions of water. They also showed that
the entropy and differential heat of hydration were independent
of temperature below 0.06 g water/g cellulose, these points
being strong arguments in favor of the hypothesis that water
is bound by chemical forces. Their data showed a smooth
transition between the water which was adsorbed with high
evolution of heat and that water which involved lesser-to-zero
amounts of heat evolution, zero being reached at about 0.2 g
water/g cellulose.

In 1947-52, Magne et al. (11, 12) measured amounts of
freezing and nonfreezing water in moist cellulose at -4.5°C.
They found that all water was nonfreezing up to about 0.04 g/g
native cotton, that about half of the water between 0.04 and
0.15-0.20 g/g was nonfreezing, and that all of the water above
0.15-0.20 g/g was freezing. They found, also, that all of the
freezing water was released by desiccation before any of the
nonfreezing water was released. A fairly good linear relationship was obtained between the amount of initially adsorbed
water (i.e., that up to the appearance of freezing water)
and the noncrystalline fraction of the cellulose. Water
initially adsorbed was considered to be hydrogen-bonded to
cellulosic hydroxyl groups.

Following extensive studies of specific volume and
density of moist cellulose, Hermans (13), in a monograph in
1946, dispelled the concept that initially adsorbed water was
compressed to high density (see above). He showed that
density of cotton rose slightly to a maximum at 0.02-0.03 g
water/g cotton, that it dropped rapidly thereafter, and that
at 0.10-0.12 g/g the apparent compression of water in cellulose
came to an end. His explanation of these observations was
that the initial macroscopic specific volume of the cotton
fiber consists of the volume occupied by cellulose molecules
plus a certain fraction of empty space, which is not penetrated
by the nonaqueous liquid medium used in the measurement. As
water molecules are adsorbed and packed among cellulose
chains, part of the empty space is occupied by water, and
the increase in volume of the fiber is less than additive.
These empty spaces in cotton are completely occupied at
0.02-0.03 g water/g cellulose. At higher water contents (ca.

0.10 g/g cotton), the sorbing surfaces are covered with a
monolayer of water molecules and no further empty spaces
exist. From this point onward, sorption assumes the character
of capillary condensation, and volumes of water and cellulose
are additive. The same interpretation is summarized in more
recent literature by Meredith (14), who stated that these
data provide basis only for distinguishing between the first
monolayer and subsequent capillary water.

The significance of publications by Rees (15) and Guthrie
(16) in 1948-9 on heats of adsorption of moisture in cellulose
is well summarized in a review by Rees (17). Differential
heat of sorption (Q_L) is essentially the same for all cellulosic
fibers, the relationship of Q_L and free energy of sorption
(ΔG) to humidity being shown in Figure 1. The difference
between the heat and free energy terms represents an excess
energy that shows by how much the energy of binding of water
molecules to cellulosic surfaces exceeds the sum of energies
required to remove a molecule of water from the water phase
and to break cellulose-to-cellulose hydrogen bonds. This
excess energy ($Q_L - \Delta G$) is shown graphically in Figure 2.
Rees concluded that: (1) Excess energy is greatest at low
relative humidities, indicating that water molecules are more
strongly attracted to cellulose at low regains. As more water
is sorbed, the attractive force decreases because adsorbed
water molecules exert a repulsive force or because multi-
layers of water molecules are formed.   (2) The water initially
adsorbed has an excess energy of about 90 cal/g, which is
about equal to the latent heat of fusion of ice. Thus, these
adsorbed water molecules may be expected to have degrees of
orientation and association comparable to those of ice. The
fact that the initial heat of sorption is approximately the
same as the heat of formation of the hydrogen bond has been
considered confirmation that water is sorbed by this mechanism.

From a more detailed study of heat of wetting of cotton,
Morrison and Dzieciuch (18) concluded in 1959 that adsorbed
water forms a complete monomolecular layer of immobilized
water molecules at about 0.03 g water/g cellulose, corresponding
to a definite break in the differential heat curve. Iyer and
Baddi (19) confirmed this conclusion and showed that differential
heats of sorption were lower for cellulose preswollen by
solvent exchange (and subsequently dried) than for the original
cellulose over the range of moisture pickup corresponding to
the formation of the monomolecular water layer. These results
are consistent with the possibility that release of strain
from microstructural elements of dried and collapsed cotton
fibers contribute significantly to the heat released when
water is sorbed.

In 1965, Ramiah and Goring (20) found that thermal
expansion coefficients of water-swollen pellets of cellulose

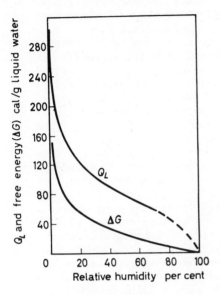

Figure 1.   *Relation of differential heat of absorption of liquid water (Q_L) and free energy (ΔG) to relative humidity (17)*

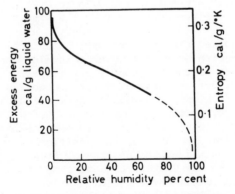

Figure 2.   *Relation of excess energy ($Q_L - \Delta G$) and entropy decrease [$S = (Q_L - \Delta G)/T$] to relative humidity (17)*

and related materials were several times the expansion coefficients measured in the dry state. They proposed that the
hydroxyl-containing surfaces of the carbohydrate molecules act
as structure breakers and enhance local concentration of the
unbonded species of water, which has a much higher coefficient
of thermal expansion than clusters of water molecules (21).
Goring's (22) model for the carbohydrate-water interface is
shown in Figure 3. Goring (22) and Ramiah and Goring (20)
pointed out that the anomalously high thermal expansion in
aqueous media is due to the high expansion coefficient of the
perturbed layer of water and also to the transformation of
some of the unbonded water in the perturbed layer to the less
dense normal or unperturbed water as temperature is raised.
This interpretation made use of recent theories of water
structure proposed by Frank and Wen (23) and Nemethy and
Scheraga (21). Ramiah and Goring (20) indicated that their
results provided new credence for the earlier concept of Filby
and Maass (9), except that the density of interfacial water is
increased by perturbation of the water structure rather than
by compression or adsorption. From thermal expansion coefficients, Neal and Goring (24) estimated the amount of perturbed
water for cotton linters to be 0.04 g/g, a value generally
similar to those already noted for bound water.

Most recently, information concerning the concept of
bound water has come from nuclear magnetic resonance (NMR)
spectroscopy. From study of the change of widths at half
value of peaks in high resolution spectra as a function of
water content of cellulose, Ogiwara et al. (25) discussed
evidence that water in cellulose is present in two distinctly
different states of binding. The content of bound water was
reported to be 0.10 g/g cotton and 0.15 to 0.25 g/g wood pulp,
the latter being influenced greatly by the kind and state of
the fibers.

Employing pulsed NMR spectroscopy, Child (26) observed
that molecular motion of sorbed water molecules depended upon
the physical state of the cellulose, particularly the degree
of crystallinity. Over a range of water content up to 0.055
g/g Whatman CF1 (a highly crystalline hydrocellulose) and 0.09
g/g cotton linters, primary sorption sites were filled by
water molecules. Sorbed water on cellulose was found to be
very strongly bound, as shown by the position of the minimum
in relaxation times and by the absence of freezing of all of
the sorbed water on the Whatman CF1 and some of the water in
the cotton linters until about 243°K.

Carles and Scallan (27) used high resolution NMR spectroscopy and devised a method different from that of Ogiwara
et al. for estimating the amount of bound water. Because of
experimental difficulties, only upper limits of bound water
were estimated; these were 0.15 g/g cotton, 0.23 g/g wood, and

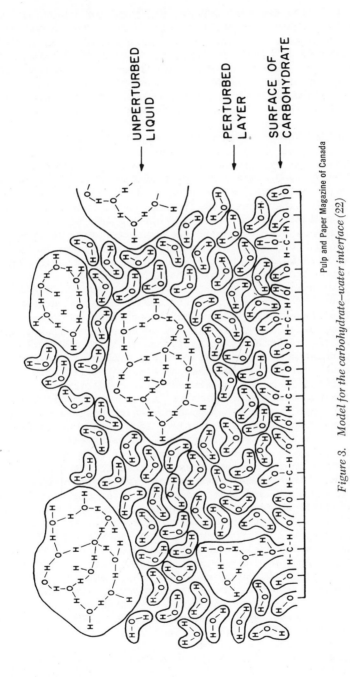

UNPERTURBED LIQUID

PERTURBED LAYER

SURFACE OF CARBOHYDRATE

Pulp and Paper Magazine of Canada

Figure 3. Model for the carbohydrate–water interface (22)

0.30 and 0.33 g/g for two wood pulps. Carles and Scallan observed that the presence of cellulose caused the water peak to shift to higher magnetic fields. Such a shift can be due to the breaking of hydrogen bonds, i.e., to a displacement of equilibrium from the normal distribution of clusters toward a higher concentration of monomeric water molecules. They concluded that water on the surface of the cellulose involved hydrogen bonds that are weaker than those in clusters of water molecules.

Friox and Nelson (28), using a pulsed NMR technique, reported detection and identification of four types of water in cellulose: (1) primary bound, up to 0.09 g/g cotton linters, (2) secondary bound, from 0.09 g/g to 0.15-0.20 g/g, which together with primary bound, they equate to nonfreezing water, (3) free, which they equate to freezing water, and (4) bulk, which is considered to be the water external to the cell wall. These authors designated the transition between primary and secondary bound water as a point of plasticization that is associated with swelling of the cellulosic structure to allow increased mobility of cellulose chains.

The foregoing information, drawn from divergent types of measurements and approaches, constitutes persuasive argument for the reality of the existence of bound water on accessible surfaces of cellulose. While it may be considered discouraging that there is so little quantitative correlation among the results generated from the different approaches, it is pertinent that the various methods assess slightly different features of the association between water and cellulose. It is encouraging, however, that there is a general pattern of consistency that runs throughout the results discussed above.

Some evidence noted above points toward two substantially different degrees of strong binding of water to cellulose. Such a situation is qualitatively consistent with the recent discovery that there are two types of accessible surfaces in cotton fibers, that these exist in purified native cotton in the ratio 0.36:0.64, and that the abundance of free hydroxyl groups available for donor and acceptor hydrogen bonding on these two surfaces is quite different (29, 30). The smaller of these two types, which is probably the more readily accessible, has the greater number of hydroxyl groups available for hydrogen bonding per unit of accessible cellulosic surface. Thus, the highest values of excess energy and the strongest associations of water and hydroxylic surfaces may be attributed to the interaction of water with these most readily accessible surfaces; the less strongly bound water may be that associated with surfaces that are less readily accessible and less populated with free hydroxyl groups.

Hermans' concept (see above) concerning penetration of water into the cotton fiber in three stages (i.e., initial

penetration into empty spaces and onto related surfaces,
penetration to cover all readily accessible surfaces with a
monomolecular layer, and subsequent deposition of capillary
water) remains reasonable. But results of Ramiah and Goring
(20) provide new substance for the existence of perturbed
water with a higher than normal density on cellulosic surfaces.
Similarity in the numerical value (0.04 g/g) estimated by Neal
and Goring (24) for the perturbed layer of water in cotton
linters and values reported above for bound water suggest that
these may be one and the same, or that the perturbed water may
constitute a portion of the total bound water. The most
accessible surfaces, to which Hermans referred, are likely
those associated with empty spaces, because stress in the
microstructural elements does not allow perfect lateral
packing. Release of strain in segments of microstructural
elements as a result of plasticization by sorbed water and
separation of microstructural units appears to contribute to
the overall heat effect in a manner that influences excess
energy, which is plotted in Figure 2.

Nonsolvent Water

Early investigators in this field (1c, 13b, 31) were
concerned with that portion of water in cellulose (and other
swollen gels) that did not act as solvent for added salts and
other compounds of low molecular weight. They assumed that a
portion of the accessible water was so strongly bound to the
cellulose that it offered no solvent action for the solute.
These studies were conducted concurrently with those of bound
water (preceding section), often with the expectation that the
two phenomena were the same and without the distinction that
we make in this manuscript between nonsolvent water, discussed
in this section, and bound water, already discussed.
Champetier (32) initiated this research in the early
1930s by soaking dry cellulose fibers in solutions of sodium
thiosulfate (mol wt of anhydrous salt 158), pressing portions
of the liquid out of the fibers with progressively increasing
pressures, and analyzing the exudate and residual fibers. The
concentrations of solutes in exudates were higher than in the
original solution, corresponding to 0.05-0.06g nonsolvent
water/g cellulose for cotton linters and ramie and 0.11-
0.13g/g for mercerized fibers.
Tankard (33) applied this method to a variety of cellulose
fibers, applying higher pressures than Champetier to reduce
the amount of water associated with a pressed sample as low as
0.20 g/g. His data points required shorter extrapolation to
the horizontal axis (Figure 4). He found some dependency of
results upon the initial concentration of the salt solution,

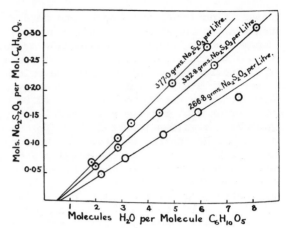

Figure 4. Composition of pressed samples of bleached cotton impregnated with solutions of sodium thiosulfate (33)

but generally confirmed Champetier's results. Values of nonsolvent water were 0.05, 0.06, 0.08, 0.11, and 0.13 g/g for cotton, linen, dried mercerized cotton, undried mercerized cotton, and rayon, respectively. More recently, two kinds of problems have been encountered with this method when it was extended to other salts. (1) For the sodium chloride-rayon system (34), extrapolated lines representing different initial concentrations of salt intercepted the horizontal axis at substantially different points. (2) For other rayon systems involving sodium or cadmium sulfate, the points representing data from different pressures and a given initial concentration of salt did not lie on a straight line (34). Geiger and Nobst (34) observed that values for nonsolvent water varied with the electrolyte and its concentration, that the apparent nonsolvent water decreased with increasing concentration of the electrolyte, and that there was no evidence of well-defined hydrates of cellulose.

In 1946, Hermans (13b) reported values of nonsolvent water obtained by measuring densities of cellulose samples in aqueous solutions with increasing concentrations of sodium chloride or glucose. Values of nonsolvent water calculated for various concentrations of solute were extrapolated to zero solute concentration. He reported 0.06 and 0.10g/g cotton for measurements involving solutions of sodium chloride (mol wt 58.5) and glucose (mol wt 180), respectively. Hermans expressed reservations concerning the significance of these results in view of the dependency of the value of nonsolvent water upon molecular weight of the solute. In this case, glucose was considered to be a large molecule that was restricted in penetration by its size, whereas water molecules and common

inorganic ions were considered capable of free circulation in
the pores of cellulose fibers.

Barkas (35) measured selective absorption of water by
wood from solutions of sugars by using an interferometer to
determine changes in concentration. Since his results indicated
a 3-fold higher amount (ca. 0.20g/g) of nonsolvent water than
expected, these measurements were repeated by Stamm and
Hansen (36) with solutions of sodium chloride, glycerol, and
sucrose. Their results showed that measurements like those of
Barkas, which were conducted with solutes in concentrations
that did not depress the relative vapor pressure, do not
measure the true surface-bound water. By analyzing the data
in another way, they concluded that a constant value of 0.03g
absorbed water/g cellulose is approached in equilibrium
with reductions in vapor pressure exceeding 25%.

Heymann and McKillop (37) investigated the lyotropic
series of salts and attributed negative values of nonsolvent
water to absorption of salts, the order being

$$CNS^->I^->IO_3^->Br^->NO_3^->Cl^->acetate>SO_4^{--} \quad \text{for anions and}$$

$$NH_4^+>K^+>Li^+>Na^+, \text{ and } Ba^{++}>Ca^{++}>Sr^{++}>Mg^{++} \quad \text{for cations.}$$

Bien and Lindenberg (38) varied concentrations of sodium
thiosulfate from 0.1242 to 682.52g/1 for measurements of
nonsolvent water. Their results, which are shown by the curve
in Figure 5, coincide with results of Tankard (see above),

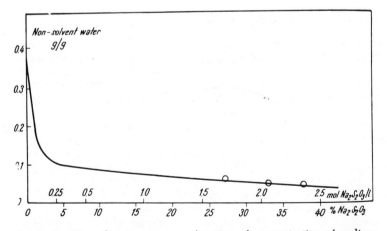

*Figure 5. Non-solvent water as a function of concentration of sodium
thiosulfate solutions contacted with α-cellulose. The curve is from Bien
and Lindenberg (38) and the data points from Tankard (33).*

which involved high concentrations of solute and which are
designated in the figure by circles. At low concentrations of
solute, nonsolvent water increased rapidly, with decreasing
solute concentration approaching a value of 0.38g/g cellulose
at zero concentration of solute. This value is many times
higher than that estimated for nonsolvent water and actually
approaches the amount of water required to completely saturate
the fiber pores.

Results summarized in this section illustrate several
points. Early investigators assumed that common inorganic
ions could penetrate cellulose fibers and circulate in pores
as freely as water, and that reasonable values for nonsolvent
water would coincide with values measured for bound water,
about 0.02 to 0.2g/g cellulose. Some of the measured values
for nonsolvent water were credible, since they fell around
0.05g/g cotton. However, the course of this research has
shown that reasonable values are forthcoming only with certain
electrolytes, that results with the most acceptable solute
(sodium thiosulfate) are concentration dependent (a consequence of zeta potential or Donnan effects), and that many
salts are apparently adsorbed on cellulose. The fundamental
weakness of this approach for discerning the presence of bound
water on cellulosic surfaces lies in the fact that electrical
forces can have great influence on the outcome of results with
electrolytes, and in the fact that the assumption concerning
the free access of ions to all pores that are available to
water is in error. It is not really clear what these experimentally measured values represent. One value of this research
is that it led up to the research described in the following
section.

Solute Exclusion by Molecular Size

Aggebrandt and Samuelson (39) were the first to describe
use of solutions of homologous series of polymer molecules
to assess degrees of penetration of solutes into porous
cellulosic fibers. Some of their data for purified cotton and
for polynosic fibers are plotted in Figure 6. Because the
history of the term "nonsolvent water" associates it with
bound water, it is appropriate to modify terminology and
emphasize that Aggebrandt and Samuelson measured the amount of
water that is inaccessible to their specific solutes. The
intimation at this point is that inaccessible water is in
smaller pores than will accommodate the solute, but that
bound water is not to be excluded as a possible explanation.
Curves in Figure 6 illustrate that the amount of water that is
inaccessible to a specific solute increases with the molecular
weight of the solute, and that inaccessibility for a given
solute varies with the cellulosic fiber. Polyethylene glycols

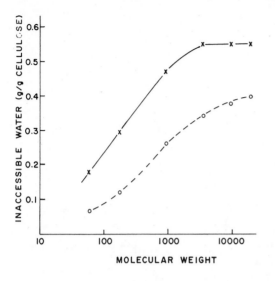

Journal of Applied Polymer Science

Figure 6. Inaccessible water in cotton (○ --) and polynosic fibers (× —) as a function of molecular weight of each polyethylene glycol used in the measurement (39)

were more suitable molecular probes than electrolytes, since concentration had a negligible effect upon the measured value for inaccessible water in the former case, but did affect values measured with sodium polymetaphosphates. Tarkow and Feist (40) obtained data and curves generally similar in shape to that of the upper curve in Figure 6 by using a series of polyethylene glycols to measure inaccessible water in holocellulose, cellophane, and wood.

Stone and Scallan (41) made extensive use of solute molecules covering a broad range of molecular weights to assess inaccessible water in various celluloses. Some of the results of Stone et al. (42) are summarized in Figure 7. Inaccessible water is plotted against molecular diameters of sugars and high molecular weight linear dextrans. Molecular diameters of the solutes were calculated from diffusion coefficients according to the Einstein-Stokes formula. Stone and Scallan explained their results as those of using feeler gauges to probe and measure pores in the 4 to 1000A range. If all of the water originally associated with a porous body is accessible to a small molecule, it will contribute to dilution of the solution by virtue of an increased volume available to the solute (case A, Figure 8). As progressively larger molecules are involved (cases B & C) the smaller pores and, finally, all of the pores become inaccessible to the solute molecules. Water in the inaccessible pores is then unavailable for dilution of the solute. Hence, differences in concentration must be measured with high accuracy, for which Stone and Scallan employed a differential refractometer. From curves such as illustrated in Figure 7, information is available

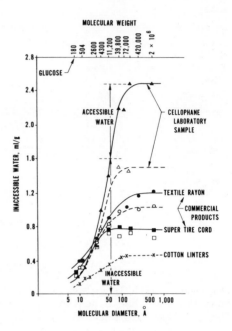

Tappi

Figure 7. Volume of water that is inaccessible in various cellulosic substrates to molecules of increasing size. (——) never-dried; (– – –) dried and rewetted cellulose. The curve for cotton linters (43) was added to the original figure (42).

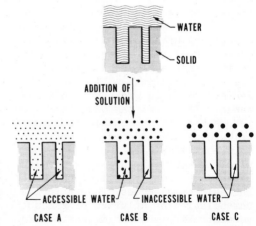

Tappi

Figure 8. Illustration of the principle of solute exclusion with molecules of three sizes and pores of two sizes (42)

concerning (a) total water within the cellulose (i.e., water
inaccessible to large solutes), (b) maximum pore size (in
terms of molecular diameter, Fig. 7 or molecular weight, Fig.
6), (c) median pore size, and (d) accessible water
(i.e., total water of swelling minus inaccessible water). As
shown in Figure 7, about 0.1-0.2 ml water/g cellulose is
contained in pores that are inaccessible to the glucose
molecule (mol wt 180). Stone <u>et al</u>. (<u>42</u>) suggested that this
water was intermolecular water rather than interfibrillar
water and that possibly it was bound water. In a review
paper, Boesen (<u>31</u>) proposed that a pore of 8 A could be
spanned by just 2 water molecules, which might constitute the
bound water that would not be available for solvent action.
There is, however, no experimental evidence that curves such
as in Figure 7 will not proceed to lower values of inaccessible water for solutes of lower molecular size.

The most recent contributions concerning interactions of
solutes with cellulose are described in the work of Rowland
and Bertoniere (<u>44</u>), who employed a gel permeation method
developed by Martin <u>et al</u>. (<u>45</u>). The latter authors passed
water-soluble solutes of various molecular weights through
columns of chopped cellulose, measured characteristics of the
columns and elution volumes of the solutes, and calculated
features such as elution volumes relative to glucose (R_g),
internal water volume in the cellulose (V_i), and the fraction of
internal water accessible to the solute (A_w). For a variety
of solutes on a purified cotton column, A_w is plotted as a
function of molecular weight of solute in Figure 9. Data
points for sugars of molecular weight 180-666 (curves A and B)
provide the basis for straight line extrapolations to $A_w \cong$
1.0 at mol wt 18. Data points for polyethylene glycols of
molecular weights 62-1000 (curve C) are the basis for extrapolation of the curve to $A_w \cong$ 1.0 at mol wt 18. The same
data are plotted as a function of molecular diameter of
solutes in Figure 10. Lack of coincidence of the two curves
in this figure is believed to be due, in part, to approxima-
tions in estimating molecular diameters. However, curves for
the stubby saccharide chains and for the slender polyethylene
glycol chains extrapolate smoothly to $A_w \cong$ 1.0 at molecular
diameter of 4, which approximates that of the water molecule.
The implications of the extrapolations in Figures 9 and 10 are
that, as a saccharide or glycol type of solute decreases in
molecular weight and size to approach those of water, all of
the internal water becomes available as solvent water. These
results suggest that the unavailability of internal water to
function as a solvent for the sugars or saccharides is based
solely on the inadequacy of small pores to accommodate the solute,
i.e., these solutes show no evidence for nonsolvent water or
bound water in an accessible pore. This type of behavior is

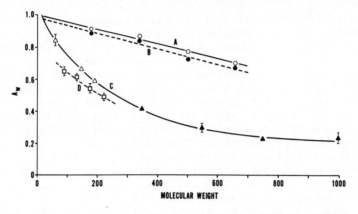

Figure 9. Fraction of total internal pore water that is available in chopped cotton cellulose to a solute (A_w) as a function of molecular weight of the solute. Curves A and B pertain to data from the series of sugars (glucose, maltose, raffinose, stachyose). Two separate lines are shown (line A for $\bigcirc$; line B for $\bullet$) representing the widest range of experimental data on separate series of runs. Curve C connects points for ethylene glycol and polyethylene glycols. Curve D connects points for mono-, di-, tri-, and tetraglymes (44).

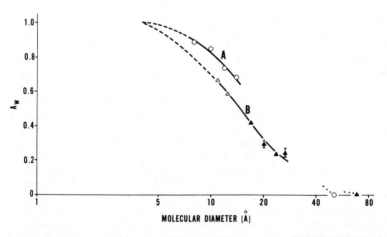

Figure 10. Fraction of internal pore water in chopped cotton cellulose that is available to a solute (A_w) as a function of logarithm of molecular diameter of the solute. Curve A refers to sugars and B to polyethylene glycols (44).

not inconsistent with the existence of bound water on the
surface of cellulosic pores. According to the thermal expansion measurements of Ramiah and Goring (20) and Neal and
Goring (24), glucose and various forms of cellulose are
capable of interacting with water in proportion to their
individual accessibilities. Therefore, it may be expected
that bound water on the surface of cellulose will still be
available as solvent water to saccharide solutes such as
glucose, maltose, etc. The situation for polyethylene glycols
is discussed below.

Glymes, i.e., methyl ethers of mono-, di-, tri-, and
tetraethylene glycols, were eluted from purified chopped
cotton columns (see Fig. 9, curve D) as if their molecular
diameters were larger or their degrees of sorption were lower
than those of polyethylene glycols of comparable molecular
weight. Others (41, 46) have established that neither polyethylene glycols nor sugars (or dextrans) show evidence of
sorption on cellulose. An alternate and more plausible
explanation is that glymes, having no free hydroxyl groups,
are less capable than glycols of disrupting bound water at the
surfaces of cellulosic pores. With less than all the water in
each pore available as solvent, the result is that of smaller
effective pores for the glymes. Because the higher glycols
have decreasing donor-hydrogen bonding capacity (i.e., proceeding from ethylene glycol to di-, tri-, and polyethylene
glycols), it is expected that the capability of glycols to
utilize water at the surface of cellulose as solvent decreases
with increasing molecular weight. Thus, as molecular weight
of polyethylene glycols increases from that of ethylene
glycol, it is proposed that the solute confronts an increasing
shell of bound or nonsolvent water at the cellulose-water
interface.

For information concerning sorption of small molecules on
cellulosic surfaces, Rowland and Bertoniere (44) showed that
patterns of elution of solutes were similar from columns of
chopped cotton and from Sephadex G-15 (a crosslinked dextran).
They studied elution of solutes from the latter column because
differences in elution volumes were larger and could be
measured more precisely on this column. The norm, which was
taken as the basis for discriminating between sorption and
repulsion, was the elution of hydroxylic compounds, specifically the line from methanol (M) to ethylene glycol (EG) to
glucose (GL) in Figure 11. R_g values (elution volume of solute
relative to that of glucose) higher than those of the reference
line were taken to indicate positive sorption and lower values
to indicate negative sorption or repulsion from the hydroxylic
polysaccharidic surfaces. Strong sorption was found for
polyamines, ethylenediamine (ETA) and diethylenetriamine

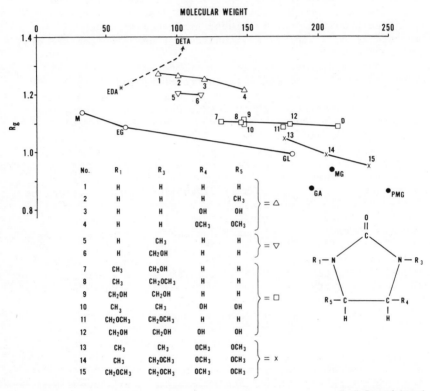

Textile Research Journal

Figure 11.   Elution volumes from a Sephadex G-15 column for various solutes relative to the elution volume of glucose (R_g) plotted as a function of molecular weight. M = methanol, EG = ethylene glycol, GL = glucose, MG = methyl glucuronate, CA = glucuronic acid, EDA = ethylene diamine, DETA = diethylenetriamine, D = methylenebis-1-[3-methyl-(2-imidazolidinone]. Imidazolidinones are identified in the tabulation and designated by numbers in the plot (44).

(DETA). Progressively decreasing sorption occurred for
imidazolidinones having (a) one free proton on each amide
nitrogen (data points 1-4), (b) a single free proton between
two amide nitrogens (data points 5 and 6), and (c) no free
protons on amide nitrogens (data points 7-12-D). The decrease
in sorption is parallel to decreasing ability of the solute to
hydrogen-bond to the hydroxyl groups of Sephadex.

Introduction of methyl groups onto ring hydroxyls of
imidazolidinones (data points 8, 13-15) and glucose (PMG,
pentamethyl glucose) reduced R_g more than expected for the
increase of molecular weight, an effect that falls in line
with that observed between glymes and glycols. A carboxyl
group at C(6) in glucose caused negative sorption, as indicated by a comparison of points for glucuronic acids (GA),
glucose (GL), and methyl glucuronate (MG) in Figure 11.

It is evident from results summarized in this section
that the primary factor controlling penetration of a solute in
aqueous solution into cellulosic pores is a sieving action,
i.e., discrimination on the basis of molecular size. But a
secondary effect, which can be quite large, depends upon the
ability of the solute to disrupt bound water at the cellulose-
water interface so that it becomes available as solvent. All
water in accessible pores of cotton cellulose appears to
be available as solvent water to saccharides and other solutes
having high proportions of groups capable of strong donor and
acceptor hydrogen bonding. Water-soluble solutes that are
characterized by limited hydrogen bonding in comparison to
saccharides find that only a fraction of the total water in an
accessible pore is available as solvent. Solutes that form
stronger donor and acceptor hydrogen bonds than are formed by
saccharides evidently find all water in an accessible pore
available as solvent; furthermore, these solutes interact with
cellulosic and polysaccharidic surfaces in proportion to the
strength and number of hydrogen bonds that may be formed.
Permeation of water-soluble solutes in cellulosic pores is
influenced by electrostatic charge, with cationic and anionic
charges contributing to positive and negative sorption,
respectively.

Structure of Water near Polar Surfaces.

Liquid water possesses distinctive structural features
that are attributable to retention of a large degree of
ice-like-ness. In 1933, Bernal and Fowler (47) proposed that
the long range hydrogen-bonding order of ices was broken when
it melted, that the liquid still retained a high degree of
short range order, and that ions increased or decreased
internal coherence and regularity of structure. In 1957,
Frank and Wen (23) suggested that water consists of flickering

clusters of hydrogen-bonded molecules in which the ice-like-ness
is the result of a cooperative phenomenon. That is, when one
hydrogen bond between molecules forms, several or many bonds
form to make a chain or cluster, and when one bond breaks in
the chain, the whole cluster breaks or dissolves. At one
instant there exists a matrix or solution in which ice-like
clusters are distributed in unbonded water molecules. Nemethy
and Scheraga (21) expanded this theory and treated it quantitatively, considering that the size and extent of clustering
decreased with increasing temperature and that clusters
continuously formed and disappeared, with an average lifetime
of about 10^{-10} to 10^{-11} sec. They calculated that, on
average, a cluster contains 57 molecules of water at 20°C and
21 molecules at 100°C (21), and that at any given instant 70%
of the water molecules are incorporated in clusters (48).
Although there are other theories of the structure of water,
this flickering cluster theory is the most widely accepted.

Goring (22) discussed the effect of cellulose and other
wood constituents on the structure of water and proposed that
carbohydrate surfaces perturb the layer of water next to the
surface in such a way that clustering is diminished, a concept
that has already been illustrated in Figure 3. He visualized
that hydroxyl groups on the carbohydrate lack the spatial
symmetry found in the water molecules; hence, they cannot
generally become part of a cluster, and the vicinal layer of
water is perturbed to contain a high proportion of unclustered
water molecules.   Drost-Hansen (49) made an extensive review
of information concerning the nature of water-solid interfaces
and postulated a 3-layer model for the structure of water near
polar surfaces. Figure 12 shows this model. Molecules

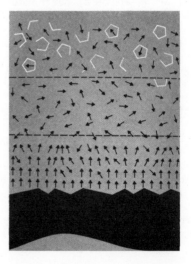

Industrial and Engineering Chemistry

*Figure 12. Model for the struc-
ture of water near polar surfaces*
(49)

immediately adjacent to the polar surface are oriented by
dipole dipole interaction, this type of order possibly
extending over a few molecular diameters. The second zone or
layer represents a disordered transition between ordered
vicinal water structure and bulk water. A third layer is that
of bulk water, in which the pentagonal circuits and partial
pentagonal outlines are intended to convey only the presence
of geometrically identifiable structural entities (clusters)
which flicker into and out of existence throughout the bulk
phase. This model differs from that proposed by Goring (22)
and illustrated in Figure 3 in that it introduces a layer of
oriented or structured water molecules on the polar surface.

Drost–Hansen's model for the structure of water near the
surface of a polar solid bears a similarity to the structure
of water about ions having high surface charge densities (23,
50). Such ions are surrounded by "A" and "B" regions of
water, the former referring to the highly structured, immobilized water in the primary hydration sphere immediately
adjacent to the ion, and the latter to randomly oriented water
that is farther from the nucleus and is not involved in
cluster formation. This composite is surrounded by normal
bulk water.

At least two questions arise in consideration of these
two and other models (51) for the water–cellulose interface.
The first question concerns the ability of the hydroxylic
surface of a carbohydrate, whether in water solution or an
insoluble interface, to polarize or hydrogen–bond water
molecules into a layer corresponding to the ordered vicinal
layer in Drost–Hansen's model or the "A" region of an ion.
Goring's model does not include this layer, but depicts the
surface of a carbohydrate as generally similar to the surface
of the layer of immobilized water ("A" region) on the ion
(52). The second question relates to the nature, primarily
the mobility, of the water molecules in the disordered transition
layer (zone 2) of Drost–Hansen's model, the perturbed surface
layer of Goring's model, and the "B" region of ions. Dobbins
(51) refers to the "B" shell of water molecules as being very
fluid, mobile water. Yet, current indications are that the
perturbed layer measured by Neal and Goring (24) is the same
as, or possibly a part of the bound water measured by other
techniques.

Whichever model proves to describe the water–carbohydrate
surface most accurately, it is reasonable to expect a gross
similarity in the interaction between water and cellulose at
the liquid–solid interface and between water and a soluble
saccharide such as glucose. This being the case, it may be
anticipated that there will be no evidence for bound water as
a result of interaction of a water–soluble solute with cellulosic surfaces when the solute and the surface are capable

of equal interactions with water. On the other hand, evidence
for bound water may be expected when the solute is less
capable of competing with the solid in the interface for the
structuring of water.

Conclusions

This report has undertaken to review the interaction of
water with cellulosic surfaces and to develop to the extent
that is reasonable at this time an overall perspective concerning the cellulose-water interface. In an area such as
this in which the structure of water is still open to various
interpretations and concepts (49) and the precise nature of
accessible surfaces of cellulose has only been touched upon in
recent years (29,30), any pretense of a statement of perspective borders on pure speculation. Nevertheless, there is
merit in taking a broad view of this field with the purpose of
building on the consistencies that exist. In this light,
tentative conclusions and overall perspectives are offered as
points for verification and departure.

A network of channels and pores is built into cellulose
at the time the solid substrate is generated, i.e., growth in
the case of a natural fiber or extrusion in the case of a
man-made product. On drying, the channels and pores collapse
in proportion to the extent of desiccation; some empty spaces
remain adjacent to the surfaces of microstructural elements
that are most strained and on which the D-glucopyranosyl units
(and hydroxyl groups) are most highly disrupted from perfect
alignment and lateral order. It is these extremely small
pores into which water, but not nitrogen, may be able to
filter with minimum need to break intermolecular hydrogen
bonds in the cellulose. Hydrogen bonding of free water
molecules on these surfaces could generate the maximum heat
effect (5 kcal/mol) and the minimum change in fiber size or
apparent density. Throughout this early stage of hydration of
cellulose, and possibly continuing into later stages, the
release of strain in microstructural elements contributes to
the heat of interaction of cellulose with water. This heat
of interaction must be modified by other effects such as that
for breaking cellulose-cellulose hydrogen bonds and that for
expanding the interfibrillar pores.

At least for the native cotton fiber, there is evidence
for two quite different types of accessible surfaces: one
having a higher population of free (i.e., noninter- or intramolecular bonded) hydroxyl groups per unit of surface and
being less orderly associated with adjacent surfaces, and the
other having quite highly ordered hydrogen bonded hydroxyl
groups and being quite well associated with adjacent lateral
surfaces. Both these types of surfaces may be considered

polar and capable of interaction with water. However, they
differ in the extreme by having as many as three free hydroxyl
groups for donor and acceptor hydrogen bonding on the one
hand, and by having little more than one free hydroxyl group
for donor and acceptor bonding plus two hydroxylic oxygens
(already internally hydrogen bonded) available only as acceptors.
Chemical evidence for the two types of surfaces shows a sharp
demarcation between the two, yet it is not unlikely that other
means for sensing these two types of surfaces may be less
clean cut. Measurements of freezing and nonfreezing water by
calorimetric or NMR methods appear to detect two degrees of
strong association of water with cellulosic surfaces, but more
quantitative data are needed.

Penetration of a water-soluble solute into a cellulosic
or polysaccharidic pore is controlled by the size of the pore
relative to the size of the solute. In the case of linear
molecules, the size of the solute must be the consequence of a
random coil. Association of water at the cellulose-water
interface reduces the effective volume of a pore or a channel,
and hence allows a smaller volume available to a solute unless
that solute is capable of disrupting this association. This
being the mechanism of penetration of a water-soluble solute,
the primary controlling factor is the distribution of pore
sizes in the substrate. The secondary factor is a dependency
upon the solute and relates to its ability to interact strongly
with bound water at the water-cellulose interface. The result
of operation of these two factors is that for solutes there is
not a unique amount of bound water on a cellulosic or polysaccharidic surface, but, rather, each solute will sense or
confront an amount of bound water that increases in inverse
proportion to the capability of the solute to interact with
water by the same mechanism.

Much additional quantitative information is needed to
clarify the nature of bound water on cellulose, validity or
meaning of measurements of bound water obtained by the
various methods, and variations in bound water as a function
of type of cellulosic surface.

Literature Cited

1. Valko, E. I., in "Chemical Aftertreatment of Textiles," (a) pp. 6–8, (b) Tables II and III, (c) pp. 50–53, Wiley-Interscience, New York, 1971.
2. Porter, B. R., Crr, R. S., Text. Res. J. (1965) 35, 159.
3. Hunt, C. M., Blaine, R. L., Rowan, J., J. Res. Natl. Bur. Stand. (1949) 43, 547.
4. Forziati, F. H., Brownell, R. M., Hunt, C. M., J. Res. Natl. Bur. Stand. (1953) 50, 139.
5. Klenkova, N. I., Ivaskin, G. P., J. Appl. Chem. USSR (1963) 36, 378.
6. Porter, B. R., Rollins, M. L., J. Appl. Polym. Sci. (1972) 16, 217.
7. Stone, J. E., Scallan, A. M., in "Consolidation of the Paper Web," Vol. 1, pp. 145–166, Br. Pap. and Board Makers' Assoc. Inc., London, 1967.
8. Rowland, S. P. in "Recent Advances in Fibre Science," Vol. II, Academic Press, London, in press.
9. Filby, A. E., Maass, O., Can. J. Res. (1932) 7, 162.
10. Stamm, A. J., Loughborough, W. K., J. Phys. Chem. (1934) 39, 121.
11. Magne, F. C., Portas, H. J., Wakeham, H. J., J. Am. Chem. Soc. (1947) 69, 1896.
12. Magne, F. C., Skau, E. L., Text. Res. J. (1952) 22, 748.
13. Hermans, P. H., "Contribution to the Physics of Cellulose Fibres," (a) pp. 73–89, (b) pp. 103–106, Elsevier, Amsterdam, 1946.
14. Meredith, R., in "Moisture in Textiles," pp. 141–159, Interscience, New York, 1960.
15. Rees, W. H., J. Text. Inst. (1948) 39, T351.
16. Guthrie, J. C., J. Text. Inst. (1949) 40, T489.
17. Rees, W. H., in "Moisture in Textiles," pp. 51–58, Interscience, New York, 1960.
18. Morrison, J. L., Dzieciuch, M. A., Can. J. Chem. (1959) 37, 1379.
19. Iyer, S. R. S., Baddi, N. T., Cellul. Chem. Technol. (1969) 3, 561.
20. Ramiah, M. V., Goring, D. A. I., J. Polym. Sci. Part C (1965) 11, 27.
21. Nemethy, G., Scheraga, H. A., J. Chem. Phys. (1962) 36, 3382.
22. Goring, D. A. I., Pulp Pap. Mag. Can. (1966) 67 (11), T159.
23. Frank, H. S., Wen. W.-Y., Discuss. Faraday Soc. (1957) 24, 133.
24. Neal, J. L., Goring, D. A. I., J. Polym. Sci. Part C (1969) 28, 103.

25. Ogiwara, Y., Kobute, M., Hayoshi, S., Mitomo, N. J. Appl.
    Polym. Sci. (1969) 13, 1689; ibid. (1970) 14, 303.
26. Child, T. S., Polymer (1972) 13, 259.
27. Carles, J. E., Scallan, A. M., J. Appl. Polym. Sci.
    (1973) 17, 1855.
28. Friox, M. F., Nelson, R., Macromolecules (1975) 8, 726.
29. Roberts, E. J., Rowland, S. P., Text. Res. J. (1972) 42, 217.
30. Rowland, S. P., Roberts, E. J., J. Polym. Sci. A-1
    (1972) 10, 2447.
31. Boesen, C. E., Cellul. Chem. Technol. (1970) 4, 149.
32. Champetier, G., C. R. Hebd. Seances Acad. Sci. (1932) 195
    280.; Ann. Chim. (Paris) (1933) [10] 20, 5.
33. Tankard, J., J. Text. Inst. (1937) 28, T263.
34. Geiger, E., Nobst, H., Helv. Chim. Acta (1961) 44, 1724.
35. Barkas, W. W., Proc. Phys. Soc. (London) (1936) 48, 1.
36. Stamm, A. J., Hansen, L. A., J. Phys. Chem. (1938) 42, 209.
37. Heymann, E., McKillop, G. C., J. Phys. Chem. (1941) 45, 195.
38. Bien, D. V., Lindenberg, A. B., C. R. Hebd. Seances Acad.
    Sci. (1963) 257 (16) 2283.
39. Aggebrandt, L. G., Samuelson, O., J. Appl. Polym. Sci.
    (1964) 8, 2801.
40. Tarkow, H., Feist, W. C., Tappi (1968) 51, (2) 80.
41. Stone, J. E., Scallan, A. M., Cellul. Chem. Technol.
    (1968) 2 343.
42. Stone, J. E., Treiber, E., Abrahamson, B., Tappi (1969)
    52, (1), 108.
43. Stone, J. E., Scallan, A. M., Donesor, E., Ahlgreen, E.,
    in "Cellulases and their Application" pp. 219–241, Advan.
    Chem. Ser. No. 95, Amer. Chem. Soc., Washington, D. C.,
    1969.
44. Rowland, S. P., Bertoniere, N. R., Text. Res. J.,
    (1976) 46, 770.
45. Martin, L. F., Blouin, F. A., Bertoniere, N. R., Rowland,
    S. P., Tappi (1969) 54 708.
46. Nelson, R., Oliver, D. W., J. Polym. Sci., Part C (1971)
    36, 305.
47. Bernal, J. D., Fowler, R. H., J. Chem. Phys. (1933)
    1, 515.
48. Nemethy, G., Scheraga, H. A., J. Phys. Chem. (1962)
    66, 1773.
49. Drost-Hansen, W., Ind. Eng. Chem. (1969) 61 (11), 10.
50. Franks, F., Chem. Ind. (London) (1968) 560.
51. Dobbins, R. J., Tappi (1970) 53, (12), 2284.
52. Goring, D. A. I., private communication.

3

Copolymerization of Vinyl Monomers with Cotton Studied by Electron Spin Resonance Spectroscopy

OSCAR HINOJOSA

Southern Regional Research Center, Agricultural Research Service,
U.S. Department of Agriculture, New Orleans, LA 70179

Electron spin resonance (ESR) spectroscopy investigations of free radicals generated in cotton cellulose by γ-irradiation have been previously made to determine the type of free radicals produced (1,2). Studies to determine the effects of solvents on the trapped radicals in γ-irradiated cotton cellulose have also been carried out (3,4). Short-lived free radicals such as those generated during polymerization and graft copolymerization reactions were also investigated using special techniques and conditions for trapping and detection by ESR (5-10).

ESR investigations of cellulosic free radicals, propagating radicals in polymerization reactions, and free radical initiated grafting reactions with cotton cellulose are summarized in this paper.

Free Radical Formation

Production of free radicals in the solid state and in systems which may be frozen during the course of the reaction allows detection of trapped radicals by ESR (1,5). Although free radicals trapped in the solid state at low temperatures generally exhibit a diffuse hyperfine structure (hfs), some information about their structure may be obtained from such ESR spectra (2). Additional information about stability and structure of free radicals trapped in the solid state may be obtained by monitoring changes in hyperfine structure and intensity of ESR spectra as the system is subjected to changes in temperature or exposed to solvents (7-10).

[60]Co γ-Radiation Initiation. Of the free radical generating systems used to produce free radicals in cotton cellulose, [60]Co γ-radiation yielded the greatest number of stable free radicals. Stability of the [60]Co γ-radiation generated free radicals in cotton cellulose is due to high crystallinity of

cellulose (1). In dry cellulose, the amorphous fraction of the cellulosic structure traps a large number of radicals.

^{60}Co γ-Radiation generates free radicals throughout the cotton cellulose matrix, i.e., radicals are produced in both the amorphous and crystalline regions. Radicals trapped in the crystalline regions are inaccessible to water and may remain trapped for years under ambient conditions of temperature and humidity (11).

Trapped radical spectra of cotton celluloses I and II, pre-dried and irradiated in a nitrogen atmosphere, are almost identical (Figure 1). Most of the free radicals formed in the irradiated celluloses were trapped in the accessible or less ordered regions of the cellulosic structures (3). About 80% of the radicals formed in irradiated cellulose I and about 90% of those formed in irradiated cellulose II (mercerized cotton cellulose) were scavenged by contacting the samples with water (Figure 2).

Decay of free radicals in the irradiated celluloses in pure methanol was less than in water. About 60% of the radicals formed in irradiated cellulose I and only about 5% of those formed in irradiated cellulose II were scavenged by contacting the samples with methanol for 30 sec (Figure 3). When a methanol (75 vol-%)-water (25 vol-%) solution was used, free radical decay took place in cellulose II to the same extent as in cellulose I (12).

Dipolar aprotic solvents also terminated free radicals in γ-irradiated cellulose, but at a much slower rate than methanol and water (4). The apparent rates of diffusion into cellulose I were dimethyl sulfoxide > dimethylformamide > acetonitrile. When water, comprising less than 50 vol-%, was added to the dipolar aprotic solvents noted above, the relative rates of diffusion were acetonitrile-water ≫ dimethyl sulfoxide-water, dimethylformamide-water. Reversal in diffusion rates of the pure solvents compared with the water-solvent combinations may reflect differences in the intramolecular association (solvation) for each of the solvents with water.

Photoinitiation. Irradiation of predried, purified cotton cellulose I with light from a Rayonet Photochemical Reactor* with 90% of the radiant energy output in the 3500 Å range resulted in formation of free radicals which generated singlet type ESR spectra. When the cellulose was irradiated wet with water, or subsequently wet after irradiation, no detectable ESR signal was generated (14).

Formation of free radicals in light-irradiated cellulose appears to take place only in the amorphous regions; no ESR detectable signal remains after contacting the irradiated sample with water.

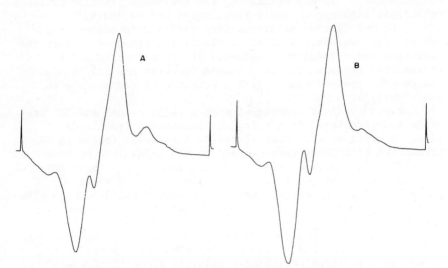

Figure 1. ESR spectra of dried cellulose irradiated in nitrogen. (A) cellulose I; (B) cellulose II. Magnetic field sweep, 100 gauss, left to right.

Figure 2. ESR spectra of irradiated celluloses after contact with water at 25°C. (A) Cellulose I; (B) cellulose II. Magnetic field sweep, 100 gauss, left to right.

Celluloses photosensitized with ferric chloride, irradiated at liquid nitrogen temperature with light from a high-pressure mercury lamp, generated complex ESR spectra which have been resolved as combinations of single-line, two-line, and three-line spectra (14). The radical yield in photosensitized rayon cellulose, upon irradiation, was about 10 times that of irradiated, untreated rayon cellulose (14).

ESR investigations of free radicals generated in rigid glasses of alcohols photosensitized with ferric chloride have been carried out at near liquid nitrogen temperatures (7,15). The ESR spectra generated in each of the rigid glasses of alcohol photosensitized with ferric chloride have been carried out at near liquid nitrogen temperatures (7,15). The ESR spectra generated in each of the rigid glasses of alcohol increased in intensity after photolysis was discontinued. As temperature of the rigid glasses of alcohol was increased, the intensity of the ESR spectra continued to rise until radical recombination became the predominant reaction.

Free radicals generated in the photosensitized alcohols were used to initiate polymerization reactions of vinyl monomers. Propagating radicals in the alcohol-monomer photosensitized system were investigated by ESR (8,10).

Hydroxyl Radical Initiation. Hydroxyl radicals generated by the Fe^{++}/H_2O_2 system (16,17,18) have been used to generate free radicals in cotton cellulose (5). The cellulose was immersed in a 0.01 $\underline{M}$ $FeSO_4$ solution and dried in a stream of dry nitrogen. The Fe^{++} impregnated dried cellulose was placed in a quartz sample tube, 0.3 $\underline{M}$ H_2O_2 was drawn onto the cellulose, and immediately liquid nitrogen was drawn through the wet sample. A triplet ESR spectrum was generated by the free radicals trapped in the cellulose-ice matrix at -110°C (Figure 4).

The free radicals were unstable and decayed beyond detectable limits at temperatures as low as -60°C. The triplet spectrum was attributed to free radicals formed on the cellulose when hydrogen atoms were extracted by hydroxyl radicals which were produced by the reaction (16,17,18)

$$H_2O_2 + Fe^{++} \longrightarrow OH^- + \cdot OH + Fe^{+++}$$

Polymerization Reactions

[60]Co γ-Radiation Initiation. Grafting of methacrylic acid (MAA) onto γ-irradiated cotton cellulose proceeded rapidly from water solutions of the monomer (19). Cotton cellulose yarn which had been irradiated in the dry state to a 1 megarad dose with [60]Co γ-radiation was reacted with aqueous MAA (30 vol-%) solution for 3 min at 25°C (6). The unreacted monomer was

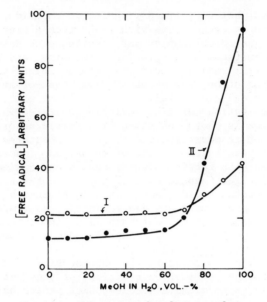

Figure 3. Effect of methanol–water solution on the concentration of free radicals in irradiated celluloses I and II after immersion for 30 sec at 25°C. Concentration determined at −150°C.

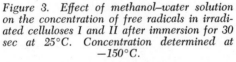

Figure 4. ESR spectra of free radicals generated in cellulose I by the Fe^{+2}/H_2O_2 system, recorded at −110°C. Magnetic field sweep, 100 gauss, left to right.

removed by washing with deaerated water, exchanging with acetone, and drying in a nitrogen atmosphere at 25°C. After recording ESR spectra of the dired cellulose-MAA copolymer, the sample was washed with aerated water, again exchanged with acetone, and dried with nitrogen at 25°C.

A typical ESR spectrum of dried cellulose I, irradiated in nitrogen, is shown in Figure 5A. The ESR spectrum of the cellulose copolymer, washed in deaerated water, consisted of two sets of lines (Figure 5B), one due to cellulosic free radicals which were not accessible to the solvents, the other due to the propagating radical of MAA. The ESR spectrum of the copolymer washed with aerated water, Figure 5C, was identical to that generated by trapped cellulosic radicals in irradiated cellulose which had been treated with water and then dried (3). Apparently the poly-(methacrylic acid) radical was scavenged by oxygen. Using a time-averaging computer attachment, the ESR spectrum C in Figure 5 was subtracted from that of B to obtain the one in D. The ESR spectrum of the free radicals in the copolymer scavenged by oxygen (Figure 5D) was almost identical to that reported by Abraham et al. (20) for γ-irradiated polymethyl methacrylate. The set of five lines which dominates the spectrum in Figure 5D indicates that, as with lauryl methacrylate and methacrylamide propagating radicals (8), the radical

$$- \overset{H}{\underset{H}{C}} - \overset{\bullet}{\underset{\underset{CH_3}{|}}{C}} - COOH$$

exists in the copolymer in the structural conformation, allowing only one of the methylene hydrogens to interact strongly with the unpaired electron. Only traces of the four-line spectrum were evident in the ESR spectrum of Figure 5D.

Earlier ESR investigations on the effects of solvents on trapped cellulosic radicals are cited in this paper (3,4,12). The effects of methanol-water solutions on the free radicals trapped in γ-irradiated cotton cellulose I and II were of particular interest because data obtained by electron spin resonance correlated well with that from grafting studies (12).

Figure 3 shows the effects of methanol-water solutions on the extent of free radical decay in γ-irradiated cotton cellulose I and II, whereas Figure 6 shows the effects of these solutions on the extent of grafting of ethyl acrylate (9 vol-%) onto similar samples after 60 min at 25°C. From water, the extent of grafting was greater with cellulose I than with cellulose II, although the extent of free radical decay was less in cellulose I. From methanol the extent of grafting was greater with cellulose II than I, and free radical decay in cellulose II was less than in I.

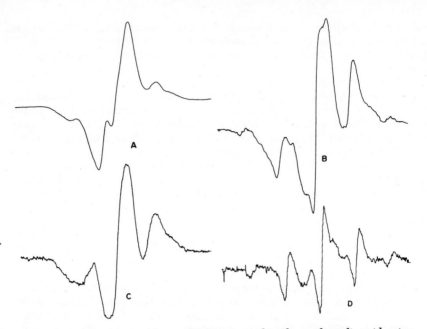

Figure 5.   ESR spectra of free radicals generated in the methacrylic acid–γ-irradiated cellulose I grafting system. (A) Irradiated, predried cellulose I; (B) cellulose–poly(methacrylic acid) copolymer; (C) cellulose–poly(methacrylic acid) copolymer reacted with oxygen; (D) free radical scavenged by oxygen (B-C). Magnetic field sweep, 100 gauss, left to right.

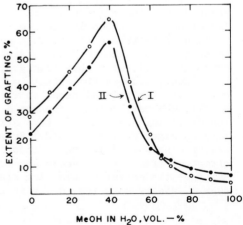

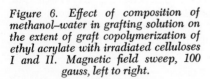

Figure 6. Effect of composition of methanol–water in grafting solution on the extent of graft copolymerization of ethyl acrylate with irradiated celluloses I and II. Magnetic field sweep, 100 gauss, left to right.

Extent of grafting was the same for both cellulose I and II
when the grafting solution was methanol (65 vol-%)-water (35
vol-%). Free radical decay was the same for both celluloses
when methanol (75 vol-%)-water (25 vol-%) was used.

The increase from 25 vol-% to 35 vol-% water from the
point where equal free radical decay occurred in both celluloses
(Figure 3) to that where equal extent of grafting occurred
(Figure 6) may be the result of the added 9 vol-% ethyl acrylate
monomer in the grafting solution. Ethyl acrylate was a poor
swelling agent for cellulose (21).

The maximum extent of graft copolymerization of ethyl
acrylate (9 vol-%) took place in methanol (40 vol-%)-water
(60 vol-%) for both irradiated celluloses (Figure 6). The
boundary condition for complete miscibility of ethyl acrylate
(9 vol-%) also developed at this methanol to water ratio. The
grafting maximum observed may be due to the increased amount of
monomer available for reaction at the boundary condition combined
with the accelerative effect of water. Because water is a poorer
solvent for poly(ethyl acrylate) than methanol, it would tend to
cause coiling and decrease mobility of the growing poly(ethyl
acrylate) chains, thus reducing the probability of chain
termination (22).

Photoinitiation. Concentration of stable free radicals in
cotton cellulose irradiated with ultraviolet light is too low for
postirradiation grafting reactions to be carried out in the same
manner as with cotton exposed to high energy irradiation.
Photoinitiated graft polymerization reactions with cotton cellulose required irradiation of the cellulose in the presence of the
monomer. Reine et al. reported the copolymerization of acrylamide, diacetone acrylamide, methacrylamide and N,N-methylene-
bisacrylamide with cotton cellulose initiated by near ultraviolet
light (23,24). The cellulose was padded with aqueous solutions
of the monomer and then irradiated with light from a Rayonet
Photochemical Reactor[37], which gave a source of radiant energy
with about 90% of the light in the 3500 Å range.

Copolymerization took place only while cotton cellulose
impregnated with monomer was irradiated (23). Photoinitiation
in air, compared with initiation in nitrogen, inhibited copolymer
formation. Apparently oxygen terminated the free radicals on the
end of the growing polymer chains, as in copolymerization of
methacrylic acid with γ-irradiated cotton cellulose (6).

The ESR spectra of cotton cellulose samples which were
saturated with water and aqueous solutions of acrylamide, diacetone acrylamide, and methacrylamide and then photolyzed for 60
min at 40°C were recorded at 22°C and are shown in Figure 7.
The ESR spectra of photolyzed cellulose saturated with water
(Figure 7A) and with 0.5 M acrylamide (Figure 7B) show little

evidence of free radical formation. On the other hand, the
spectra of photolyzed cellulose saturated with 0.5 $\underline{M}$ diacetone
acrylamide (Figure 7C) and with 0.5 $\underline{M}$ methacrylamide (Figure 7D)
show indications of free radical formation (13). When water or
aqueous solutions of the monomers were photolyzed in the absence
of cellulose, there was no detectable ESR signal.

The ESR spectra of cotton cellulose samples that were
saturated with aqueous solutions of the monomers, dried, and
then photolyzed for 60 min at 40°C and recorded at 22°C are
shown in Figure 8. Photolyzed, dried cellulose generated a
singlet spectrum (Figure 8A). A similar sample, containing
acrylamide generated a three-line spectrum (Figure 8B); that
containing diacetone acrylamide, a doublet spectrum (Figure 8C);
and that containing methacrylamide, a five-line spectrum (Figure
8D). When the pure monomers were photolyzed for 60 min at 40°C,
poorly resolved free radical spectra were generated.

The hyperfine structure of the ESR spectra of the propagating radicals trapped in the rigid cotton cellulose copolymer
matrix indicated that there was restricted rotation about the
C_α - C_β bond (8,10,25). Addition of an initiating free
radical to the double bond of the monomers should yield the
propagating radicals:

$$R - \overset{\overset{\displaystyle H}{|}}{\underset{\underset{\displaystyle H}{|}}{C}} - \overset{H}{\underset{\bullet}{C}} - CONH_2, \quad R - \overset{\overset{\displaystyle H}{|}}{\underset{\underset{\displaystyle H}{|}}{C}} - \overset{H}{\underset{\bullet}{C}} - \overset{O}{\overset{\|}{C}} - N - \overset{\overset{\displaystyle CH_3}{|}}{\underset{\underset{\displaystyle CH_3}{|}}{C}} - \overset{\overset{\displaystyle H}{|}}{\underset{\underset{\displaystyle H}{|}}{C}} - \overset{O}{\overset{\|}{C}} - CH_3,$$

$$R - \overset{\overset{\displaystyle H}{|}}{\underset{\underset{\displaystyle H}{|}}{C}} - \overset{\overset{\displaystyle CH_3}{|}}{\underset{\bullet}{C}} - CONH_2$$

The triplet ESR spectrum of the acrylamide propagating
radical indicated that the unpaired electron interacted with only
one of the methylene hydrogens. Interaction with both methylene
hydrogens would have resulted in a more complex spectrum (9,10).
Propagating radicals formed in rigid glasses of acrylate monomer
solutions were found to exist in two conformations (9,10). In
one, the unpaired electron interacted with only one of the
methylene hydrogens.

The doublet ESR spectrum generated by the diacetone acrylamide propagating radical indicated that the unapried electron
interacted with only one hydrogen. Both methylene hydrogens
were out of the plane of interaction with the unapried electron
(8,10,13).

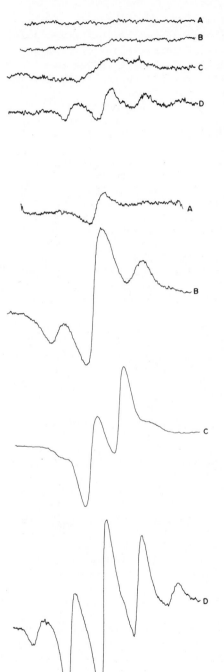

Figure 7. ESR spectra of cotton cellulose I saturated with aqueous monomer solutions and photolyzed for 60 min at 40°C, recorded at 22°C. (A) Water only; (B) 0.5M acrylamide; (C) 0.5M diacetone acrylamide; (D) 0.5M methacrylamide. Magnetic field sweep, 100 gauss, left to right.

Figure 8. ESR spectra of cotton cellulose I photolyzed for 60 min at 40°C and recorded at 22°C. Legends same as Figure 7; cellulose dried prior to photolysis.

The methacrylamide propagating radical generated a five-line ESR spectrum, attributed to interaction of the unpaired electron with the three methyl hydrogens and only one of the methylene hydrogens (7,8). Rigidity of the dry cellulose copolymer matrix at 22°C apparently restricted the trapped propagating radicals to only one conformation.

Propagating radicals in vinyl monomer polymerization reactions initiated by light in rigid glasses of monomer-alcohol solutions photosensitized with ferric chloride provided an excellent system for investigation of the effects of structural conformation of free radicals on their ESR spectra (8,10). The five-line spectrum generated when a methyl methacrylate (MAA)-methanol rigid glass containing ferric chloride was irradiated for 2 min at -170°C shows evidence of a triplet spectrum due to .CH_2OH (Figure 9A). When temperature of the irradiated glass was increased to -160°C for 2 min, then decreased to -170°C, intensification of the five-line spectrum was recorded (Figure 9B). On increasing the temperature to -150°C for 2 min, then decreasing it to -170°C, four additional lines began to appear in the spectrum (Figure 9C). After further warming to -140°C and then decreasing to 170°C, a nine-line spectrum was evident (Figure 9D).

When the same procedure was applied to a rigid glass of lauryl methacrylate (LMA)-methanol containing ferric chloride, a five-line spectra similar to that recorded for MMA (Figure 9B) was recorded (7). Although irradiated glasses of both LMA-methanol and MMA-methanol were subjected to the same temperature changes, the ratio of intensity of the four lines to that of the initial five lines was much lower in the LMA spectrum.

Rigid glasses of methacrylamide (MA)-methanol containing $FeCl_3$ also have been irradiated with ultraviolet light. The ESR spectrum recorded initially was similar to that in Figure 9A. As the temperature of the irradiated glass was increased, the spectrum recorded was clearly a five-line spectrum similar to that recorded for MMA-methanol (Figure 9B). Continued increases in temperature of the irradiated MA-methanol glass did not increase the number of lines of the ESR spectrum as was the case with MMA and LMA. Propagating radicals that would generate a nine-line spectrum were not detected when MA was polymerized.

Hyperfine splitting of the propagating radicals in the polymerization of methacrylate monomers that generated five-line spectra were about 0, ± 22, and ± 44 gauss. The hyperfine splittings of propagating radicals that generated four-line spectra were about ± 11 and ± 33 gauss from the center of the spectra. Free radicals generating four-line spectra were detected only after formation of those generating five lines (Figure 9C). The g-values for the centers of the spectra were about equal to that for free spin. Ingram et al. (25) proposed

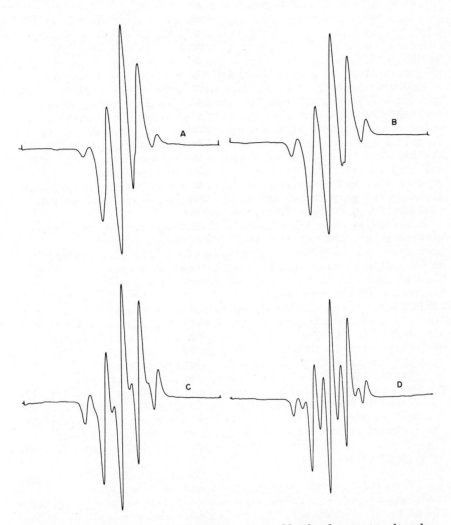

Figure 9. ESR spectra of free radicals in ferric chloride–photosensitized metha-nol–methyl methacrylate glass photoirradiated for 2 min at −170°C. (A) Spectra recorded at −170°C; (B) after warming to −160°C for 2 min, spectra recorded at -170°C; (C) after further warming to −150°C for 2 min, spectra recorded at −170°C; (D) after further warming to −140°C for 2 min, spectra recorded at −170°C. Magnetic field sweep, 250 gauss, left to right.

$$
\begin{array}{c}
\text{H} \quad \cdot \\
- \text{C} - \text{C} - \text{O} - \text{R} \\
\text{H} \quad \text{HCH}_3
\end{array}
$$

as the structure for propagating radicals detected in photo-
polymerizations of methyl methacrylate in peroxide or azobi-
sisobutyronitrile photosensitized methanol-monomer rigid glasses.
Two sets of lines, a five-line set and a weaker four-line set,
composed the nine-line spectrum. The five-line set was attributed to interaction of the unpaired electron with one of the
methylene hydrogens and the three hydrogens of the methyl group.
The remaining four lines were explained on the basis that some of
the free radicals had structural conformations such that neither
of the methylene hydrogens interacted strongly with the unpaired
electron and only the methyl group interacted with the unpaired
electron to generate a four-line spectrum.

Recording of a five-line ESR spectrum with the irradiated
glasses in the absence of a four-line spectrum (Figure 9B)
indicates that at lower temperatures the propagating radicals
in the rigid glasses were in a structural conformation that
allowed only one of the methylene hydrogens and methyl group to
interact with the unpaired electron. As the temperatures of the
rigid glasses were increased, rotation about the $C_\alpha - C_\beta$ bond
took place so that in some of the propagating radicals neither of
the methylene hydrogens interacted with the unpaired electron;
evidently a freely rotating methyl group interacted with the
unpaired electron to generate a four-line spectrum.

Steric hindrance due to chain entanglement, bulky ester
groups, or hydrogen bonding as proposed for methacrylamide (7,8)
would tend to favor one structural conformation of the propagating radical over others. The structural conformation assumed by
the monomers as the temperature was lowered to form the rigid
glasses probably determined initial conformation of the propagating radicals.

Hydroxyl Radical Initiation. Graft copolymerization
reactions of vinyl monomers with cotton cellulose have been initiated by generating hydroxyl radicals in the presence of cotton
cellulose and monomer, using the Fe^{++}/H_2O_2 system (26,27).
Although the proposed mechanism of reaction involved a hydroxyl
radical abstraction of a hydrogen atom from the cellulose, no
evidence was obtained for the hydroxyl radical or the radical
generated on the cellulose.

Electron spin resonance investigations of the reactions
between the hydroxyl radicals generated by the Fe^{++}/H_2O_2 system
using Ti^{4+} in solution as an indicating ion, the ESR spectrum
of the hydroxyl radical-Ti^{4+} complex was recorded (28).

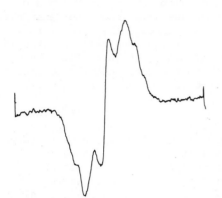

Figure 10.   ESR spectra of free radicals trapped in the cellulose I–Fe^{+2}/
H_2O_2–acrylonitrile system, recorded at
−110°C.   Magnetic field sweep, 250
gauss, left to right.

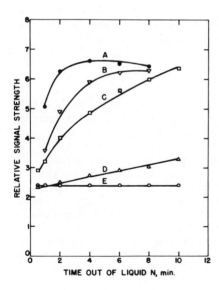

Figure 11.   Effect of temperature on
formation of free radicals in the cellulose I–Fe^{+2}/H_2O_2–acrylonitrile system.
(A) −30°C; (B) −40°C; (C) −50°C;
(D) −60°C; (E) −70°C.

Cotton cellulose immersed in 0.1 $\underline{M}$ FeSO$_4$, dried in a flowing stream of nitrogen, was placed in a quartz tube, and 0.3 $\underline{M}$ H$_2$O$_2$ saturated with acrylonitrile monomer was drawn onto the cellulose. Immediately, liquid nitrogen was drawn through the tube, freezing the wet cellulose. The ESR spectrum of the free radicals trapped in the frozen matrix was recorded at -110°C (Figure 10). The spectrum generated in the presence of the acrylonitrile monomer was more intense than that generated in the cellulose in the absence of the monomer (5).

Free radicals generated during the graft copolymerization reaction were more stable than cellulosic free radicals. The effect of temperature on the formation of free radicals initiated in the cellulose/Fe^{++}-H$_2$O$_2$/acrylonitrile system is shown in Figure 11. Dry cellulose containing ferrous ion was wet with 0.03 $\underline{M}$ H$_2$O$_2$, saturated with acrylonitrile, and immediately frozen in liquid nitrogen. At -70°C or below the free radical concentration remained constant. When the temperature was increased above -70°C, free radical concentration increased with time. Above -40°C, free radical concentration approached a maximum value.

ESR results indicate that cellulosic free radicals generated by the hydroxyl radicals are easily terminated at temperatures above -60°C. In the absence of monomer, the cellulosic free radicals are probably terminated by reaction with hydroxyl radicals. However, in the presence of monomer, the hydroxyl radicals attack both the cellulose and the monomer, thus generating two types of free radicals. The cellulosic free radicals can initiate chain polymerization reactions, as well as terminate reactions which would otherwise result in homopolymer formation. In either case, a cellulose - poly (acrylonitrile) graft is produced.

Abstract

Graft polymerization reactions of vinyl monomers with cotton cellulose were initiated by free radicals produced in cotton by cobalt-60γ-radiation, ultraviolet (uv) radiation, and oxidation-reduction reactions. Electron spin resonance (ESR) spectroscopy was used to investigate reactions of initiating radicals and propagating radicals in graft polymerization reactions. Effects of solvents on stability of free radicals in γ-irradiated cotton cellulose were correlated with their effects on extent of grafting of ethyl acrylate onto irradiated cotton. The ESR spectra of methacrylic acid (MAA) propagating radicals trapped in the copolymer matrix at room temperature when the graft polymerization of MAA onto γ-irradiated cotton was stopped were similar to the ESR spectra of free radicals trapped in γ-irradiated methyl methacrylate polymer. Propagating radicals in the uv-radiation initiated graft polymerization of acrylamide, methacrylamide, and diacetone acrylamide generated different ESR spectra for each system. Changes in the ESR spectra of free radicals generated in ferric chloride-photosensitized polymerization reactions reflected changes in conformational structure of the propagating radicals. ESR spectra of initiating and propagating radicals in the polymerization of acrylonitrile onto cotton initiated by the ferrous ion-hydrogen peroxide system were recorded.

Literature Cited

1. Arthur, J. C., Jr., Mares, T., and Hinojosa, O., Text. Res. J. *36*, 630-635 (1966).
2. Arthur, J. C., Jr., Hinojosa, O., and Tripp, V. W., J. Appl. Polym. Sci. *13*, 1497-1507 (1969).
3. Hinojosa, O., Nakamura, Y., and Arthur, J. C., Jr., J. Polym. Sci. Part C *37*, 27-46 (1972).
4. Reine, A. H., Hinojosa, O., and Arthur, J. C., Jr., J. Polym. Sci. Part B *9*, 503-507 (1971).
5. Arthur, J. C., Jr., Hinojosa, O., and Bains, M. S., J. Appl. Polym. Sci. *12*, 1411-1421 (1968).
6. Hinojosa, O. and Arthur, J. C., Jr., J. Polym. Sci. Part B *10*, 161-165 (1972).
7. Harris, J. A., Hinojosa, O., and Arthur, J. C., Jr., Polym. Prepr. Amer. Chem. Soc. Div. Polym. Chem. *13*, 479-484 (1972).
8. Harris, J. A., Hinojosa, O., and Arthur, J. C., Jr., J. Polym. Sci. Polym. Chem. Ed. *11*, 3215-3226 (1973).
9. Harris, J. A. Hinojosa, O., and Arthur, J. C., Jr., Polym. Prepr. Amer. Chem. Soc. Div. Polym. Chem. *15*, 491-494 (1974).
10. Harris, J. A., Hinojosa, O., and Arthur, J. C., Jr., J. Polym. Sci. Polym. Chem. Ed. *12*, 679-688 (1974).
11. Dilli, S., Ernst, I. T., and Garnett, J. L., Aust. J. Chem. *20*, 911-927 (1967).
12. Nakamura, Y., Hinojosa, O., and Arthur, J. C., Jr., J. Polym. Sci. Part C *37*, 47-55 (1972).
13. Reine, A. H., Hinojosa, O., and Arthur, J. C., Jr., J. Appl. Polym. Sci. *17*, 3337-3343 (1973).
14. Ogiwara, Y., Hon, N., and Kubota, H., J. Appl. Polym. Sci. *18*, 2057-2068 (1974).
15. Hinojosa, O., Harris, J. A., and Arthur, J. C., Jr., Carbohyd. Res. *41*, 31-39 (1975).
16. Baxendale, J. H., Evans, M. G., and Park, G. S., Trans. Faraday Soc. *42*, 155-169 (1946).
17. Haber, F. and Weiss, J., Naturwissenschaften *20*, 948-950 (1932).
18. Haber, F. and Weiss, J. Proc. Roy. Soc. (London) *A 147*, 332-351 (1934).

19. Byrne, G. A. and Arthur, J. C., Jr., J. Appl. Polym. Sci. 14, 3093-3103 (1970).

20. Abraham, R. J., Melville, H. W., Ovenall, D. W., and Whiffen, D. H., Trans. Faraday Soc. 54, 1133-1139 (1958).

21. Nakamura, Y., Hinojosa, O., and Arthur, J. C., Jr., J. Appl. Polym. Sci. 13, 2633-2641 (1969).

22. Trommsdorff, E., Kohle, H., and Lagally, P., Makromol. Chem. 1, 169-198 (1948).

23. Reine, A. H. and Arthur, J. C., Jr., Text. Res. J. 42, 155-158 (1972).

24. Reine, A. H., Portnoy, N. A., and Arthur, J. C., Jr., Text. Res. J. 43, 638-641 (1973).

25. Ingram. D. J. E., Symons, M. C. R., and Townsend, M. G., Trans. Faraday Soc. 54, 409-415 (1958).

26. Richards, G. N., J. Appl. Polym. Sci. 5, 539-544 (1961).

27. Bridgeford, D. J., Ind. Eng. Chem., Prod. Res. Dev. 1, 45-52 (1962).

28. Bains, M. S., Arthur, J. C., Jr., and Hinojosa, O., J. Phys. Chem. 72, 2250-2251 (1968).

*Mention of companies or commercial products does not imply recommendation by the U. S. Department of Agriculture over others not mentioned.

Liquid Ammonia Treatment of Cotton Fabrics

S. ALLAN HEAP

International Institute for Cotton, Manchester, England

The last few years have seen the development and commercial introduction of a brand new finishing technology in the use of anhydrous liquefied ammonia as a setting agent for cotton fabrics.

IIC has been sponsoring background research on several aspects of this process, mainly at the University of Stuttgart and the Norwegian Textile Institute, and I would like to discuss two topics from this programme today:-
1. The influence of the ammonia content of the fabric upon its deformability,
2. Easy-care finishing of ammonia treated fabrics; a comparison of the low-add-on crosslinking technique with the normal padding method.

But first, by way of introduction, a few data which have already been published in the German language but may not have been seen here, and which draw some comparisons between NH_3 and caustic soda treatments.

Figure 1 illustrates the swelling (change in thickness) of an unrestrained poplin fabric as a function of time and the concentration of ammonia. Two points are immediately obvious; the very rapid rate of the reaction and the sensitivity to the presence of moisture. When we expand the time scale by speeding up the chart, it is clear that for anhydrous ammonia, essentially all the swelling takes place within the first fifteen seconds.

Figure 2 shows a comparison between anhydrous ammonia and caustic soda in the yarn untwisting test. Ammonia shows a clearly faster rate of swelling, but a lower equilibrium value. Although the equilibrium swelling of the fibres is less in NH_3 than in NaOH, fabric shrinkage tends to be about the same when little or no restraint is applied. The actual difference depends upon the fabric construction and presumably can be explained by assuming that fibres are prevented from reaching their maximum degree of swelling, especially in caustic soda. Indeed, the caustic swollen fabric is much more easily prevented from shrinking by the application of a restraining force (Figure 3).

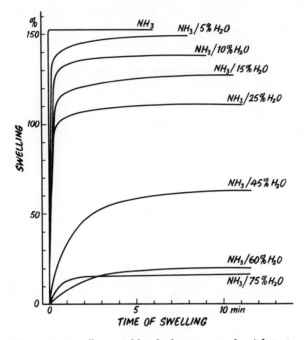

Figure 1.   *Swelling of bleached cotton poplin fabric in liquid ammonia/water ($\sim -40°C$)*

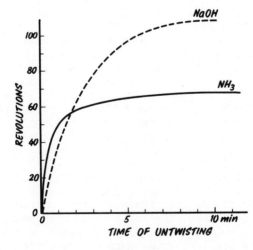

Figure 2

When the fabric is held to constant dimensions, the force
generated by ammonia swelling is generally much larger than that
caused by caustic soda (Figure 4). Furthermore, the application
of a pretension to the fabric, before contact with the swelling
agent produces a marked reduction in the swelling force generated
by NaOH, but has apparently almost no influence on the NH$_3$ system (Figure 5).

The large influence of tension upon the degree of swelling
of cotton fibres in caustic soda is, of course, well documented,
so the apparent insensitivity of the ammonia system to tension
was rather surprising. It has led us provisionally to conclude
that the ammonia cellulose complex is rather different from alkali cellulose, especially in its mechanical properties, with little capability for stress decay. The practical consequence of
this behaviour is that it is somewhat more difficult to control
the dimensions of a fabric in the ammonia process than in mercer-
ising.

Figures 6 and 7, which picture the length changes during typical swelling cycles will serve to illustrate the point a little
further.

Figure 6 is supposed to model a slack swelling and restretch
ing cycle. Note the similar degree of shrinkage with a faster
rate for NH$_3$. The fabric was then loaded with 1Kg per cm. before removal of the swelling agent. The caustic-swollen sample
immediately stretched significantly, with a further restretching
as soon as the water rinsing bath was applied. The ammonia
swollen sample, however, extended far less on first applying the
load, and there was a clear delay after the start of evaporation
before restretching began.

In Figure 7, the cycle illustrated is one where a pretension
is applied before swelling. This tension was sufficient to more
or less eliminate shrinkage in NaOH, but there was still a fair
degree of shrinkage in NH$_3$. Once again, during evaporation of
NH$_3$ there was a delay period during which no extension occurred.

Concentration Of NH$_3$ On The Fabric.

The thought naturally arises that this block to the extensibility of ammonia swollen fabric should be related to the concentration of ammonia remaining in the fibres. Figure 8 shows
the values obtained from the instantaneous elongation experienced
by slack swollen samples, as a function of the load applied and
the ammonia content at the instant of application of the load.
Three levels of ammonia are shown to illustrate the extremes
and an intermediate in the family of curves. Clearly, the highly swollen material is very resistant to elongation, and this
must be a basic fibre property since the fabric structure will
be jammed at full swelling. Only when the fibre swelling is
reduced sufficiently to create space in the fabric will elongat-

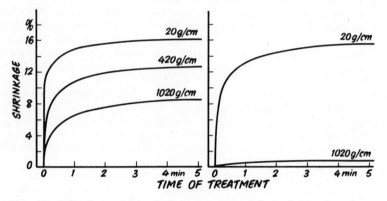

Figure 3.   Shrinkage of bleached cotton poplin fabric: (left) in liquid ammonia ($\sim -40°C$); (right) in 20% aqueous NaOH (20°C)

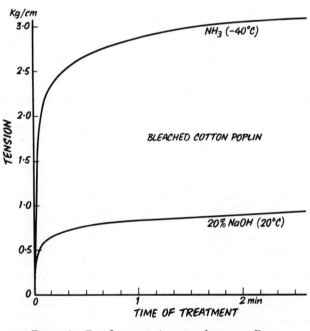

Figure 4.   Development of tension during swelling

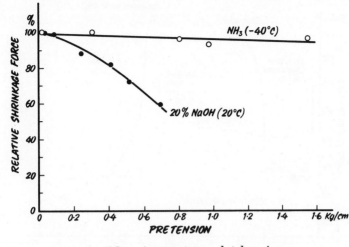

Figure 5.   *Effect of pretension on shrinkage forces*

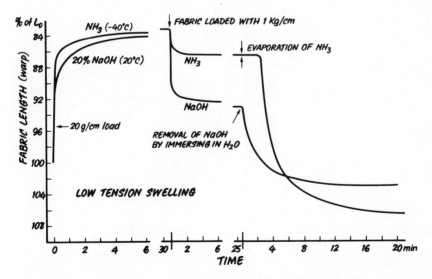

Figure 6.   *Shrinkage and elongation of cotton poplin fabric during NH₃ and NaOH treatments*

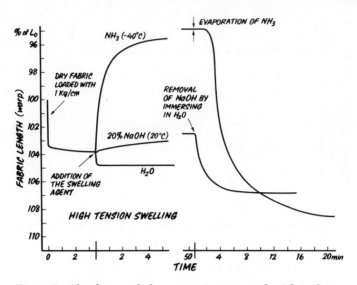

Figure 7.   Shrinkage and elongation of cotton poplin fabric during
NH$_3$ and NaOH treatments

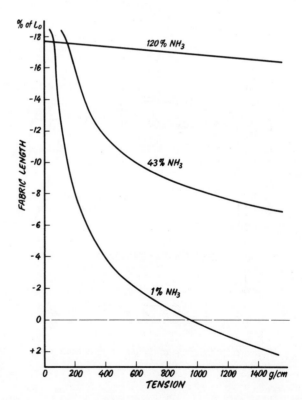

Figure 8. Restretching of
slack-swollen cotton poplin
(warp)

ion become possible at reasonable loads. There is also the
possibility that at some intermediate ammonia content the fibre
itself becomes capable of easy elongation as the ammonia cellulose complex is broken down. Both mechanisms (fabric jamming
and fibre extensibility) will presumably be affected by the
manner of ammonia removal - in particular, one might expect
differences between the cases where ammonia is removed by
"dry" evaporation on the one hand, or by replacement with water
on the other. Up to now, we have studied only the evaporation
systems in this respect.

Figure 9 shows a typical result when one applies a constant
load during evaporation of the ammonia. Restretching begins at
an ammonia concentration of about 55%, and one can suppose this
figure to indicate approximately the point at which one is beginning to remove ammonia from within the fibres rather than simply
evaporating interstitial liquid. We have other circumstantial
evidence pointing to a figure in the region of 50% for the within fibre liquid.

This 50% NH_3 figure does not correspond to the critical
point as conventionally defined during drying processes, when
the rate of drying and the fabric temperature changes abruptly
due to the greater difficulty of removing more tightly bound
liquid. Figure 10 shows that, for one set of circumstances, we
found this critical point to be in the region of 35% NH_3. This
latter value happens to agree pretty well with a calculated
three moles of NH_3 per glucose residue.

Recently, we have been considering the possibility that a
50-60% level of add-on may be all that is technically needed to
produce the desirable effects of ammonia treatment and we have
made a fairly large number of studies in this area. So far,
the results are inconclusive and not particularly encouraging.

Easy-Care-Finishing.

A range of samples was prepared on continuous pilot scale
equipment by applying increasing levels of DHDMEU/$MgCl_2$ to
ammonia treated, mercerised, and control fabrics. On the one
hand, the usual padding technique was used to apply the cross-
linking liquor, and on the other hand, the new Low-Add-On (LAO)
system was used. In the LAO system, the amount of liquor applied can be controlled at such a level (30-35%) that essentially
no migration ensues during drying and a more uniform distribution of crosslinking is obtained in the final fabric. A
wide range of qualities were processed which all gave similar
results, therefore, just one set of results is presented here
today.

The mercerised samples gave results very similar to those
of the controls and therefore, these are not included.

Generally speaking, the use of the LAO system gave better
crease recovery angles and/or better abrasion resistance for

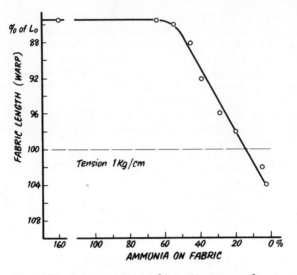

Figure 9.   *Degree of restretching of cotton poplin as a function of ammonia concentration on the fabric*

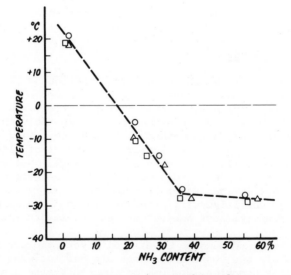

Figure 10.   *Fabric temperature during drying*

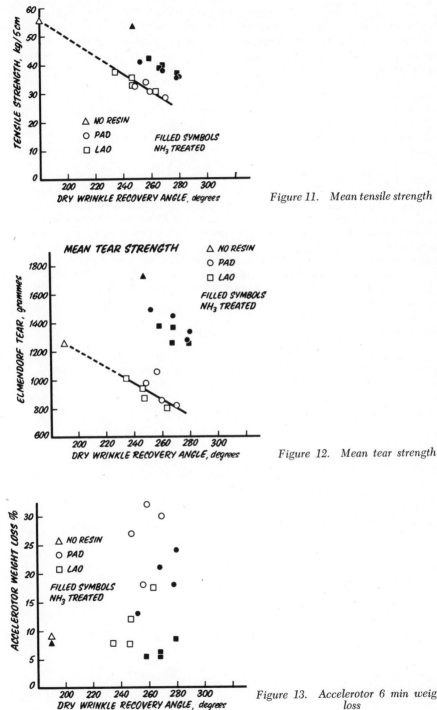

Figure 11. Mean tensile strength

Figure 12. Mean tear strength

Figure 13. Accelerotor 6 min weight loss

the same solids add-on of crosslinking agents but tensile and
tear strength were about the same as the controls.

The ammonia treated samples showed consistenly better crease
recovery, tensile strength, tear strength and abrasion resistance
for a given solids add-on.

The combination of an ammonia pretreatment and the LAO system gave the best results of all. Figures 11, 12 and 13 sum-
marise the tensile, tear and Accelerotor weight loss figures for
a sheeting fabric of the European type (about $150g/m^2$), as a
function of the dry crease recovery angles - the so called
balance of properties which every cotton finisher has to optimise.
The most startling results are those for tear strength and abrasion resistance where the combination of ammonia pretreatment
and MA finish allowed crease recovery angles of about 280 degrees
with mechanical strength not much worse than the untreated control. This improvement can be attributed firstly to the very
effective setting effect of the ammonia treatment (which considerably reduces the inter-yarn friction, thus improving tear
strength and crease recovery), and secondly to the high efficiency of utilisation of the crosslinking agent due to the improved
uniformity of distribution of the crosslinker brought about by
the use of the LAO finishing system.

Acknowledgement.

Grateful thanks are due to Dr. Karl Bredereck, Mr. Harald
Jensen, and Mr. Bob Leah for ideas and experimental work in
Stuttgart, Bergen and Manchester respectively.

Synthesis and Testing of Biodegradable Fiber-Forming Polymers

S. J. HUANG, J. P. BELL, J. R. KNOX, H. ATWOOD, K. W. LEONG,
K. NATARAJAN, J. PAVLISKO, M. ROBY, and N. SHOEMAKER

Departments of Chemistry and Chemical Engineering, Biological Science Group, and
Institute of Materials Science, University of Connecticut, Storrs, CT 06268

Recent literature in the field of biodegradability of synthetic polymers is mostly concerned with the problem of preventing or retarding attack on synthetic polymers and plastics by micro-organisms (1-9). Potts and coworkers reported in 1973 an extensive study on the biodegradability of synthetic polymers by micro-organisms (10). They reported that aliphatic polyesters and polyester based polyurethanes were the only classes of synthetic high molecular weight polymers found to be biodegradable in a study embracing a large number of synthetic polymers such as polyesters, polyamides, polyoleffins, and polyurethanes. Unfortunately the degradable aliphatic polyesters generally lack the desirable physical properties necessary for many applications. The microbial degradation of cellophane and amylose films has been studied by Carr and coworkers (11, 12).

It has been reported by several workers that low molecular weight normal paraffins and low molecular weight polyethylene supported some microbial growth (10, 13-15). Efforts have been directed toward the synthesis of photodegradable polymers so that segments from photodegradation of the polymers might become biodegradable (16-18). Attempts have also been made to improve the biodegradability of polymer composites by mixing biodegradable biopolymers such as starch with nondegradable synthetic polymers such as polyethylene (19).

Currently there are very few reported studies on truly biodegradable synthetic polymers that have the desirable physical properties necessary for the production of a wide range of biodegradable plastics, films, and fibers. Bailey and coworkers have reported that some copolymers of α-aminoacids and longer aminoacids were metabolized by soil micro-organism (20). It has been reported by Gilbert and coworkers that Borax, a polyacrylonitrile based resin, was utilized by micro-organism (21). Polyenamine was found to be degradable (22). Biodegradable polyurethane has

been obtained from the modification of cellulose (23). Poly-
glycolate is being used as surgical suture.

It became apparent from the above mentioned literature that
useful biodegradable polymers will have to come from new synthetic approaches designed to incorporate biodegradable structural
units into polymer chains having desirable physical properties.
Biodegradable fiber forming polymers should find uses in surgical
inplants, sutures, controlled release drugs, fertilizers, fungi-
cides, nematocides, mulch, etc..

Our efforts in biodegradable polymers have been directed
toward two areas. Firstly, we are modifying biodegradable polymers to improve their physical properties so that useful biodegradable plastics, films, and fibers can be produced. Secondly,
we are designing, synthesizing, and testing new polymers that
might be biodegradable and have the desirable physical properties.

Biodegradation Methods

Most of the above mentioned biodegradation studies involve
soil burial tests or culturing on agar-immersed samples. While
our degradation testing includes these methods, we have developed
procedures for exposing polymer materials to concentrated enzyme
solutions in order to accelerate the degradation reaction and to
be able to establish the chemistry and kinetics of a single reaction in the absence of side reactions originating in the micro-
organism. Details of our biodegradation methods have been reported recently (24).

Results

Cross-linked Gelatin. Gelatin, an animal by-product, is
available in quantity and is relatively low priced. It is water
soluble and consists of protein chains of Mn 30,000 - 50,000.
Among the aminoacid components of gelatin are lysine and arginine. The amino side groups of lysine and arginine residues provide suitable sites for modifications of gelatin. Our goal has
been to produce a material which is water insoluble yet pliable
enough to be used as fibers, ribbons, or sheets. The material
would at the same time be easily biodegradable since the main
component is protein. Water insoluble materials have been obtained by cross-linking of gelatin with various reagents (25).
We studied the cross-linking reactions of gelatin with diacid
chlorides, dialdehydes, and diisocyanates and found that diisocyanates are most suitable for our purpose. We have succeeded in
cross-linking gelatin using different conditions: interfacial
cross-linking, bulk cross-linking, and cross-linking of drawn
fibers.

Draw fibers of gelatin were prepared by blending a plasticizer and water with gelatin prior to extrusion at 60°C since melt extrusion is not suitable due to the thermal instability of gelatin. The tensile properties of the fibers vary with the nature of the plasticizer. Glycerine produced a relatively weak but elastic fiber, whereas glycol increased the modulus but gave very brittle tensile behavior. Diethylene glycol incorporated the hugh modulus of the ethylene glycol with the high elongation of the glycerine into much more acceptable tensile properties. The fibers were cross-linked by treatment with 3% solution of 1,6-diisocyantohexane in toluene at 60°C for 1/2 hr. The cross-linked fibers are insoluble in water and have much improved tensile properties, Table 1.

Table 1.   Tensile Properties of Gelatin Fibers[a]

Plasticizer	Tensile, psi	
	Before Cross-link.	After Cross-link.[b]
Glycerine	1,000	3,200
Ethylene glycol	1,800	2,100
Diethylene glycol	7,000	13,600
Triethylene glycol	3,300	4,500
Polyethylene glycol Mn - 200	6,600	10,000

a. Gelatin: plasticizer : water = 2 : 1 : 1.

b. Cross-linked with 3% 1,6-diisocyanatohexane in toluene at 60°C for 1/2 hr.

Removal of the plasticizer and water prior to the cross-linking by washing the fibers with ethanol further improved the properties of the fibers. Fibers prepared with diethylene glycol, elongated 75%, and washed with ethanol followed by cross-linking have a tensile strength of 29,580 psi.

All the cross-linked gelatin fibers were found to be degradable by proteolytic enzymes such as papain, subtilisin, and trypsin. Up to 90% degradation as compared with the degradation of untreated gelatin was observed. Elongation of the fibers before and after cross-linking showed no effect on the biodegradability.

New Polymers.

1.Polyamides. Our initial testing showed that nylon–6 and nylon–6,6 resist enzyme hydrolysis. Since proteolytic enzymes are specific in cleaving peptide linkages adjacent to either hydrophobic or hydrophilic substituents we decided to synthesize polyamides with substituents, anticipating that the introduction of the suitable substituent would make the polyamide more susceptible to enzyme cleavage.

Benzylated polyamides, nylons–n,6Bz (n = 2,4,6,8), were prepared by the interfacial polymerization of α–benzyladipoyl chloride with alkylenediamines. All but the nylon–2,6Bz are fiber forming. Unfortunately, the biodegradability of the nylons was found to be extremely low. However, a copolymer (nylon–6,10–co-nylon–6,6Bz) was found to be hydrolyzed by papain.

$$-[-NH(CH_2)_nNHCOCH_2CH_2CH_2CHCO-]-$$
$$CH_2Ph$$

Nylon–n,6Bz

n = 2	sp. 145°C	Mn 13,400
n = 4	140	29,100
n = 6	120	19,900
n = 8	105	8,500

Nylon–6,3Bz, prepared from hexamethylenediamine and benzylmalonic acid, was found to be degradable by chymotrypsin — 20% hydrolysis after 10 day exposure. However, we have not been able to prepare polymers of high enough molecular weight that is fiber forming.

$$-[-NH(CH_2)_6NHCOCHCO-]-$$
$$CH_2Ph$$

nylon–6,3Bz

mp 140–145°C

Mn 2,000

Fiber forming poly(2-hydroxy-1,3-propylene sebacamide) and poly(1,2-propylene sebacamide) were found to be degraded readily by the fungi <u>Aspergillus niger</u> and <u>Aspergillus flavus</u>. A fiber forming 1/1 copolymer prepared from 2-hydroxy-1,3-propylenediamine and 1,2-propylenediamine and sebacyl chloride was degraded by both protease K and subtilisin. The copolymer has a mp 200 - 210 and Mn 13,000.

$$-\!\!\left[\!\!\begin{array}{c} NHCH_2CHCH_2NHCO(CH_2)_8CO \\ | \\ OH \end{array}\!\!\right]\!\!-$$

poly(2-hydroxy-1,3-propylene sebacamide)

dec. $225°C$ Mn   20,000

$$-\!\!\left[\!\!\begin{array}{c} NHCH_2CHNHCO(CH_2)_8CO \\ | \\ CH_3 \end{array}\!\!\right]\!\!-$$

poly(1,2-propylene sebacamide)

mp 223-228$°C$ Mn 8,300

2. <u>Polyurea.</u> Lysine methyl and ethyl esters were converted into polyureas by the reaction with 1,6-diisocyanatohexane. The polyureas are degradable by chymotrypsin and subtilisin and supported the growth of <u>Aspergillus niger</u>.

$$-\!\!\left[\!\!\begin{array}{c} NH(CH_2)_4CHNHCONH(CH_2)_6NHCO \\ | \\ COOR \end{array}\!\!\right]\!\!-$$

R = methyl and ethyl

polyureas

R = methyl   mp 106-108$°C$ Mn 5,900

R = ethyl   mp 125-129$°C$ Mn 17,900

The introduction of proper substituent does improve the biodegradability of polyamides and polyureas. However, the racemic
substituted polymers tend to have low crystallinity and softening points. The use of optically pure monomers should give stero-
regular polymers of high crystallinity and high softening points.
The biodegradability of the right optically active monomer will
also give polymers of much higher biodegradability than the racemic polymers. However, with the exception of α–aminoacids optically pure monomers are generally not available. Since our results mentioned so far and that of Bailey indicated that copolymers are generally more degradable than the corresponding homo-
polymers we decided to prepared copolymers with various linkages
instead of various substituents.

3. Poly(amide–ester–urethane). Polycaprolactone was reported to supported fungi growth (10). However, its poor phys-
cal properties (mp 60°C and low tensile) limit the use of this
polymer. We have converted polycaprolactone into a new poly-
(amide–ester–urethane) by reacting it with ethanolamine and
repolymerizeing the resulting polyester–amidediol with 1,6–di-
isocyanatohexane. The resulted copolymer has a nitrogen content
of 1.8%, indicating one of each 19 caprolactone units was reacted
to the ethanolamine. Only a very slight melting peak was observed at 320–330°K by DSC, due to residue crystalline segments
of polyester.
The polymer was extruded into a monofilament at 95°C. The
ultimate percentage elongation of the drawn fiber was 350% , and
the undrawn, 1,000%. The tensile strength of the drawn fiber
was around 17,000 psi. The original polycaprolactone has tensile
strength well below 2,000 psi.

$$\underset{}{\text{---} [O(CH_2)_5 CO]_x^{-} NHCH_2 CH_2 OOCNH(CH_2)_6 NHCO \text{---}}$$

poly(amide–ester–urethane)

The copolymer was found to support the growth of Aspergillus
flavus and Penicillium funiculosum. Ten–day exposure to urease
resulted in 25% degradation. Renin, an enzyme produced by the
Aspergillus strains, also degraded the copolymer but it was not
as effective as urease.

4. <u>Poly(amide-urethane)</u>. A poly(amide-urethane) was prepared from ethanolamine, sebacyl chloride, and 1,6-diisocyanato-hexane. The crystalline and fiber forming copolymer was found to be degradable by protease-K. It represent a very promising class of polymer since it combines the desirable physical properties with biodegradability.

$$\text{---}\text{OCH}_2\text{CH}_2\text{NHCO}(\text{CH}_2)_8\text{CONHCH}_2\text{CH}_2\text{OOCNH}(\text{CH}_2)_6\text{NHCO}\text{---}$$

Poly(amide-urethane)

Summary

Modification of gelatin drawn fibers by cross-linking gave fibers of much improved properties. Substituted polyamides and polyureas were prepared and some of them are suitable for biodegradable fibers. Copolymers of various linkages are very promising biodegradable polymers.

Acknowledgement

The financial supports from U.S. Army Natick Laboratories, National Science Foundation, and The University of Connecticut Research Foundation are gratefully acknowledge.

Literature Cited

1. Kaemf, G., Papenroth, w. and Holm, R., Farbe Lack (1973), <u>59</u>, 9.
2. Monk, D. W. Text. Res. J. , (1972), <u>42</u>, 741.
3. Osman, J. L. Klausmeier, R. E. and Jamison, E. I. Mater. Proc. Int. Biodeterior. Symp., (1971), <u>2</u>, 66.
4. Fields, R. D. and Rodriguez, F.,"Proc. 3rd Int. Biodegradation Symp.", Sharpley and Kaplan, Eds., 775, Applied Science Publishers, London, 1976.
5. Tirpack, G. SPE J., (1970), <u>26</u>, 26.
6. Darby, R. T. and Kaplan, A. M., Appl. Microbiol., (1968), <u>16</u>, 900.
7. Wassell, C. J., SPE Trans., (1964), 193.
8. Jen-Hao, L. and Schwartzm A., Kunstoffe, (1960), <u>51</u>, 317.
9. Huek, H. J., Plastics, (1960), 419.
10. Potts, J. E. Clendining, R. A., Ackart, W. B. and Niegisch, W. D., "Polymers and Ecological Problems", Guillet, Ed., 61, Plenum Press, N. Y., 1973.

11. Engler, P. and Carr, S. H. J. Polym. Sci. Polym. Phys. Ed., (1973), 11, 313.
12. Bradley, S. A. Engler, P. and Carr, S. H. Appl. Polym. Symp., (1973), 22, 269.
13. Merdinger, E. and Merdinger, R. P. Appl. Microbiol., (1970), 20, 561.
14. Barna, P. K. et. al., Appl. Microbiol., (1970), 20, 657.
15. Miller, T. L. and Johnson, M. J. Biotechnol. Bioeng., (1966), 8, 567.
16. Guillet, J., "Polymers and Ecological Problems", Guillet, Ed., 45, Plenum Press, N. Y., 1973.
17. Cooney, J. D. Colin, G. and Wiles, D. M. Am. Soc. Test. Mater. Spec. Tech. Publ., (1973), 533, 17.
18. Scott, G. , Chem. in Brit., (1973), 9, 267.
19. Griffin, G. J. L., Ger., (1973), 2333440.
20. Bailey, W., "Proc. 3rd Int. Biodegradation Symp.", Sharpley and Kaplan, Eds., 765, Applied Science Publishers, London, 1976.
21. Gilbert, S. G., Giacin, K. J., Van Gordon, T., Vahidi, A. and Giacin, J. R. Coating and Plastics Reprints, (1974), 34, 114.
22. Kim, S. L., Diss. Abstr. Int. B., (1974), 35, 1121.
23. Kim, S., Stannett, V. and Gilbert, R. D., J. Polym. Sci. Polym. Lett., (1973), 11, 731.
24. S. J. Huang, J. P. Bell, J. R. Knox, el. al.,"Proc. 3rd Int. Biodegradation Symp.", Sharpley and Kaplan, Eds., 731, Applied Science Publishers, London, 1976.
25. Sinclair, R. G., Environ. Sci. Technol., (1973), 7, 955.

Reaction of Wood Pulp with α,β-Amic Acids

I. Synthesis of Possible Spinnable Derivatives

LARRY C. WADSWORTH and JOHN A. CUCULO

Fiber and Polymer Science Program, Department of Textile Chemistry,
North Carolina State University, Raleigh, NC 27607

In view of the shortage of petrochemicals used
for the production of synthetic fibers, it is no
surprise that renewed emphasis is being placed on
cellulose chemistry, a field which has received
sagging interest for the past twenty years. In the
coming years, our oil reserves will become increasingly scarce, or nonexistent, but cellulose is today, and
in the future will remain the most abundant of raw
materials. But far more important, cellulose is a
continually replaceable raw material (1). Trees or
other plants currently under study, can be replanted
as soon as existing mature trees are consumed. The
rotation cycle for pulp can be as little as 15 years
or even less (2).

Granted that greater use of cellulose as a
source of textile fibers could mean lesser or minimal
dependence upon petrochemicals, fabrics made from
cellulosics such as rayon and cotton have great aesthetic appeal, primarily greater wearing comfort due
to the inherent hydrophylic properties of cellulose.
Yet, the production of rayon in the United States and
elsewhere is decreasing largely because of the unfavor-
able economics of meeting pollution standards and from
competition with other fibers (3).

An alternative to the viscose process has been
proposed by Cuculo (4) through the reaction of cellulose with amic acids. The product envisioned is a
cellulose half-acid ester. Limited solubility of the
derivatives has been obtained in dilute alkali. With
increasing degree of substitution (DS), the solubility
of the cellulose half-acid ester should go through a
transition of insolubility to solubility in dilute
alkali, water, water-alcohol mixtures, hydrocarbon-

alcohol mixtures, and finally, organic solvents, similar to the transition described by Peters (5) for
cellulose ethers. The ester part of the derivative,
however, would be subject to saponification in aqueous
alkali, dependent upon alkali concentration and temperature and derivative structure.

Ideally the cellulose half-acid ester could be
converted into a water soluble salt, and wet extruded
as a fiber, or film into an acid, or other non-solvent
coagulating bath. This procedure offers the advantage of allowing conditions to be chosen for preventing saponification of the derivative during the solubilization step, thereby opening up many possibilities
for producing cellulosic fibers with enhanced properties, since many amic acid derivatives which impart
desired properties can be utilized. One important
application could be the production of inherently
flame-retardant fiber by reacting cellulose with amic
acid derivatives containing bromine or phosphorous.

Yet, the production of sufficiently high DS
cellulose acid ester to produce wet-spinnable derivative need not be a limitation for the reaction. A
four-fold increase in water absorbency (6) has been
obtained in the reaction of rayon fabric with succinamic acid with a DS of 0.3. Research is now in progress in which amic acids containing bromine are
being reacted with cellulosic fabrics for the production of flame-retardant fabrics (7). This has already
been demonstrated in the laboratory for the latter
case. The potentials for modifying nonwovens by this
method are also quite fascinating. For example, wood
pulp could be reacted with amic acids prior to nonwoven fabric production to produce highly absorbent
padding and backing materials.

In the present work, degrees of substitution
ranging from 0.3 to 0.7 were obtained in the reaction
of various wood pulps ranging from high to low degrees
of polymerization (DP) with succinamic acid, ammonium
succinamate, and N,N-diethyl succinamic acid in pad-
bake reactions. Rather low DS values (DS approximately 0.1) were obtained in the Barratte-type reactions of dry and "never-dried" wood pulps with succinamic acid. Structural proof of the cellulose hemisuccinate derivative was obtained by infrared analysis.
DP determinations accompanied all DS analyses so that
reaction conditions could be appropriately varied to
obtain high degree of substitution with minimum degradation.

Experimental

Reactants. Succinamic acid was synthesized from succinic anhydride as described by Allen (8).

Ammonium succinamate was synthesized from succinamic acid. Succinamic acid, 500 g, was dispersed in acetone to a total volume of 2 ℓ in a 4 ℓ beaker. The succinamic acid was slightly soluble in acetone. Ammonia gas was slowly bubbled through the reaction media for 2 1/2 hours with continuous stirring. The reaction was slightly exothermic, but required no external cooling. The crystals which formed were filtered under vacuum, washed five minutes with acetone without vacuum, and filtered dry under suction. The procedure was repeated two times, and the crystals were spread out in a tray to dry. A 95% yield was obtained. Purity and identification were determined by melting point (109° to 110°C) and infrared analysis.

N,N-diethyl succinamic acid was synthesized from succinic anhydride by Bowman (9). N,N-diethylamine, 55 ml, from Matheson Co., Inc. was purified by simple distillation. Succinic anhydride was obtained from Armageddon Chemical Co. The amine was dissolved in 40 ml of acetone (Fisher Laboratory Grade) and added to a suspension of 100 grams of anhydride in 100 ml of acetone. The reaction was initially exothermic (maximum temperature 40°C). The solution was evaporated to near dryness. To remove the yellow tint, 100 ml of acetone and approximately 2 g of Norite B, decolorizing carbon were added and the mixture heated to a boil. The mixture was allowed to steep for about five minutes, and filtered warm to yield a clear solution. The filtered solution was then heated to a boil and carbon tetrachloride was added to the point of incipient turbidity. Finally the solution was cooled in the freezer, and the resulting crystals were filtered, and spread out in a tray to dry. An 81% yield was obtained. Purity and identity were determined by melting point (82° to 84°C) and by infrared analysis.

Cellulose Source. The following dissolving pulps were obtained from ITT Rayonier, Inc. in dry sheet form with the intrinsic viscosities (I.V.) specified in dl/g: Rayocord-X-F, I.V.-9.2; Cellunier-F, I.V.-3.72; Rayselect-J, I.V.-3.32. All were Southern Pine and pulped by the Sulfite Process (10).

"Never-dried" Cellunier-P (Hemlock) and "never-dried" Cellunier-F (Southern Pine) were also obtained from ITT Rayonier (11).

Pretreatment Conditions. The dry pulp sheets, as received, were first shredded with water in a commercial blender at high speed for 90 seconds. The pulp slurry was then poured into a Buchner funnel, and suction applied. Pulp which was not to be mercerized was then washed for five minutes with acetone before suction was applied. This step was repeated twice, and the pulp spread out on aluminum foil, and air-dried at room temperature. The moisture content of the pulps to be mercerized were determined so that the sodium hydroxide concentration (approximately 20%) could be prepared to result in an equilibrium value of 17.5% to compensate for the dilution effect of the wet pulp. The samples were placed in the refrigerator at 7.5°C for 24 hours. The mercerized cellulose was then washed free of caustic and acidified with 10% acetic acid. After washing free of acid, the cellulose was acetone washed and air-dried.

Both the "never-dried" pulps were sulfite pulped and were acidic to litmus paper. As soon as received, the pulps were washed with water on a Buchner funnel. The washings were repeated until the filtrate was determined neutral by a yellow to blue color change when one drop of 0.1N NaOH and two drops of a 0.1% solution of bromocresol purple indicator were added to 100 ml of filtrate. Portions of both wet, neutralized pulps were sealed in polyethylene bags and placed in the refrigerator until ready for use. Portions of both wet, neutralized pulps, 250 grams (approximately 6:1 water to pulp content), were further washed three times each with methanol, ethanol, isopropanol, and acetone. The pulps were then air-dried at room temperature.

Nonwoven Mat Formation. A cyclindrical handsheet mold (6 in x 16 in) was utilized to make the cellulose mats. A round fiberglass screen was cut slightly larger than the handsheet mold diameter and placed onto the mat forming screen of the mold. The cylinder was filled with water and 1 gram of cellulose which had been shredded in a commercial blender at high speed for 90 seconds, was added. The water-cellulose slurry was agitated, the lower water valve to the mold opened, and a uniform cellulose mat was formed on the fiberglass screen with a weight of 1.62 oz/yd^2 (707 grn/yd^2)

Another fiberglass screen was placed on top of the cellulose mat to form a sandwich and was then removed from the mold.

Amic Acid Treatment Solutions. Succinamic acid pad baths were prepared by dissolving 54% succinamic acid on the weight of the solution (o.w.s.) in deionized distilled water. Heat was required to maintain succinamic acid solubility (90°C + 5°C). When catalyst was utilized, 1.62% ammonium sulfamate (o.w.s.) was added to the bath. Succinamic acid solutions were prepared in the same manner for the Baratte reactions.

The aqueous ammonium succinamate pad bath was prepared by dissolving 61.9% ammonium succinamate in deionized distilled water, and heating to 85°C + 5°C. When specified, 1.62% ammonium sulfamate catalyst (o.w.s.) was added. The melt baths were prepared, simply by heating ammonium succinamate to slightly above its melting point of 110°C.

The N,N-diethyl succinamic acid melt pad bath was prepared by heating to slightly above its melting point of 84°C.

Pad-Bake Technique. The handsheet sandwiches were stapled around the circumference to confine the cellulose mat. After an immersion time of 90 seconds at the specified pad temperature, the handsheet was removed, blotted between two pulp sheets, and squeezed between pad rolls to a pickup ratio of approximately 4 to 1.

The samples were immediately placed in a plastic bag after padding to keep them wet until the entire series was padded (not longer than 20 minutes). The samples were then suspended with paper clips on a ring stand which was immediately placed into the oven. The bake oven was raised to 3°C above the specified bake temperature to allow for temperature drop during the opening and closing of the oven door, and the cooling effect caused by the heating of the metal ring stand. Throughout the bake reactions, the temperature was maintained at the specified temperature + 3°C. The oven was a Precision Scientific Company I Isotemp with forced air draft.

Baratte reactions were performed in a Buchi Rotavapor. Ten grams of pulp were placed into a 500 ml round bottom flask and 100 grams of short glass rods (approximately 1.5 x 1.0 cm) were added to the flask to enhance uniform tumbling of the pulp throughout the reaction. When Baratte reactions were performed on "never-dried" pulps, sufficient wet pulp was utilized

to be equivalent to 10 grams of dry pulp. The amic
acid solutions were then added to the flask, and the
flask was rotated in a silicone oil bath maintained
at the temperature corresponding to that of the
equivalent pad solution in the pad-bake reactions, for
a period of 15 minutes to allow for sufficient satur-
ation of the substrate with the amic acid. Than a
second oil bath at the specified reaction temperature
was placed under the rotating flask.

Experimental Analyses. The determination of
pendent carboxylic acid content by the ion-exchange
reaction between calcium acetate and the carboxylic
acid groups, and the determination of total carboxyl
carbonyl and ester carbonyl by the modified Eberstadt
method have been previously described (8).
In addition to determining the carboxylic acid
content by the calcium acetate method using Cramer's
correction factor (8, 12), free carboxyl content was
also determined by the cation-exchange reaction
between the silver cation and the carboxyl proton
as described by Davidson and Nevel (13) with the
exception that the volume of silver meta-nitrophenolate
treatment solution was increased from 100 to
300 ml.
The calculations of free, total, and crosslink
degrees of substitution were performed using the
formulas developed by Johnson, et al. (14).
Intrinsic viscosities were determined on the
saponified derivatives using ASTM Procedure D1795-62
(15), and degrees of polymerization were calculated
using the Mark-Houwink equation and the K and a values
of Newman, et al. (16).
Nitrogen and sulfur analyses were performed by an
independent laboratory using the flash combustion
technique and the Schoniger test for the two analyses,
respectively.
Infrared analyses of the wood pulps and derivatives were performed with potassium bromide pellets
utilizing a Perkin Elmer 337 Grating Infrared Spectro-
photometer. A Wiley mill was utilized to disintegrate
the pulp to aid in the preparation of more uniform
pellets. The regenerated cellulose films were simply
run without further preparation.

Results and Discussion

Reactants. The structures of the α,β-amic acids
reacted with wood cellulose are given in Table I.
Degradation of the cellulose chain is shown in this

paper to occur in the reaction of cellulose with
succinamic acid, particularly in the presence of
ammonium sulfamate catalyst. It was theorized that
degradation could be minimized by reacting cellulose
under the more alkaline conditions effected by the
use of ammonium succinamate reactant. N,N-diethyl
succinamic acid was selected to eliminate a competing
imide side reaction (17), and thereby increases the
amount of product converted to cellulose half-acid
ester.

Infrared Analyses of Cellulose Hemisuccinate
Derivatives. The main product of the reaction is a
cellulose half-acid ester with the evolution of
ammonia:

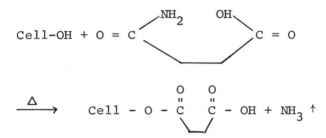

The mechanism of the reactions with alcohols is
thought to involve a cyclic anhydride intermediate (18,
19, 20) and was the subject of a recent Ph.D. dissertation (17).
        The infrared spectrum of a cellulose hemisuccinate
produced from the reaction of mercized Rayocord-X-F
wood pulp with succinamic acid is shown in curve A of
Figure 1a. The number of succinic acid groups per
anhydroglucose unit as expressed by the free DS is
0.38. The broad absorption peak centered at 3400 cm^{-1}
is typical of the OH stretching assigned to cellulose.
The sharper absorption band at 2900, also assignable
to cellulose, is due to CH stretching (21). The
strong absorption peak at 1720 cm^{-1} which is not
observed in native cellulose is due to the overlap
of the carboxyl carbonyl and the ester carbonyl. If
this is truly the structure, then converting the
pendant carboxyl group into a carboxylate anion should
result in the resolution of the single peak into two
peaks with the carboxylate anion absorbing at lower
energy, thereby providing proof of structure. This is

Table I.   Reactants

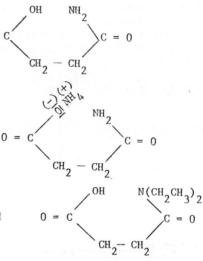

Succinamic acid

Ammonium succinamate

N,N-diethyl succinamic acid

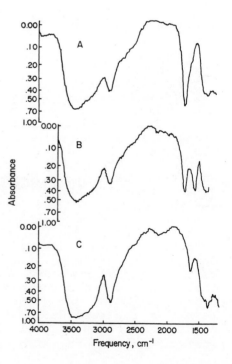

Figure 1a. IR spectra: (A) cellulose hemisuccinate; (B) sample A washed with 10% sodium bicarbonate; (C) sample A saponified

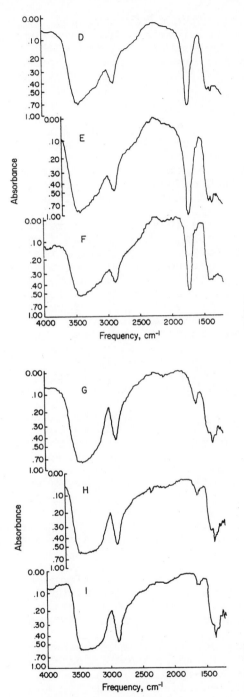

Figure 1b. IR spectra of Rayselect-J pulp reacted with (D) succinamic acid, (E) ammonium succinamate, and (F) N,N-diethyl succinamic acid

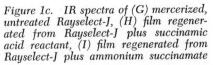

Figure 1c. IR spectra of (G) mercerized, untreated Rayselect-J, (H) film regenerated from Rayselect-J plus succinamic acid reactant, (I) film regenerated from Rayselect-J plus ammonium succinamate

confirmed in curve B in which the derivative was
washed with 10 percent sodium bicarbonate. This same
effect has been shown with cellophane reacted with
succinamic acid (17). In the curve C, the absorption
spectra after saponification of the derivative by the
modified Eberstadt method is shown (12, 22), and is
identical to that of pure cellulose. The peak at
1635 is due to absorbed water (21).

Curves D, E, and F (Figure 1b) represent mercerized Rayselect-J reacted with succinamic acid with
catalyst, ammonium succinamate without catalyst, and
N,N-diethyl succinamic acid respectively. All three
curves appear identical which offers strong support
that the three reactants yield the same cellulose
hemisuccinate derivative.

Curve G, Figure 1c, is the IR spectrum of mercerized, unreacted Rayselect-J pulp. Curves H and I are
spectra of cellulose films formed by dissolving the
cellulose-hemisuccinate derivatives in 10% sodium
hydroxide at -10°C, and coagulating the cellulose by
the addition of acetone. The reactants from which
the cellulose-hemisuccinate derivatives were formed
prior to solubilization and subsequent regeneration
of cellulose were succinamic acid and ammonium
succinamate, curves H and I, respectively. These two
spectra are identical to that of pure cellulose,
curve G, and it is no surprise that the derivatives
are saponified in the 10% sodium hydroxide.

Effect of Treatment Conditions. From the photo-
graphs in Figure 2, it can be seen that the mercerized cellulose handsheet has a more open texture and
is less matted down than is the same weight of unmercerized Rayocord-X-F wood pulp. It was shown that
the mercerized cellulose resulted in almost twice the
degree of substitution as was obtained with unmercerized cellulose.

The effects of the various pretreatment stages as
well as the subsequent baking, and saponification and
acid neutralization of the pad-bake controls are
depicted in Table II. Overall, none of the pretreat-
ments given the wood pulps had any notable effect on
I.V., or DP as calculated from I.V. Baking without
reactant at 180°C for 15 minutes and saponification
followed by acid neutralization resulted in only minor
reduction of DP values.

The negative DS values obtained are to be expected for untreated pulp. The formulas used in calculating the DS values make the assumption that no substituent other than cellulose half-acid ester or the

Table II. Pad-bake controls

A. Conditions

| Sample designation | | | | | | | | |
Rayocord-X-F	Rayselect-J	Cellunier-F	As received[a]	Shredded[b]	Merc.	Handsheet	Baked 180°C/15 min	Sapon./acid neut.
1	7	13	X					
2	8	14	X	X				
3	9	15	X	X				
4	10	16	X	X	X	X		
5	11	17	X	X	X	X	X	
6	12	18			X	X	X	X

B. Experimental data

	I.v., dl/g[c]	DP[d]	DS Total	DS Free	DS Crosslink
1	6.98	1184			
2	7.37	1249			
3	7.29	1235			
4	7.06	1196			
5	6.32	1070			
6	5.49	931	−0.01	0.00	−0.01
7	3.23	547			
8	3.29	558			
9	3.30	559			
10	3.21	544			
11	3.07	520			
12	2.84	481	−0.01	0.00	−0.01
13	3.74	633			
14	3.86	654			
15	4.31	730			
16	3.94	667			
17	3.48	589			
18	3.29	557	−0.03	0.02	−0.05

[a] Dry sheets as received from ITT Rayonier, Inc. were prepared for intrinsic viscosity determination according to ASTM Procedure D1795–62.

[b] Shredded with water in a commercial blender at high speed for 90 seconds.

[c] Intrinsic viscosity determined by ASTM Procedure 1795–62.

[d] DP calculated from Mark-Houwink equation using the k and a values of Newman, Loeb, and Conrad (16).

the crosslink segment is present on the substrate.
Crosslinking DS was determined by the amount by which
the total saponification equivalent was greater than
twice the pendant carboxyl determination (14). Thus,
at very low degrees of reaction, or with no reaction
as with the controls, negative DS values are likely
to be encountered because any experimental errors
are greatly magnified by those built-in assumptions.

The effect of bake time at bake temperatures
ranging from 150°C to 180°C is shown in Figure 3.   DS
increases with temperature, but less drastically beyond 160°C. With all temperatures, DS appears to
level off at intermediate bake times of 20 minutes
from 150°C to 170°C and 15 minutes at 180°C. A
similar levelling-off of DS with bake time at 150°C
was shown by Cuculo (6) in the reaction of succinamic
acid with rayon fabric, and by Johnson (23) after
three minutes at 170°C.

The effects of treatment conditions on DS and DP
are given in Table III. Three wood pulps were utilized and some experiments were performed in two to
five separate trials, effecting many replications of
the same conditions. The free DS values in samples
19-23 differ very little; however, the first two
total DS values are notably lower than those of
samples 21 through 23. The total saponification equi-
valents of samples 19 and 20 were determined by the
alcoholic alkali method (22) in which 95% ethanol was
used as a swelling agent to aid in the penetration of
sodium hydroxide, but in all remaining experiments
water was substituted for the ethanol since it was
reported by Allen (8) that water was a better swelling
agent for the cellulose half-acid ester than was
ethanol, although he found no difference in DS by the
substitution of water for ethanol.

Eliminating the catalyst in samples 24, 30 and
35, has no detectable effect in total DS. Catalyst
has been reported to decrease the amount of cross-
linking and shift more of the product to the desired
half-acid ester (8). Cuculo (6) has found that acidic
catalyst increases the extent of reaction when short
bake times and temperatures are utilized. With the
bake conditions of 180°C for 15 minutes employed in
this work, however, the presence of catalyst had no
significant effect on total, free or crosslinking DS.

Samples 25 and 31 were both baked at 150°C for
22 minutes with acid catalyst, and both had lower DS
values compared to the average of all the experiments
at 180°C for 15 minutes. Samples 26 and 32 were not
mercerized prior to treatment, and resulted in DS

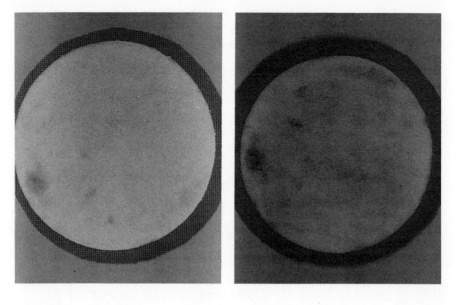

(a)   (b)

Figure 2. Handsheets of (a) unmercerized Rayocord-X-F and (b) mercerized Rayo-cord-X-F

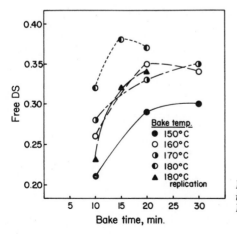

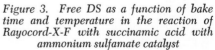

Figure 3. Free DS as a function of bake time and temperature in the reaction of Rayocord-X-F with succinamic acid with ammonium sulfamate catalyst

Table III. Pad-bake reactions of wood pulps with succinamic acid

A. Conditions

Sample designation Rayocord-X-F	Rayselect-J	Cellunier-F	Shredded	Merc.	Handsheet	Catalyst	Padded Dry	Padded Wet	Baked 150°C/22 min	Baked 180°C/15 min
19–23	27–29	33–34	X	X	X	X	X			X
24	30	35	X	X	X	none	X		X	X
25	31		X	X	X	X	X		X	
26	32	36	X	none	X	X	X	X	X	X
		37	X	none	X	none	X			X

B. Experimental data

Sample	DS Total	DS Free	Crosslink	I.V., dl/g	DP
19	0.39[a]	0.38	0.01	1.92	325
20	0.41[a]	0.32	0.09	2.37	402
21	0.48	0.40[b]	0.08	1.39	235
22	0.62	0.46	0.16	2.50	424
23	0.61	0.42	0.19	1.56	264
24	0.47	0.41	0.20	3.52	596
25	0.27	0.30[b]	0.17		
26		0.22[b]	0.05		
27	0.51	0.44[b]	0.07	1.51	256
28	0.65	0.46	0.19	1.06	180
29	0.68	0.46	0.22	0.69	116
30	0.70	0.47	0.23	1.60	272
31	0.46	0.37[b]	0.09	1.44	245
32	0.30	0.26[b]	0.04	2.28	386
33	0.62	0.43	0.19	1.31	222
34	0.62	0.48[b]	0.14	1.66	281
35	0.65	0.48	0.17	1.97	334
36	0.46	0.38	0.08	1.49	252
37	0.31	0.23	0.08		

[a] Total saponification equivalent determined by the alcoholic alkali method (22); in the remaining analyses, distilled water was substituted for the ethanol.

[b] Carboxyl content determined by absorption of silver from silver meta-nitrophenolate solutions (13); calcium acetate method (8, 12) used for other carboxyl analyses.

values on the order of approximately one-half those
obtained on the mercerized pulps. Not surprisingly,
this strongly indicates that accessibility could be
the limiting factor for DS. Wood pulp sample number
36 was pre-wet with water (4:1 pickup ratio) prior to
padding to determine if the wet substrate would result
in improved penetration by the reactant. When compared to samples 25 and 31 which received the same
treatment conditions except being padded dry, there
were no differences in DS values. Although no benefit was derived from padding the wet sample in this
particular case, the fact that there was no loss in
DS presents the advantage of being able to react wet
pulp, likely after the final washing stage after
pulping or mercerization.

The effects of treatment conditions on DP are
very striking in Table III when compared to the untreated control values in Table II. The DP of Rayocord-X-F was reduced from 1196 in the handsheet to an
average value of 321 after treatment. These samples
were baked at 180°C for 15 minutes, and resulted in a
73% decrease in chain length. Under the same conditions, a 66% decrease in DP resulted with Rayselect-J
and a 62% decrease with Cellunier-F. Appreciable
degradation also occurred at the less severe bake
conditions of 150°C for 22 minutes. Removing the
catalyst in experiments 24, 30, and 35 resulted in
notably less degradation in all three trials, without
significantly affecting DS. High DP values are
obtained on pulps not mercerized prior to treatment,
but the corresponding DS values are low.

Degradation was first suspected in the work by
noting sample discoloration upon treatment. Normally,
the more severe the treatment conditions, the darker
the brown discoloration. Subsequent work with ammonium succinamate reactant led to high DS with only
slight discoloration.

The wood pulps treated under severely degrading
conditions in Table III may be approaching a level-off
DP. According to Battista, et al. (24), level-off DP
is dependent upon the severity of the degradation conditions, and they give the average level-off DP of
bleached sulfite pulps as ranging from 280 to 200,
while that of mercerized wood pulp ranges from a DP of
90 to 70. Level-off DP cellulose has been shown to
exhibit higher lateral order, and it has been hypothe-
sized with strong supporting evidence that under acid
hydroylis, the amorphous regions are hydrolyzed leaving only the highly ordered and well-defined crystalline regions (24, 25). Detailed structural analysis

by X-ray or other methods, have not yet been performed
on the cellulose half-acid ester derivative, but will
be the subject of future investigations.

The effects of treatment conditions on the DS and
DP of wood pulps reacted with ammonium succinamate and
N,N-diethyl succinamic acid are given in Table IV.
Samples 38 and 44 were padded with aqueous ammonium
succinamate with catalyst and baked at 150°C for 22
minutes. The free DS values of the two were 0.45 and
0.47 as compared to 0.45 for the sample baked at 180°C
for 15 minutes. Thus, bake conditions more severe
than the former appear to be unnecessary for ammonium
succinamate. Sample 45, which was padded wet, ex-
hibited slightly higher total and free DS values than
did sample 39 which was padded dry. Again, under the
reaction conditions employed, the presence of catalyst
was of little significance.

The pad-bake reactions of mercerized Cellunier-F
with ammonium succinamate melts yield rather low DS
values when padded dry and pre-wet with water, resulting in free DS values of 0.16 and 0.19, respectively.
The low DS values were likely due to poor penetration
of the reactant since the ammonium succinamate was
rather viscous.

N,N-diethyl succinamic acid did not react with
either of the pulps when padded dry; however, when
the cellulose mats were pre-wet with water, DS values
of 0.32 and 0.36 were obtained with two different wood
pulps. This was the most pronounced effect observed
with the reactant by prewetting the substrate prior
to padding. Apparently with the bulkier N,N-diethyl
succinamic acid, pre-wetting of the substrate with
water is much more important.

As shown in Table V, the Baratte reaction of N,N-
diethyl succinamic acid with mercerized Cellunier-F
results in approximately the same free carboxylic acid
DS, 0.31, as in the pad-bake reactions. In this
Baratte reaction, the pulp was pre-wet to 500% moisture content prior to adding the melted N,N-diethyl
succinamic acid, and the flask was rotated over an oil
bath at 145°C for 15 minutes before applying the
vacuum to remove the water. Apparently pre-wetting
the pulp had the same beneficial effects. Sample
number 51 was also pre-wet, but was placed in the oven
at 110°C for 38 hours. Free DS the most important
parameter, was only slightly greater than that obtained with the Baratte reaction, but the total DS was
much higher, and was reflected primarily in increased
crosslinking.

Table IV.   Pad-bake reactions of wood pulps with ammonium succinamate and N, N-diethyl succinamic acid

A. Conditions

Sample designation Rayselect-J	Cellunier-F	Reactant	Shredded	Merc.	Handsheet	Catalyst	Padded Dry	Padded Wet	Baked 150°C/22 min	Baked 180°C/15 min
38	44	61.9% amm. succ.	X	X	X	X	X		X	
39	45	61.9% amm. succ.	X	X	X	X	X			X
40		61.9% amm. succ.	X	none	X	X		X		X
41		61.9% amm. succ.	X	X	X	none	X			X
	46	amm. succ. melt	X	X	X	none	X			
	47	amm. succ. melt	X	X	X	none		X		
42	48	N, N-diethyl melt	X	X	X	none	X			X
43	49	N, N-diethyl melt	X	X	X	none		X		X

B. Experimental Data

Sample	DS[a] Total	DS[a] Free	Crosslink
38	0.53	0.45	0.08
39	0.50	0.45	0.05
40	0.29	0.25	0.04
41	0.56	0.49	0.07
42	-0.02	0.07	-0.09
43	0.32	0.32	0.00

Sample	I.V., dl/g	DP
38	1.57	266
39	1.80	305
40	2.27	385
41	2.37	401
42	2.87	486
43	2.21	374
44	1.97	335
45	1.94	329
46	3.02	511
47	3.04	515
48	3.50	592
49	2.52	428

[a] Carboxyl content determined by absorption of silver from silver meta-nitrophenolate solutions (13).

Table V. Baratte reactions of wood pulps with N, N-diethyl succinamic and succinamic acids

A. Conditions

Sample designation		Reactant	Dry sheets			"Never-dried" pulp			Catalyst
Cellunier-F	Cellunier-P		Shredded	Merc.	Wet	Washed Alcohol	Washed Acetone	Air-dried	
50[a]		N,N-diethyl melt	X	X					none
51[b]		N,N-diethyl melt	X	X					none
52[c]		54% succ. acid				X	X	X	none
53[d]		54% succ. acid				X	X	X	X
54[d]		54% succ. acid				X	X	X	X
55[e]		54% succ. acid			X				X
56[e]		54% succ. acid			X				X
	57[c]	54% succ. acid				X	X	X	none

B. Experimental data

	DS[f]			I.V.,dl/g	DP
	Total	Free	Crosslink		
50	0.34	0.31	0.03	2.72	462
51	0.49	0.34	0.15	1.57	267
52	0.11	0.09	0.02	3.55	602
53	0.13	0.10	0.03	3.32	563
54	0.08	0.08	0.00	3.30	560
55	0.09	0.09	0.00	3.66	620
56	0.06	0.06	0.00	3.64	618
57	0.10	0.08	0.00	3.50	592

[a] Baratte reaction at 145°C for three hours under nitrogen and aspirator vacuum; remaining Baratte reactions at 160°C for ninety minutes.

[b] Pulp saturated with amic acid in Erlenmeyer flask, heated 110°C for 38 hours.

[c] Stream of nitrogen gas forced into rotating flask throughout reaction, aspirator vacuum applied.

[d] Reaction performed under reflux conditons, no nitrogen, no vacuum.

[e] Steam forced into rotating flask during reaction.

[f] Carboxyl content determined by calcium acetate method (8,12).

Baratte reactions of "never-dried" pulps and "never-dried" pulps which had been solvent exchanged with alcohols all yielded rather low DS values of approximately 0.1 when reacted with 54 percent succinamic acid. The reactions were performed both with and without: catalyst, aspirator vacuum, and nitrogen atmosphere. The lowest DS 0.06, was obtained when steam was forced into the rotating flask throughout the reaction. Hydrolysis of the succinamic acid to the less reactive monoammonium succinate (17) obviously has a greater possibility in the Baratte reactions than under pad-bake conditions where the water is quickly removed after performing the beneficial effect of swelling the cellulose.

The rather high DP values resulting from Baratte reactions were of little consequence considering the low degrees of reaction obtained.

Solubility Determinations. Sample number 28, pad-baked with 54% succinamic acid with catalyst, and sample number 41, pad-baked with 61.9% ammonium succinamate were dissolved at a concentration of 0.5% cellulose hemisuccinate in 10% sodium hydroxide at -10°C. Both had total DS values of approximately 0.6. Sample number 28 appeared soluble after 30 minutes, and had a clear, but amber color. After approximately one hour, sample 41 yielded a clear, colorless solution. After three hours at -10°C, the samples were placed in the lower part of the refrigerator at 7.5°C and left overnight. Upon standing, some particulate matter, smaller than fibers in size, were noticed. The solutions were filtered through a medium porosity glass frit, and the cellulose was regenerated with the addition of acetone. The sample was then centrifuged, and the acetone and aqueous mixture was decanted. At this point, some fractionation of the cellulose was suspected because with both samples, a ring of precipitant was observed suspended above the solid fraction at the bottom of the centrifuge tube. These upper phases were separated and weighed, and represented 0.8% of sample 28 and 4.1% of sample 41 that were originally dissolved. The coagulated samples were washed with water until neutral, centrifuged, and poured into aluminum weighing dishes, and upon drying overnight at room temperature formed films. The films were translucent, and somewhat brittle, but appeared to be strong. Although diligent efforts were not made to save all the material, 55% of sample 28 which was originally dissolved and 57% of sample 41 were converted to films.

Cellulose hemisuccinates with a DS of 0.4 and higher have been dissolved by Allen and Cuculo (26) and in this work at a concentration of 0.5% derivative in 10% sodium hydroxide at temperature of -10°C, 2°C, and 7.5°C. Solubilities at higher concentrations of derivative were not evaluated, although 5% cellulose hemisuccinate has been dissolved by Allen (26) in 10% sodium hydroxide at room temperature. The derivative however, was produced by racting rayon, which has a much lower DP and is more accessible than wood pulp, with succinamic acid with an acid catalyst. These conditions have been shown to result in severe chain degradation in the present work. The exact nature of these solutions, if in fact they are true solutions, warrant further studies, preferably with such detailed and precise methods as light scattering.

Degree of Polymerization. The objective of this present work is to obtain a high degree of reaction with minimum degradation in the reaction of α,β-amic acids with wood pulp. With sufficiently high DS the derivatives should dissolve in dilute alkaline solutions, and possibly in non-saponifying solutions. Improved solubility at the expense of cellulose chain degradation, however, is not desired. It has been shown (27, 28, 29, 30) that low and medium DP cellulose of high accessibility will dissolve in 9 to 10 percent sodium hydroxide at -5°C.

Figures 4, 5, and 6 clearly show that there is only slight degradation of the wood pulp controls, even when subjected to the same baking and saponification treatments as received in the reaction and subsequent analyses. The reductions in DP upon treatment with succinamic acid in the presence of catalyst are striking. Increases in DP of approximately 100 anhydroglucose units (AGU) were noted with all three pulps upon the removal of the catalyst. In Figure 5, ammonium succinamate with catalyst resulted in approximately the same DP as succinamic acid without catalyst, and as shown in Figure 6, the ammonium succinamate with catalyst resulted in a slight increase in DP. Figure 7 illustrates the effects of removing the ammonium sulfamate catalyst and of the substitution of ammonium succinamate on the DP of the saponified derivative and on the DP of the regenerated films. The number at the top of each bar represents the total DS of the original derivative. Removal of the catalyst increases the DP from 180 to 270. The use of ammonium succinamate with catalyst resulted in an increase to a DP of 305. A further increase in DP to

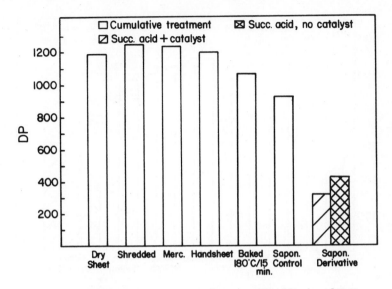

Figure 4.   Effect of treatment conditions on DP of Rayocord-X-F

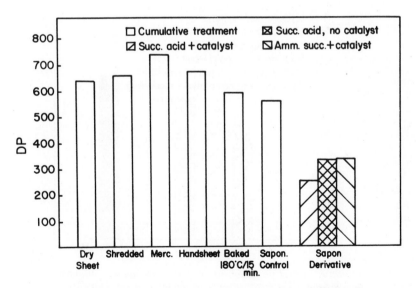

Figure 5.   Effect of treatment conditions on DP of Cellunier-F

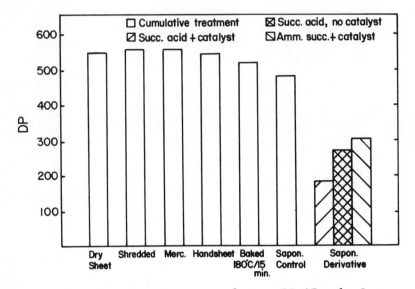

Figure 6.   Effect of treatment conditions on DP of Rayselect-J

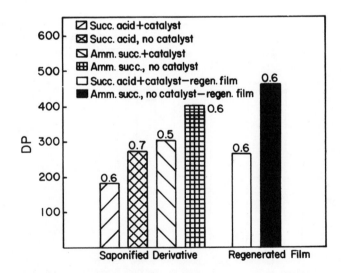

Figure 7.   Effect on DP of Rayselect-J of ammonium sulfamate catalyst and of the substitution of ammonium succinamate for succinamic acid

401 was obtained by removing the catalyst from ammonium succinamate, and still at a DS of 0.6. The DP
values of the regenerated films reflected the same
trend except they were a little higher due to the
fractionation that was noted during the coagulation
and washing steps. Highly significant was the fact
that the DP of the regenerated film produced from the
reaction of ammonium succinamate with wood pulp was
493, and almost as much as that of the starting wood
pulp.

The DP loss of wood cellulose as a function of
total DS in the reaction of wood pulp with succinamaic
acid is shown in Figure 8. Although the coefficients
of determination (r^2) indicate a relatively good fit,
the high degree of scatter can be accounted for by
virtue of the fact that the data were gathered over a
two-year period with four different wood pulps. The
plots show that DP loss with succinamic acid is less
without catalyst, but is still appreciable at higher
DS.

In Figure 9, DP loss with ammonium succinamate
with catalyst is almost identical to that of N,N-
diethyl succinamic acid without catalyst. Removal of
the catalyst from ammonium succinamate, results in
almost a complete levelling off of DP loss with increasing DS. Although there were only three points
in the latter plot, the value of r^2 was quite good.

Nitrogen and Sulfur Analysis. Nitrogen and
sulfur analyses were performed on the samples shown in
Table VI. The absence of significant sulfur content
in the sampes which had been catalyzed with ammonium
sulfamate catalyst indicates that the sulfur had not
combined chemically with the cellulose. The slightly
higher nitrogen content of the samples reacted with
ammonium succinamate indicated that some half-amide
ester (8) may have been produced.

Carboxyl Determinations. A comparison of carboxyl determinations by silver absorption and by calcium
acetate methods is given in Table VII. The determination of carboxyl content by the calcium acetate method
using Cramer's correction factor (8, 12) requires an
exact one gram of sample, whereas the determination of
carboxyl group by silver absorption was performed on
0.2 to 0.5 grams. Whenever sample size was a limitation, carboxyl content was determined by silver absorption. Sufficient quantities of the samples in Table
VII were produced to allow for a comparison of the two
methods. The silver absorption method was found to

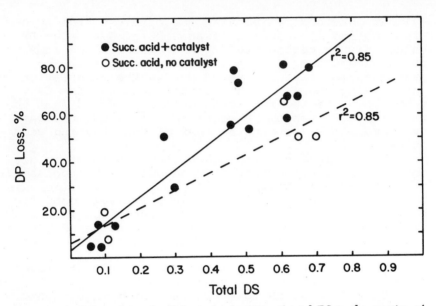

Figure 8. DP loss of wood cellulose as a function of total DS in the reaction of wood pulp with succinamic acid with and without ammonium sulfamate catalyst

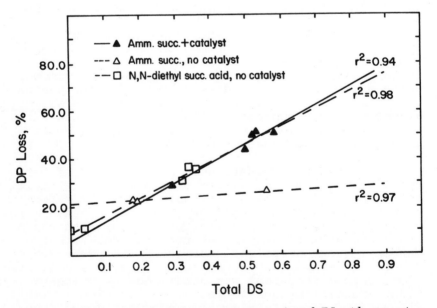

Figure 9. DP loss of wood cellulose as a function of total DS with ammonium succinamate with and without catalyst and with N,N-diethyl succinamic acid

Table VI. Nitrogen and sulfur analysis

Sample no.	Reactant	Catalyst	Experimental data	
			Nitrogen, %[a]	Sulfur, %[b]
27	54% succ. acid	X	< 0.2 < 0.2	< 0.2 < 0.2
39	61.9% amm. succ.	X	0.44 0.49	< 0.2 < 0.2
41	61.9% amm. succ.	no	0.38 0.30	< 0.2 < 0.2
43	N,N-diethyl melt	no	< 0.2 < 0.2	— —

Note: Pad-bake reactions performed on Rayselect-J pulp.

[a] Flash combustion technique.

[b] Schöniger test.

Table VII.

Comparison of carboxyl determinations by silver absorption and by calcium acetate methods

Sample no.	Silver absorption Free DS[a]	Calcium acetate Free DS[b]	(Silver abs. - Ca. Ac.) Free DS
22	0.53	0.46	0.07
24	0.45	0.41	0.04
28	0.46	0.46	0.00
30	0.54	0.47	0.07
33	0.47	0.43	0.04
35	0.56	0.48	0.08
37	0.24	0.23	0.01
52	0.08	0.08	0.00
53	0.10	0.10	0.00
54	0.08	0.08	0.00
55	0.09	0.09	0.00
56	0.06	0.06	0.00
57	0.09	0.08	0.01
		$\overline{X}$	$\overline{0.02}$

[a] Carboxyl content determined by absorption of silver from silver meta-nitrophenolate solutions (13)

[b] Carboxyl content determined by calcium acetate method (8, 12).

result in higher DS values - on the average of 0.02 higher than those of the calcium acetate method, however, the differences appeared to be greater with the higher degrees of reaction.

Plans for Future Work

Plans for future work are to perform pad-bake reactions of aqueous N,N-diethyl succinamic acid and N,N-diethyl ammonium succinamate on mercerized wood pulp. The use of liquid anhydrous ammonia because of its great swelling and plasticizing effects (31, 32, 33) on cellulose will also be investigated. The liquid ammonia itself will be considered as a solvent for the amic acid derivatives. In this application, the liquid ammonia could swell the cellulose, serve as a transport media for the amic acid, and be conveniently volatilized off as heat is applied in the bake step.

Summary

In the pad-bake reactions, total DS values of up to 0.70 were obtained in the reaction of succinamic acid with mercerized wood pulp and up to 0.58 DS was obtained in the treatment of pulp with 61.9% aqueous ammonium succinamate. The higher DS values obtained with succinamic acid reactant, however, were due to increased crosslinking; and consequently, the same limiting free DS of 0.5 was obtained with both succinamic acid and ammonium succinamate reactants. The pad-bake and Baratte reactions of N,N-diethyl succinamic acid with mercerized wood pulp resulted in free DS values of 0.34 and 0.31 respectively, with negligible crosslinking in both reactions. The Baratte reactions with succinamic acid and "never-dried" wood pulps yielded DS values of only approximately 0.1. This low extent of reaction was probably due to hydrolysis of succinamic acid to monoammonium succinate, which was favored under the Baratte conditions.

The problem of acessibility was apparent in all the reactions. With both succinamic acid and its ammonium salt, DS values obtained with the mercerized pulps were on the order of twice those obtained with the unmercerized pulps. With N,N-diethyl succinamic acid, pre-wetting the substrate prior to padding was found to make the difference between negligible reaction and an average DS of 0.34 on two mercerized pulps. The ammonium succinamate melts were very viscous and resulted in free DS values of 0.16 and

0.19 with dry and wet substrate, respectively, as
compared to 0.50 for the aqueous ammonium salt pad.
    The use of ammonium sulfamate catalyst was found
to be of little consequence for increasing the extent
of reaction, and was deleted from the pad baths without affecting free or crosslink DS; but was found to
be of major consequence in its effect on degrading
cellulose during the reaction. Significantly less
degradation occurred when the catalyst was removed
from the succinamic acid and ammonium succinamate
pad baths; nevertheless, upon removal of the catalyst
from both pad baths, succinamic acid still resulted in
appreciable degradation of the cellulose, whereas,
ammonium succinamate resulted in only minor degradation. Highly significant is the fact that ammonium
succinamate without catalyst and succinamic acid with
catalyst both resulted in a total DS of 0.6 and a
free DS of 0.5.
    Cellulose hemisuccinates prepared from succinamic
acid with catalyst and ammonium succinamate without
catalyst were dissolved at a concentration of 0.5% in
10% sodium hydroxide at -10°C. Determinations of
solubility were made with the naked eye. Films were
formed from the cellulose which was regenerated by the
addition of acetone to the solution. Infrared analyses
confirmed that the derivative had been saponified, as
was expected, and that the films were pure cellulose.
The DP of the film produced from the succinamic acid
plus catalyst reaction was 243, and was comparable to
that of the corresponding derivative; whereas, the DP
of the film produced from the ammonium succinamate
with no catalyst was 493, as compared to the unreacted
wood pulp DP of 544.

Acknowledgements

    We wish to express our appreciation to ITT
Rayonier, Inc. for funding this research and providing the wood pulps, and technical assistance; to
Dr. Bowman G. Bowman; to the faculty of the Department
of Wood and Paper Science, North Carolina State
University, and in particular, to Dr. Larry G. Griffin
for invaluable assistance. We wish also to thank the
Research Group of American Enka Company for their
technical advice and assistance.

Literature Cited

1. Goldstein, I. S., Science, (1975), 189, 847-852.
2. Davey, C. B., Prof. and Head, Forestry, N. C. State

University, Raleigh, North Carolina, Private
Communication (1976).

3. Handy, C. T., E. I. du Pont de Nemours and Co.,
Wilmington, Delaware, Private Communication (1976).

4. Cuculo, J. A., Professor, Textile Chemistry, N. C.
State University, Raleigh, N. C., Private Communication (1973).

5. Peters, R. H., Textile Chemistry, Vol. 1, 176-223,
Elsevier Publishing Co., New York (1963).

6. Cuculo, J. A., Textile Res. J., (1971), $\underline{41}$,
321-326.

7. Dagenhart, G. S., Unpublished Work (1976).

8. Allen, T. C. and J. A. Cuculo, "Cellulose Techno-
logy Research," ACS Symposium Series 10, Turbak,
Albin F., Ed., 51-74, American Chemical Society,
Washington (1975).

9. Bowman, B. G., Unpublished Work (1975).

10. Acton, W. P. ITT Rayonier, Inc., New York,
Private Communication (1974).

11. Haff, D. R., ITT Rayonier, Inc., New York,
Private Communication (1975).

12. Cramer, F. V., E. I. du Pont de Nemours and Co.,
Private Communication (1972).

13. Davidson, G. F. and T. P. Nevell, Shirley Inst.
Mem. , (1947), $\underline{21}$, 75-84.

14. Johnson, P. R., B. G. Bowman and J. A. Cuculo,
Textile Res. J., (1975), $\underline{45}$, 314-316.

15. Am. Soc. Testing Materials, Philadelphia, ASTM
Designation: D 1795-62 (Reapproved 1968), Part 21,
169-175.

16. Newman, S., L. Loeb and C. M. Conrad, J. Polym.
Sci., (1953), $\underline{10}$, 463-487.

17. Bowman, B. G., Ph.D. Dissertation, Department of
Textile Chemistry, North Carolina State University,
Raleigh, North Carolina (1975).

18. Bender, M. L., Y. Chow and F. Chloupak, J. Am.
Chem. Soc., (1958), $\underline{80}$, 5380-5384.

19. Bender, M. L., J. Am. Chem. Soc., (1960), $\underline{79}$,
1258-1259.

20. Bender, M. L., Chem. Rev., (1960), $\underline{60}$, 53-113.

21. Treiber, E., "Polymer Handbook," Brandrup, J. and
E. H. Immergut, Eds. V-98-V-100, John Wiley & Sons,
New York (1975).

22. Genung, L. B. and R. C. Mallatt, Ind. and Eng.
Chem., (1941), $\underline{13}$ (6), 369-374.

23. Johnson, E. H. and J. A. Cuculo, Textile Res. J.,
(1973), $\underline{43}$, 283-293.

24. Battista, S. C., J. A. Howsmon, F. F. Morehead and
W. A. Sisson, Ind. and Eng. Chem., (1956), $\underline{48}$ (2)
333-335.

25. Scallan, A. M., Textile Res. J., (1971), 41 647-653.

26. Allen, T. C. and J. A. Cuculo, "Proceedings of the Eight Cellulose Conference. III General Papers," Timell, T.E., Ed., 811-829, John Wiley & Sons, New York (1976).

27. Davidson, G. F., J. Textile Inst., (1934), 25, T 174-T196.

28. Davidson, G.F., J. Textile Inst., (1936), 27, T112-T130.

29. Davidson, G. F., J. Textile Inst., (1937), 28, T27-T44.

30. Rossner, U. Dtsch. Textiltech. (1966) 16 (5), 304-309.

31. Lewin, M. and L. G. Roldan, J. Polym. Sci., Part C, (1971), 36, 213-229.

32. Lewin, M., R. O. Rau and S. B. Sello, Textile Res. J., (1974), 44, 680-686.

33. Schleicher, H., C. Daniels and B. Philipp, J. Polym. Sci., Part C, (1974), 47, 251-260.

7

Hollow Fibers as Controlled Vapor Release Devices

T. W. BROOKS, E. ASHARE, and D. W. SWENSON

Conrel, An Albany International Co., 735 Providence Highway, Norwood, MA 02062

In recent years controlled release of active materials has emerged as a distinct technology in answer to a great many end-use needs in medicine, agriculture, forestry and the home. The subject has gained enough prominence to deserve a book (1), two international symposia (2), and a symposium scheduled for this centennial meeting of the American Chemical Society. A growing number of commercial products are based on controlled release formulations including such familiar items as time release oral medications, fragrance dispensing wicks and gels, and impregnated plastic pesticide strips or animal collars. Modern controlled release devices and systems such as impregnated plastic or rubber matrices, membrane envelopes, laminated poromerics and microcapsules testify to the growing level of sophistication being demanded of this technology to satisfy increasingly complex end-use requirements.

This paper will deal with the use of hollow polymeric synthetic fibers as a controlled release medium for dispensing vaporizable materials. The underlying principles of the hollow fiber approach to controlled release vapor dispensing will be discussed along with examples of how these principles can be applied to specific controlled release formulation needs and some results from actual field testing of hollow fiber dispensers for insect pheromones. In keeping with the spirit and intent of the symposium this paper provides an example of how man-made fiber technology is being wedded with other seemingly unrelated technologies to obtain products which hold promise in helping us manage our environment more responsibly.

Objectives of Controlled Release

Some of the more important objectives in developing controlled release product forms are (1) an extended period of activity for the released material, (2) longer use life for normally nonpersistent (unstable) active materials, (3) more efficient utilization of active materials, e.g., lower total dosages, (4) reduced environmental contamination, and (5) greater safety for the users of hazardous materials. Controlled release product forms meeting these objectives are becoming especially important in the pesticide field (2) where ecological considerations are dictating the abandonment of persistent materials, like the chlorinated hydrocarbons, in favor of less stable materials such as the organophosphate and carbamate insecticides. Other potential benefits of controlled release product forms include improved specificity of action on target organisms and enhanced economics of application. Thus, whatever the field of application, be it economic entomology, preventive and therapeutic medicine, or consumer products, the broad objective of controlled release is to improve the technical performance of an active material in an economical way.

Controlled Vapor Release From Hollow Fibers

Hollow fibers have been found to be a useful means of confining and mediating the controlled release of a variety of vaporizable materials. If a material is allowed to evaporate from the lumen of a hollow fiber sealed at one end and open at the other, the release curve, obtained by plotting mass released versus time, is characterized by an initial steep slope followed by an extended lower slope flat portion which approximates zero order release kinetics. This release behavior follows form with all vaporizable materials as long as they are single component or comprised of mixtures of components with comparable volatilities. Typical release curves are shown in Figure 1 for two insect pheromones and the insecticide DDVP (2,2-dichlorovinyl-0,0-dimethyl phosphate). The absolute rate of release for any given material is directly proportional to fiber internal diameter. At a given temperature release rates can be manipulated by adjustments in fiber internal diameter and the number of fibers employed. The active life for dispensing is a function of hollow fiber length, i.e., the length of the column of active material.

For design purposes only the flat portion of the release curve is used. The initial high rate or "burst effect" portion of the curve can usually be ignored since it represents only a small percentage of the total lumen charge and a relatively short period of the total dispensing life. The "burst effect" portion of the release curve for an active material can sometimes be eliminated by diluting the lumen charge with a high volatility inert. This ploy is frequently useful in dispenser designs where one wishes to dispense vapor mixtures having individual components with substantially different volatilities. Dilution can also be used to make short lived dispensers which otherwise would have to be made up in inconveniently short lengths.

Thus, for a given vaporizable material, hollow fiber controlled release dispensers can be formulated knowing only the release curve obtained with a particular fiber material and size at some specified temperature. Designing the dispenser to a specific release rate and lifetime is a simple matter of calculating the number of fiber ends needed to give the desired dose rate and the fiber length needed to achieve a prescribed life span.

The need to know the fiber material and internal diameter used in obtaining release curves deserves some explanation. It turns out that evaporation rates for many materials are sensitive to the diameter of the fiber lumen or capillary reservoir. That is, the vapor flux is not directly proportional to the square of the capillary radius for all liquid and fiber material combinations, as one might naively expect. In Table I are shown data which illustrate this phenomenon. Steady state release rates were measured on four different materials using 200 and 500 micron I.D. hollow fibers. Neutroleum-alpha is a commercial general purpose deodorizer formulation, while 4-methyl-3-heptanol (1), multistriatin (2), and a-cubebene (3) are compounds which comprise the three-com-

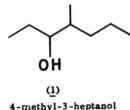

(1)
4-methyl-3-heptanol

(2)
multistriatin

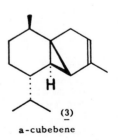

(3)
a-cubebene

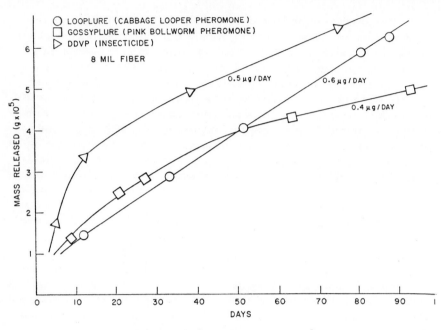

Figure 1.   Release of various materials

Table I

Comparison of Fluxes for Selected Materials
from Two Different Hollow Fiber Sizes[a]

Material	Flux, cm/day[b] 200μ I.D.	Flux, cm/day[b] 500μ I.D.	Flux Ratio 200μ: 500μ	Absolute Release Rate μg/day/end 200μ	Absolute Release Rate μg/day/end 500μ
Neutroleum-alpha[c]	1.8×10^{-2}	1.8×10^{-2}	1	5.9	37.4
cubeb oil[d]	5.8×10^{-3}	1.5×10^{-2}	2.6	1.9	30.5
multistriatin	2.1×10^{-2}	3.4×10^{-2}	1.6	6.8	69.6
4-methyl-3-heptanol	2.2×15^{-2}	3.16×10^{-2}	1.4	7.2	64.1

---

[a]Fiber material is undrawn polyester (polyethylene terephthalate). All
release measurements were made at 21 ± 1°C and 65 ± 5% relative humidity.

[b]The 200μ and 500μ fiber I.D.'s correspond to lumen cross-sectional areas
of 3.24×10^{-4} and $2.03 \times 10^{-3} cm^2$ respectively. This corresponds to a ratio
of the larger to the smaller cross-sectional area of 6.3.

[c]A proprietary general purpose deodorizer formulation comprised of a blend
of essential oils and aromatic chemicals. Marketed by Fritzsche Bros., Inc.,
New York.

[d]α-cubebene is a constituent which is extracted from the berry of the Java
pepper plant.

ponent aggregation pheromone of the smaller European elm bark beetle, Scolytus multistriatus (Marsham) (4). Comparison of fluxes of these materials from the two different sized fiber lumina reveals that release rate varies unpredictably with capillary diameter. Only with neutroleum-alpha did flux remain equal for the two diameters. With the three other materials flux ratios for 200 and 500μ diameters ranged from 1.4 to 2.6. Thus in going from the smaller to the larger diameter, release rate increased by more than the ratio of cross-sectional areas.

An explanation for this phenomenon probably lies in the surface energy relationships between the liquid charge and the fiber wall. It is known from classical physical chemistry that the vapor pressure above a liquid surface is dependent upon the radius of curvature of that surface. For different liquid-fiber material combinations the liquid meniscus-fiber wall contact angles will be different, and therefore the radii of curvature of the menisci will also differ. It is important to recognize the existence of this phenomenon when considering the design of hollow fiber controlled release formulations. In practice this subtle complication is avoided by measuring release curves with the fiber material and fiber internal diameter which will be used for a specific formulation. This is especially important with insect pheromones where biological dose-response relationships often dictate a very precise and constant release rate in order to make insect monitoring traps function properly.

Mechanism of Vapor Release from Hollow Fiber

The mechanism of vapor release from hollow fibers, if trans-wall permeation is excluded, is a simple three-step process.

1. Evaporation at the liquid-vapor interface.
2. Diffusion from the liquid-vapor interface to the open end of the hollow fiber.
3. Convection away from the open end.

A detailed discussion of the mass transport theory involved in this process is given elsewhere (3, 5). The release rate equation derived from the theory is

$$\frac{dl}{dt} = \frac{McD\,P_a^{vap}}{2\rho P}^{1/2} t^{-1/2}$$

where dl/dt, the change in meniscus level with time, is directly proportional to the dispensing rate, M is the molecular weight of the dispensed material, c is its molar density, D is the diffusion coefficient, ρ is the liquid density, P_a^{vap} is the vapor pressure of the volatile material, and P is the prevailing atmospheric pressure. The validity of the equation was examined using carbon tetrachloride as a model material. Figure 2 shows a logarithmic plot of evaporation rate versus time in which calculated and experimentally observed curves are displayed. The agreement between experiment and theory testifies quite well for the validity of the rate expression.

Release of material by permeation through the fiber wall is excluded from consideration for practical as well as theoretical reasons. In practice fiber materials are selected which are impermeable to the active material to be dispensed. This is necessary since the fiber must confine the active material during storage prior to activating release by opening the fiber end.

Hollow Fiber Controlled Release Product Forms

Controlled release vapor dispensers have been fashioned basically in two forms. In the first a parallel array of fibers is fixed to an adhesive tape. After pressure filling the active material into the fibers, the fibers are sealed ultrasonically at regular intervals along the tape. The active material must be in liquid form for the filling operation. Release is activated by cutting the tape at a point adjacent to the seals thereby opening fiber ends. A graphical illustration of this dispenser form is shown in Figure 3. This kind of dispenser is useful for the exact positioning of vapor point sources. Example uses might include the baiting of insect traps with an attractant, dispensing a vapor action insecticide to packages or containers of stored goods susceptible to insect attack, and deodorizing enclosed areas with air freshening fragrances or masking chemicals.

A second form of dispenser is made by sealing individual fibers at regular intervals and then chopping at a predetermined distance from the seal. This chopped fiber form is designed primarily for broadcasting vapor point sources over large areas. Charging chopped fibers with an active material is accomplished by immersing the fibers in the material, drawing a vacuum to remove air and other gases from the lumen, and then releasing the vacuum. Again, the

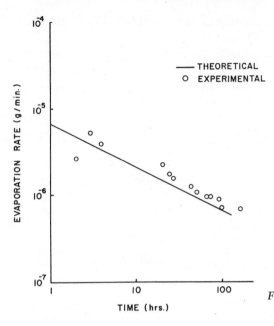

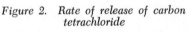

Figure 2. *Rate of release of carbon tetrachloride*

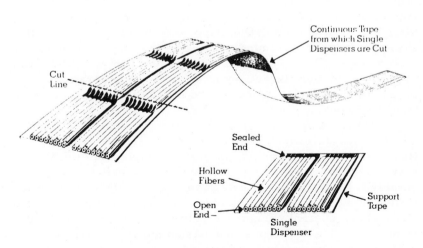

Figure 3. *Tape form hollow fiber vapor dispenser*

active material must be in a liquid form at the time of filling.
Chopped fibers charged with active material are stored in
hermetically sealed containers. Release is activated when the
container is opened. Example uses for the chopped fiber form
of hollow fiber dispenser would include broadcast dissemination
of insect sex attractant pheromones for mating disruption of
agricultural or forest insect pests (pheromones and pheromone
dispensing applications are discussed further below), insecticide dispensing, and possibly soil fumigation.

In both product forms, release rates are governed by
fiber size and the number of fiber ends while active life is
governed by fiber length. Which product form is preferred
for a given application is generally determined by the purpose
and the economics of the application.

The Application of Hollow Fiber Vapor Dispensing to Insect Pheromones

Insect pheromones are volatile organic compounds produced by insects for purposes of communication through their
highly developed olfactory sensory systems (6). These highly
specific chemical messengers serve to influence insect behavior in a variety of ways. Pheromones may function to
signal alarm, mating conduct, trail marks, oviposit, aggregation and specialized behavior in the regulation of social insect colonies. Sex attractant insect pheromones have been of
particular interest to entomologists since they raise the possibility of controlling pest insects by interdicting the sexual
communication which leads to mating and proliferation of populations (7, 8). If population suppression could be accomplished
with pheromones, of course, many of the environmental hazards associated with chemical insecticide control measures
might be avoided. Indeed environmental considerations have
been a motivating influence behind much of the research on insect pheromones.

Three basic strategies are being developed for the use of
pheromones in insect pest management. These are (1) monitoring and survey trapping, (2) mass trapping and (3) mating
disruption (8). In the first case pheromone baited traps are
employed to assist in the detection and location of infestations,
timing of insecticide applications, and monitoring of the effectiveness of control measures. The mass trapping stratagem
is designed to achieve pest population suppression by physi-
cally removing insects from the environment, a novel refine-

ment of the flypaper approach. In the mating disruption approach an area is permeated with sex pheromone in order to interfere with the insect's olfactory inter-sexual communication system. By thus subverting the mating and reproduction process it is hoped that population suppression can be achieved without resort to lethal agents.

The application of these pheromone use strategies is made a challenging task by two important factors. First, pheromones are frequently very expensive chemicals to synthesize. Those which are commercially available may cost anywhere from several hundred to several thousand dollars per pound. Second, pheromones typically possess a high order of biological activity and therefore are used in extremely minute quantities as compared, say, to conventional chemical insecticides. Application rates for mating disruption of lepidopterous species, for example, are on the order of grams per acre-season. For successful pheromone trapping the lure frequently must be metered out at a very precise rate. It is not uncommon for the optimum dose rate of a pheromone trap bait to be on the order of micrograms per day. An underdose can cause the trap to fail for lack of attractiveness while an overdose can lead to disorientation of an insect attracted to the vicinity of the trap so that he fails to find his way in. These factors necessitate a controlled release method of pheromone dispensing which is precise, reliable, and efficient. In many instances the development of pheromone technology for insect control and the development of controlled release technology have gone hand in hand. Without an adequate controlled release system it is doubtful that pheromones could ever be made sufficiently practical and economical for pest control use on a commercial scale.

Our investigations into insect pheromone dispensing with hollow fibers have involved work with more than twenty different insects. Out of this number three have been selected as illustrative examples of how the principles of hollow fiber vapor dispensing can be applied in various ways to the controlled release of pheromones.

Hollow fiber pheromone dispensers have been prepared and field tested for the trapping of the smaller European elm bark beetle, Scolytus multistriatus (Marsham), principle vector for the Dutch elm disease pathogen Ceratocystis ulni. The aggregation pheromone of the elm bark beetle is a mixture comprised of at least three compounds, 4-methyl-3-heptanol (1), 2,4-dimethyl-5-ethyl-6,8-dioxabicyclo (3.2.1) ocatane(2), and a-cubebene (a constituent of cubeb oil) (3). Compound (2) has been given the trivial name, multistriatin. The alcohol and multistriatin are beetle-produced while the a-cubebene is a host-produced synergist (4).

Release curves for the elm bark beetle pheromone constituents are shown in Figure 4. Note that release rates at steady state are nearly equal for the alcohol and multistriatin while the steady state release rate for cubeb oil, a much less volatile material, is significantly lower. At the time these experiments were conducted, the optimum release ratio for trapping baits was thought to be:

Cubeb oil	200µg/day
multistriatin	40µg/day
4-methyl-3-heptanol	40µg/day

From these specifications and the respective release curves dispensers were prepared with the following design features:

Cubeb oil	115 fiber ends
multistriatin	5 fiber ends
4-methyl-3-heptanol	5 fiber ends

All fibers were 3 cm in length which corresponds to a design life of 3 months using an overdesign factor of fifty percent. Overdesign of dispenser life is frequently practiced to guard against premature exhaustion in the field owing to unanticipated periods of exceptionally warm weather.

Dispensers with the above design were field tested in traps set out in Australia in early 1975 when U.S. beetle populations were dormant. The results of these trapping experiments are presented in Table II. The hollow fiber dispensers consistently out-captured beetles when compared to a polyethylene vial type of dispenser which is frequently employed by experimenters. Further, as the season progressed the hollow fiber dispensers improved in performance relative to the plastic vials. Since no data were collected after the fifth week, no comment can be made on total performance. The data do suggest however, that the hollow fiber dispensers adhered more closely to release design specifications than did the plastic vials. This, in turn, demonstrates the greater potential hollow fibers offer in designing dispensers for multicomponent pheromones. Most other controlled release devices lack the design flexibility afforded by the hollow fiber approach.

Experiments with elm bark beetle pheromone dispensers are continuing in the U.S. where it is hoped that spread of Dutch Elm disease can eventually be arrested by mass trapping of the beetle vector. The results of this work, including eval-

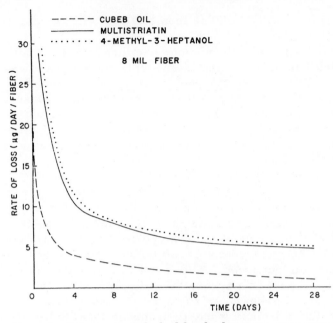

Figure 4.   Release rate of elm bark beetle pheromone components

Table II

Elm Bark Beetle Trapping Results
with Hollow Fiber Pheromone Dispensers

Trap No.	Trap Installed On Tree Species	Dispenser Type[b]	Beetle Catch on Dates (1975)			
			2/6	2/12	2/26	3/17
1	Eucalyptus saligna	PV	31	175	13	54
3[a]	Archontophoenix cunninghamiana	---	0	0	0	0
4	Ditto	HF	15	37	15	143
5	Nothofagus solanderi	PV	6	15	5	7
7	Ulmus procera	HF	3	35	53	112
8	Ditto	PV	17	99	35	193
9[a]	Prumus spp.	---	0	0	0	0
11	Ulmus procera	HF	18	144	8	220
12[a]	Quercus spp.	---	0	0	0	0
13	Eucalyptus calophylla	PV	4	5	1	9
14	Ulmus procera	HF	16	302	130	200
16	Cedrus deodara	PV	23	75	4	7
17	Ulmus procera	HF	210	786	209	990
19	Pinus radiata	PV	33	70	16	32
21[a]	Pinus ponderosa	---	0	0	0	0
22	Ulmus procera	HF	54	235	34	160
23[a]	Ditto	---	0	0	0	0
	Total Catches		430	1978	497	2127
	% of Total with HF Dispensers		73	78	90	86

[a]Control trees, traps installed without baits

[b]PV = polyethylene vials
HF = hollow fiber dispenser

uations of controlled release formulations will be reported by
other investigators (9).

A second insect pheromone chemical to which hollow fiber
dispensing has been applied is gossyplure, the sex attractant of
the pink bollworm, Pectinophora gossypiella (Saunders). The
pink bollworm is a major cotton pest in the U. S. Desert South-
west and in a number of Latin American countries where cotton
is grown. The use of pheromone baited traps to monitor for
this insect is becoming a common practice in cotton pest management programs.

Gossyplure is a 1:1 mixture of (Z, Z)-and (Z, E)-7, 11-
hexadecadienyl acetates (10). Its attracting power for male
moths is remarkable. The optimum dose rate for attraction of
pink bollworm males to a standard commercial trap is in the
range of 2.4 to 4. 0 μg/day. Gossyplure is one pheromone
which must be metered out carefully when used as a trap lure
for monitoring purposes. This point is illustrated in Figure 5.
The dose-response data were taken by field bioassay in a cotton field near Buckeye, Arizona, late in the 1974 growing season. Captured insects were all from the local wild population.
The plot of number of moths captured versus number of fibers
per trap bait shows an optimum dose rate of about 3.2 μg/day,
i. e. , eight fibers of 8 mil I. D. (200μ) (see Figure 1).

As the number of fibers is increased beyond the optimum,
trap catches drop off and tend to become erratic. This response
pattern makes it imperative that traps be baited with a pheromone dispenser that gives off a well-defined and constant dose
of the attractant. This is crucially important if the trapping
results are used for monitoring control programs.

The gossyplure experiment illustrates another useful
feature of hollow fiber controlled release devices. When a new
pheromone is isolated the entomologist often cannot specify an
optimum release rate for trap baiting since he lacks dose-
response data of the kind in Figure 5. Hollow fiber dispensers
make it convenient to obtain such data by field or laboratory
experimentation in which release rates are manipulated simply
by varying the number of fiber ends. This technique for obtaining dose-response data with pheromones promises to make
the whole process of developing such information a much easier
task.

A third example of a promising use for hollow fiber
pheromone dispensers can be drawn from a recent experiment
on disruption of the grape berry moth Paralobesia viteana
(Clemons). This insect is a very serious vineyard pest in many

of the Eastern U.S. grape growing areas. The sex pheromone of the grape berry moth is (Z)-9-dodecenyl acetate (11).

Multifiber dispensers of the pheromone were placed in a New York vineyard test plot, one per vine and 604 dispensers per acre. Individual dispensers each had nine fiber ends giving a total of 5445 fiber ends per acre. The design release rate was 3.5×10^{-7} cm^3 per day giving each point source an output of about 3.2×10^{-6} cm^3 per day. For 605 point sources and a 150-day season the nominal rate of application was 0.286g per acre-season. The true rate of application was 1.85 g per acre-season because it was necessary to make the fibers one cm in length. This length was arbitrarily chosen to make it convenient to handle dispensers in the field. The results of the grape berry moth disruption experiment are summarized in Table III. Note that orientation on pheromone baited traps was disrupted for a period of two and one-half months, after which the experiment was terminated. Disruption of E. argutanus was also observed for the same period of time. The latter insect is a local species of no economic consequence. The record of its disruption serves only as additional evidence that the technique is working. The grape berry moths in this test were lab-reared insects while E. argutanus were from the local wild population.

This is the first time, to our knowledge, that orientation disruption of a pest insect was achieved for a two and one-half month period with a single pheromone treatment. This fact, coupled with the very modest rate of application, clearly indicates that pheromone treatment with a reliable and economical controlled release system has commercial potential in agriculture. Tests planned for the 1976 season will be designed to ascertain whether disruption of the grape berry moth also protects the crop against insect-caused damage. Successful crop protection is the ultimate measure of economic value for any treatment method.

A more complete disclosure of the 1975 grape berry moth disruption experiments will be made in a separate publication by Taschenberg and Roelofs (12). These investigators conducted the disruption experiment and graciously provided us with the data in Table III, along with other background information.

Conclusion

The principles of controlled vapor release with hollow fibers have been demonstrated in a variety of ways. The con-

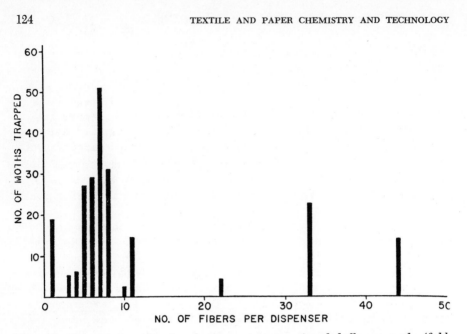

Figure 5. Dose-response data for pheromone trapping of pink bollworm moths (field bioassay)

Table III

Grape Berry Moth Orientation Disruption Tests
with Hollow Fiber Pheromone Dispensers - 1975[a]

Number of Males Captured in 6 Traps

Date		Treated Plot		Untreated Check Plot	
		GBM	E. Argutanus[b]	GBM	E. Argutanus
Jul	15	0	0	2	2
	20	0	0	19	45
	25	0	0	14	65
	30	0	0	7	39
Aug	6	2	2	28	199
	16	0	0	9	49
	26	0	1	11	26
Sept	5	0	0	15	8
	15	0	0	7	0
	25	0	0	11	0
Totals		2	3	123	433

[a] These data were gathered by Dr. E. F. Taschenberg, Vineyard Laboratory New York State Agricultural Experiment Station, Fredonia, New York.

[b] E. argutanus is a non-pest insect attracted by (Z)-9-dodecenyl acetate.

cept has been shown to have potential in specific applications
involving the use of insect pheromone for pest management
purposes. Based on the test results disclosed in this paper, it
is reasonable to expect that hollow fiber vapor dispensing will
find a number of commercial applications, some of which will
represent a substantial contribution to a safer and better environment.

Acknowledgements

The technical assistance of JoanEllen Hoar and Roger
Kitterman in preparing formulations and obtaining field test
data is gratefully acknowledged. We wish also to acknowledge
the invaluable contributions of E. F. Taschenberg and W.
Roelofs of the New York State Agricultural Experiment Station
who conducted the grape berry moth experiment, and J. W.
Peacock and R. A. Cuthbert of the U. S. Department of Agriculture Northeast Forest Experiment Station who arranged for
the elm bark beetle tests.

Literature Cited

(1) Tanquary, A. C., and Lacey, R. E., (eds.), "Controlled Release of Biologically Active Agents," Plenum Press,
New York (1974c).

(2) Cardarelli, N. F. (ed.), "Proceedings of the 1974
Controlled Release Pesticide Symposium," University of
Akron, Akron, Ohio, September 16-18, 1974; Harris, F. W.,
(ed.), "Proceedings of the 1975 Controlled Release Pesticide
Symposium," Wright State University, Dayton, Ohio, Septem-
ber 8-10, 1975.

(3) Ashare, E., Brooks, T. W., and Swenson, D. W.,
"Controlled Release from Hollow Fibers," Ibid., p. 42.

(4) Pearce, G. T., Gore, W. E., Silverstein, R. M.,
Peacock, J. W., Cuthbert, R. A., Lanier, G. N., and Simeone,
J. B., J. Chem Ecol., 1, 115 (1975).

(5) Ashare, E., Brooks, T. W., and Swenson, D. W.,
Paper presented at the American Chemical Society Centennial
Meeting, Joint Symposium on "Controlled Release Polymeric
Formulations," sponsored by Divisions of Polymer Chemistry
and Organic Coatings and Plastics Chemistry, New York,
April 19, 1976.

(6) Birch, M. C., Ed., Pheromones, Elsevier Pub. Co.,
New York (1974c).

(7) Jacobson, M., Insect Sex Pheromones, Academic Press, New York (1972c).

(8) Roelofs, W., "Manipulating Sex Pheromones for Insect Suppression" in Insecticides of the Future, Jacobsen, M., Ed., Marcel Dekker, Inc., New York (1975c) p. 41.

(9) Peacock, J.W. and Cuthbert, R.A., private communications.

(10) Hummel, H.E., Gaston, L.K., Shorey, H.H., Kaae, R.S., Byrne, K.J. and Silverstein, R.M., Science, 181 873 (1973).

(11) Roelofs, W.L., Tette, J.T., Taschenberg, E.F. and Comeau, A., J. Insect Physiol., 17, 2235 (1971).

(12) Taschenberg, E.F. and Roelofs, W. private communications.

Evolution of Man-Made Fibers

E. E. MAGAT and R. E. MORRISON

Pioneering Research Laboratory, Textile Fibers Department,
E. I. du Pont de Nemours & Co., Inc., Wilmington, DE 19898

Let us take a short trip through what may be called the golden age of man-made fibers. This review of man-made fibers deals only with fibers prepared from organic intermediates and does not include fibers spun from cellulosic derivatives. It all started with the discovery and commercialization of nylon in 1940 and reached the point today where noncellulosic man-made fibers account for more than half of the total fiber consumption and are expected to reach about two-thirds by 1980 in the United States.

The scenario can be divided into four phases:

Phase 1 - 1940-1950 - Development of nylon and intensive exploration for new fiber-forming polymers.

Phase 2 - 1950-1956 - Introduction and commercialization of major man-made fibers beyond nylon.

Phase 3 - 1956- - Development of second generation fibers.

Phase 4 - 1960- - Development of specialty fibers.

Research on the last two phases is still going strong today.

Phase I

With the discovery of nylon and its commercial introduction, fiber research all over the world shifted to a search for other synthetic polymers capable of forming fibers. Initially, the objectives

were twofold.
  (1)   To duplicate the properties and feel of
        natural fibers, the resilience of wool, the
        luxury of silk and the versatility of cotton.
  (2)   To develop a relationship between fiber
        structure and chemical composition with fiber
        properties.

Literally hundreds of polymers were prepared
during this period and spun by the new melt spinning
process specifically developed for nylon and by wet or
dry spinning used for cellulosic derivatives.

The first target met by nylon was the silk
hosiery market leading ultimately to nylon monofil
hosiery. Following the overwhelming acceptance of
nylon hosiery a second "natural" end-use was tricot
capitalizing on its excellent knittability and durability resulting in penetration of a major rayon and
acetate stronghold. Another major penetration was in
tire cord based on nylon's high strength, impact
resistance and ability to withstand repeated flexing
and stresses.

A variety of other polyamides were examined and
except for 6 nylon which was developed in Germany, 6-6
nylon emerged as the major polyamide candidate from
this era.

Research turned in the direction of polyesters
and vinyl polymers. Two major fibers emerged from
this intensive search, poly(ethylene terephthalate)
and polyacrylonitrile. Building on Carothers' work
the discovery of poly(ethylene terephthalate) fibers
by Whinfield and Dixon in England opened the door to a
new fiber which could utilize much of the melt spinning
technology developed for nylon. The polyacrylonitrile
breakthrough came with the discovery of a solvent which
could dissolve this heretofore intractable polymer and
thus yield spinnable polymer dopes.

With the preparation of hundreds of polyamides,
polyesters and polyacrylics, a sound basis for
correlating structure and fiber properties was established, opening the door to Phase II.

Phase II

As we approached 1950, the growth of man-made
fibers was proceeding at a very rapid pace. Three
nylon plants were already in operation. Polyacrylonitrile fibers introduced as Orlon® started as continuous filament yarn in 1950 and staple in 1952. The
first commercial Dacron® polyester plant went into
operation in 1953.

The objective continued to be the penetration of
existing markets. The versatility of polyester soon
became apparent leading to fibers which simulated wool,
cotton or rayon depending upon processing conditions.
Polyacrylics showed many of the characteristics of
wool and found rapid acceptance in sweaters, carpets
and blankets. It is indeed remarkable that the search
for wool-like fibers initially centered on polyamides
and polypeptides turned out to be best met by polyesters and polyacrylics which have none of the chemical
characteristics of wool.

In the mid-50's the discoveries of Ziegler and
Natta opened the door to isotactic polypropylene which
emerged as the major polyolefin fiber candidate and
became the fourth major fiber.

Intensive research and evaluation of these four
fibers led to fabrics with unique characteristics far
exceeding those of fabrics from natural fibers. The
most striking of these are:

(1) wash-wear
(2) resistance to wrinkling and recovery from
     wrinkling
(3) durability
(4) heat settability.

These unusual properties opened entirely new end-use
areas and provided the springboard for further growth
of the four major fibers.

The first two characteristics stem from the outstanding recovery properties of polyester fibers, both
wet and dry. For the first time some garments could
be worn all day in dry and wet weather without
excessive wrinkling. Wrinkles introduced during
washing could be removed simply by tumbling the

garments in a dryer. These properties could be
achieved not only with polyester alone but with blends
of polyesters with cotton and wool. Blending of polyester with resin-treated cotton provided the degree of
fabric strengthening which made the permanent-press
concept possible.

Durability of nylon and polyesters provided a new
order of magnitude to longevity of wearing apparel.
Boys' jeans could finally be outworn rather than worn
out. The durability of nylon carpets is indeed
remarkable and unmatched by any fiber.

Heat settability turned out to be a very important
attribute. Heat setting of nylon and polyester fibers
and fabrics imparts a memory of their original conformation. It started with the discovery of pre-
boarding of hosiery leading to seamless hose, spread
to permanent pleats and creases and now is the basis
of the enormous textured continuous filament yarn
market.

Phase III

Having established a sound basis with nylon,
polyester, polyacrylics and polyolefin fibers,
research shifted into a new direction. In 1956 we
entered into the era of molecular engineering as
coined by Prof. Mark. By appropriate chemical and
physical modification one was able to prepare second
generation fibers with tailor-made characteristics.
Fibers were developed based on the same basic materials
and chemistry as the parent fiber but offering novel
properties, aesthetics and performance. These technological advances have opened huge new markets and
have steadily increased demand for man-made fibers.

The general pattern was to develop building
blocks which could be superimposed on conventional
fiber technology.

Physical modification has opened up very large
markets where bulk, texture and luster were prime requirements. Improved bulk and texture were achieved
by thermal or mechanical texturing using processes
such as false twist or jet texturing. Self-crimping
yarns were obtained by combining polymers with

different shrinkage characteristics in bicomponent fibers or in mixed shrinkage yarns. These yielded fabrics with attractive aesthetics and bulk. Cross-section modification provided fabrics with an attractive luster and tactile aesthetics. Some cross-section options are shown in Fig. 1. In the field of industrial yarns, new drawing processes and crystallization sequences have led to fibers with novel morphology giving yarns with improved stability and tensile properties.

Chemical modification has added a great deal of versatility to all four basic fibers and provided solutions to major end-use limitations. This can be illustrated by examining some of the effects obtained by chemical modification of nylon. Similar advances have been made in polyesters and polyacrylics. Major advances in nylon technology are shown in Table I. Higher molecular weight has led to stronger and tougher fibers. On the other hand, lower molecular weight leads to more brittle fibers which exhibit improved pill resistance in staple fabrics. Incorporation of acidic and basic dye sites had led to increased dye versatility; antioxidants (e.g., copper and manganese salts) to better heat and light durability; antistatic modifiers to freedom from static and in some cases soil resistance through soil hiding.

Sites for acid dyes are readily controlled by changing the balance of amine and carboxyl ends in nylon. Sites for basic dyes are incorporated by co-polymerizing, for example, a small amount of sulfoisophthalic acid in place of adipic acid. When fibers with different dyeabilities are combined in one single fiber, multicolor effects can be achieved by dyeing the fabric in one single dye bath. A striking illustration is the "Sunburst" carpet containing fibers with four levels of dye affinity dyed in one single dye bath containing three types of dyes.

Research on fiber modifications is still continuing and we are witnessing the beginning of third generation fibers. An example of a fiber combining many of the most desirable building blocks is the development of Qiana® nylon which exemplifies the

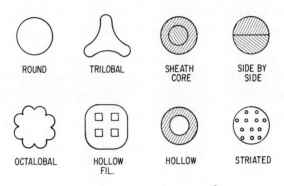

Figure 1. Cross-section versatility

TABLE I

POLYMER MODIFICATION

HIGHER MOLECULAR WEIGHT	STRONGER FIBERS
INCORPORATION OF ACIDIC AND BASIC DYE SITES	DYE VERSATILITY
ANTIOXIDANTS	HEAT DURABILITY LIGHT DURABILITY
ANTISTATIC MODIFIERS	FREEDOM FROM STATIC (SOIL HIDING)

purposeful combination of chemical and physical modifications to yield high performance self-bulking fibers. The polymer base for this polyamide which contains cyclohexane rings is designed to give high recovery properties and a high glass transition temperature far exceeding temperatures encountered in apparel end-uses. These properties account for the outstanding ease-of-care characteristics for garments of Qiana®. The self-bulking feature of Qiana® is the result of a finely tuned combination of polymer modifications and spinning technology by which some filaments in a yarn bundle have higher shrinkage than others. This shrinkage is triggered during fabric finishing, providing fabrics with a rich handle and a bulky feel as well as a myriad of interfilament capillary spaces that bring about wearer comfort. Another facet of physical modification in Qiana® is the fiber shape and the particulate additive that gives a silk-like pearlescent luster without chalkiness.

Another direction for the development of new generation fibers is the preparation of sheet structures by a process integrated with fiber spinning. This is the basis of spunbonded technology where multiple yarns are spun and laid down directly as a sheet structure or nonwoven fabric. This technology has been applied to polyethylene in Tyvek® where extremely fine fibers are interconnected in a continuous network, to polyester in Reemay® where a web of continuous filament yarns is bonded with a bonding agent and to polypropylene in Typar® where a web of coarse fibers is self-bonded.

As we complete the survey of major fibers and their second and third generation derivatives, let us take a look at the growth of man-made fibers during this initial 36 year period. The over-all picture is shown in Fig. 2. It took 30 years from introduction for the noncellulosics to catch up with cotton. In 1976 their volume is expected to be twice that of cotton. By 1980 in the United States alone shipments are expected to exceed 10 billion lbs. of noncellulosic man-made fibers as compared to 4 billion lbs. of natural fibers.

Table II shows how fast the four major fibers have
grown. Polyester is by far the fastest growing fiber
and is now second only to cotton. By 1979 it is
expected to be the number one fiber in textiles. At
these high volumes the advantages of large-scale manufacture become highly significant and enhance the
favorable competitive position of these four fibers.
The carpet industry is a good example where a fiber
started competing with wool and has now increased the
total market by several orders of magnitude. In 1976
carpets will use 1.2 billion lbs. of nylon vs. 16
million lbs. of wool. In these inflationary times the
price trend of man-made fibers is quite remarkable.
The price of polyester as compared to cotton is illustrated in Fig. 3. For a short time in 1974 polyester
staple was actually cheaper than cotton. Today they
are about equivalent, thus providing a strong driving
force for expanded use of polyester staple where performance is at a premium.

Phase IV

At about the same time as the development of
second generation fibers, research attention shifted
to fibers with an entirely different set of properties
which cannot be achieved by chemical or physical modification of the four basic generic fiber systems.
These fibers are sometimes referred to as specialty
fibers because they do not have the broad utility of
polyesters, polyacrylics, polyolefins, and polyamides
but yet they are specifically designed to fill an
important market need. Markets for these specialty
fibers are in the tens of millions of lbs. in contrast
to hundreds of millions of lbs. for the basic fibers.

Here again the initial research pattern was to
duplicate properties of fibers from basic materials
such as rubber, glass and steel or achieve extreme
performance characteristics such as heat resistance,
flame resistance and chemical resistance.

Each of these represents a development story in
itself. Each new product is the outcome of an intensive search for the desired properties, understanding

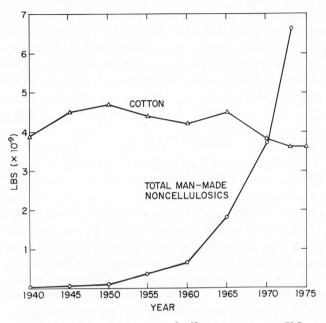

Figure 2. Growth of man-made fibers vs. cotton in U.S.

TABLE II

GROWTH OF MAJOR FIBERS (U.S.)

(MM LBS.)

	NYLON	POLYESTER	ACRYLIC	OLEFIN
1950	90	0	1	0
1960	411	75	135	14
1970	1354	1465	491	255
1976 (PROJ.)	2000	3000	600	500

(COTTON: 3600)

of the mechanical properties desired and correlation
between fiber chemical and physical structure with
fiber properties. This discussion will be limited to
four types of fibers which have reached the commercial
stage: high temperature resistant fibers, chemically
resistant fibers, elastic fibers and reinforcing
fibers.

High Temperature Resistant Fibers

The four major fibers have a maximum use temperature well below 200°C. For a number of industrial and
apparel end-uses fibers are needed which can perform
for extended periods of time at temperatures ranging
between 200° and 400°C. Extensive research has been
carried out over the past ten years aimed at defining
the relationships between polymer structure and thermal stability. The most promising heat-resistant
fiber candidates are aromatic polymers where benzene
rings are linked by amide, imide and imidazole
linkages. Typical chemical reactions for preparing
these products and fiber properties are shown in
Table III. Starting with an aromatic diamine and an
aromatic dibasic acid chloride, one obtains aromatic
polyamides. If one starts with a tetramine and the
diphenyl ester of a dicarboxylic acid, polybenzimida-
zoles are obtained. If one uses a diamine with an
aromatic acid dianhydride, the product is a polyimide;
and finally, if a tetramine is used with a bis
anhydride or a tetracarboxylic acid, a ladder polymer
is obtained which combines the properties of a
benzimidazole and an amide in a condensed heterocyclic
structure.

The major commercial fiber in this end-use is
Nomex® aramid which was introduced commercially in
1961. It is prepared by solution polymerization of a
dibasic acid chloride with an aromatic diamine
followed by solution spinning from an amide solvent.

Related to heat resistance a highly desirable goal
is flame resistance. In certain end-uses flame resistance requirements are so severe that performance
needs cannot be fully met by conventional polyacrylic,
nylon and polyester fibers even after they are flame

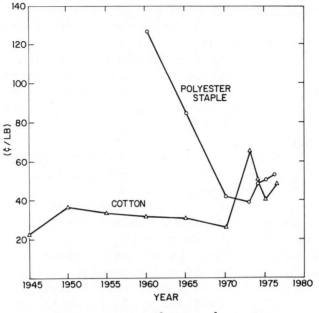

Figure 3.   Prices of polyester staple vs. cotton

TABLE III

HEAT RESISTANT FIBERS

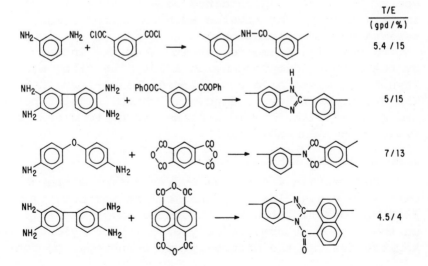

retarded. These end-uses dictate fibers with polymer
structures which are difficult to ignite and stable to
relatively high temperatures.

Nomex® meets this requirement to a high degree.
Fibers are difficult to ignite, generate little smoke
and are self-extinguishing. As a result of its flame
resistance, Nomex® is now being extensively used in
protective clothing for military and industrial uses,
and in carpeting and upholstery in aircraft. Protection from flame by Nomex® is the result of a unique
fiber and fabric behavior which produces a thick protective char upon exposure to a flame.

In certain catastrophic flame exposures such as
total immersion in flames, lightweight fabrics of
Nomex® shrink and break open thus protection beyond
that offered by Nomex® is desired. Under these
extreme exposure conditions short-term total insulation
from extremely high heat flux is the key.

Du Pont has developed a new fiber to supplement
Nomex® for such uses which is now referred to as
Nomex® III. This fiber introduced in 1971 is based on
a new aromatic polyamide and on new spinning technology. When subjected to high heat flux, Nomex® III
fabrics maintain strength, do not break open and
exhibit very low shrinkage, thereby maintaining an air
insulating layer. The protection characteristics of
Nomex® III have been obtained with no sacrifice of
important fabric attributes such as comfort, abrasion
resistance and coloration.

A new high flame resistant fiber was introduced
by the Carborundum Company in 1970. The fiber named
"Kynol" is based on a crosslinked phenol-formaldehyde.
The precursor fiber is a novolac which is later post-
crosslinked with formaldehyde and cured to give a non-
fusible, nonflammable fiber.

Chemically Resistant Fibers

For certain industrial end-uses fibers are needed
with a very high level of chemical resistance. In
1960 Teflon® fibers were introduced which capitalized
on the high inertness of polytetrafluoroethylene. The
key advance was the discovery of technology for con-

verting an intractable polymer such as polytetrafluoroethylene into a fiber. A process based on wet spinning
of Teflon® dispersed in a viscose solution followed by
heat coalescence of the Teflon® dispersion was
developed and put to commercial use.

Elastic Fibers

In the search for a sheer, strong and stable
elastic fiber the key finding was that elastic fibers
could be prepared from linear non-crosslinked polymers.
Thus, one would not have to resort to crosslinking as
in conventional rubber. The essential feature of
polymers giving elastic fibers without crosslinking is
their segmented nature. They consist of alternating
segments or blocks of "hard" high melting polymers
with "soft" amorphous polymers. The hard segment
domains dispersed in a soft segment matrix act as reinforcing filler particles to give an elastomer of high
toughness. Following an extensive program aimed at
defining the best block composition, polyurethanes were
selected as giving the best balance of product properties and processibility. In 1958 Lycra® was introduced utilizing a polyether as the soft segment. The
general scheme for preparing this type of fiber is
shown in Table IV. To form the hard block, the soft
segment is end-capped with an excess of aromatic diisocyanate to give an isocyanate terminated prepolymer.
The final step in preparing the segmented polyurethane
is the synthesis of the hard segment by chain extension
with hydrazine or a diamine. The final reaction
product is a high molecular weight polymer having
hydrogen bonding sites in the form of urethane or urea
linkages. These polymers are soluble in amide
solvents and fibers can readily be prepared by dry
spinning.
This general pattern of elastic fiber formation
has been refined over the years using optimum soft
segment structures of polyethers and polyesters,
aromatic diisocyanates and a variety of chain ex-
tenders. This has resulted in fibers of improved
functional and mechanical properties including improved
color, hydrolytic stability and UV stability, high

TABLE IV

Soft Segment

Macroglycol

$$H\left[O-CH_2CH_2CH_2-CH_2\right]_n OH$$

MW ~ 2000

End Capping

$$+ \; OCN-R-NCO$$

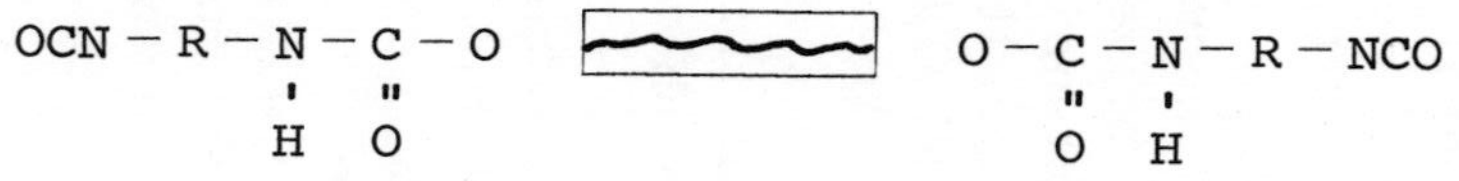

$$OCN-R-\underset{\underset{H}{|}}{N}-\underset{\overset{\|}{O}}{C}-O-\boxed{\sim\!\!\sim}-O-\underset{\overset{\|}{O}}{C}-\underset{\underset{H}{|}}{N}-R-NCO$$

Chain Extension

$$+ \; H_2N-R'-NH_2$$

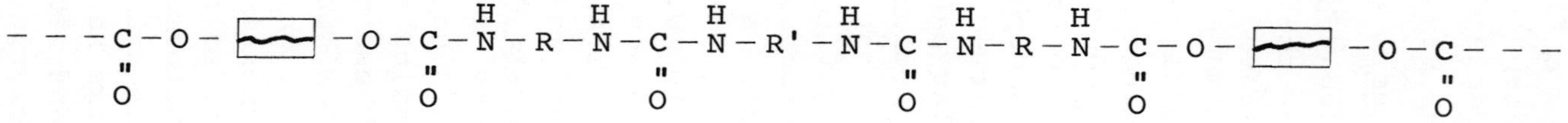

$$-\underset{\overset{\|}{O}}{C}-O-\boxed{\sim\!\!\sim}-O-\underset{\overset{\|}{O}}{C}-\underset{\underset{H}{|}}{N}-R-\underset{\underset{H}{|}}{N}-\underset{\overset{\|}{O}}{C}-N-R'-\underset{\underset{H}{|}}{N}-\underset{\overset{\|}{O}}{C}-\underset{\underset{H}{|}}{N}-R-\underset{\underset{H}{|}}{N}-\underset{\overset{\|}{O}}{C}-O-\boxed{\sim\!\!\sim}-O-\underset{\overset{\|}{O}}{C}-$$

power, high elongation and high recovery.

Reinforcing Fibers

A rapidly expanding market for continuous filament fibers is the reinforcement of rubber and resins. The reinforcement of rubber for tires is a well-established technology and provides one of the largest markets for fibers. Organic fibers have dominated the tire reinforcement field, starting with cotton and progressing through a series of synthetic fibers including rayon, nylon and polyester. In general these fibers were engineered for textile applications but were subsequently adapted by special processing to make them suitable for tires. The advent of radial tires has led to stringent new performance demands which could not be met with existing organic fibers. Glass and steel provided the required stiffness for tire belts and rapidly captured this market. While glass and steel contribute some of the desired properties, they also have their limitations. The introduction of a new high tenacity, high modulus man-made organic fiber, Kevlar® aramid, has provided new levels of properties ideally suited for tires, thus affording an organic fiber alternative to glass or steel.

Stress-strain curves of major tire reinforcement fibers are shown in Fig. 4. The high strength and modulus of Kevlar® combined with its low density provides a strong margin of superiority. Tensile strength-modulus relationships for tire fibers are graphically shown in Fig. 5. On the basis of strength, 1 lb. of Kevlar® can replace 2 lbs. of glass, nylon or polyester, or 5 lbs. of wire. Tensile strength is only one consideration in selecting a tire yarn. For belt yarns high stiffness is of major importance. The tire yarn must also offer a good balance of adhesion, flex life and ease of processibility. Kevlar® meets these requirements to a remarkable degree.

Reinforcement of resins by continuous filament fibers is receiving increased attention as the basis of the rapidly growing technology of advanced composites. Reinforcement of thermosetting resins to yield advanced composites initially started with con-

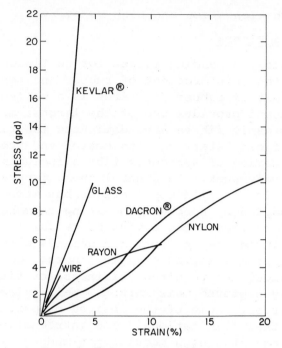

Figure 4.   Tire yarn stress–strain curves

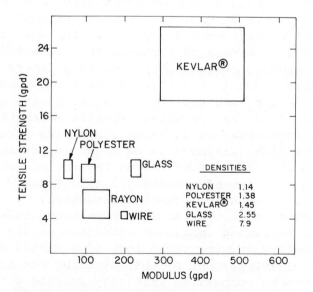

Figure 5.   Tensile strength–modulus relations for tire
fibers

tinuous filament glass. The major goal is a high
ratio of tensile strength-to-weight and a high ratio
of stiffness-to-weight to achieve the properties of
structural metals at lower weights. While glass is
quite strong, it is somewhat deficient in stiffness.
High modulus fibers of graphite and boron have sparked
a materials/design revolution by offering the possibility of preparing advanced composites matching the
properties of metals at considerably lower weights.
With the introduction of a variant of Kevlar® named
Kevlar® 49, organic fibers now compete directly with
inorganic fibers in this application. Comparative
stress-strain curves of these fibers are shown in
Fig. 6 where psi engineering units are used to compare
tensile strengths of fibers of equal cross-section. A
more realistic comparison of these fibers for advanced
composites is to plot specific strength vs. specific
stiffness as shown in Fig. 7. These values reflect
tensile properties at equal weight.

The third area of fiber reinforcement using metals
as the matrix is still in its infancy. The drive is to
incorporate high tenacity, stiff fibers in metals such
as aluminum to increase stiffness-to-weight ratio and
to improve retention of properties at elevated temperatures. Here graphite and boron continuous filament
fibers are being explored intensively as well as
experimental alumina fibers.

Let us take a quick look at the preparation and
properties of graphite and Kevlar® fibers. Graphite
fibers are prepared by thermal decomposition of a
polymeric precursor to carbon followed by high temperature conversion to graphite. Cellulose and polyacrylonitrile have provided the main source of carbon
fibers. Fig. 8 illustrates the properties obtained
upon conversion of polyacrylonitrile (PAN) continuous-
filament yarns to graphite yarns. Three process steps
are involved: thermal pretreatment, carbonization and
high-temperature treatment. In the first step the PAN
is converted to a flameproof structure originally
known as black Orlon®. Carbon fibers made by the PAN
process reach their highest tensile strength when
heated to 1400-1800°C (Graphite HT). There is direct

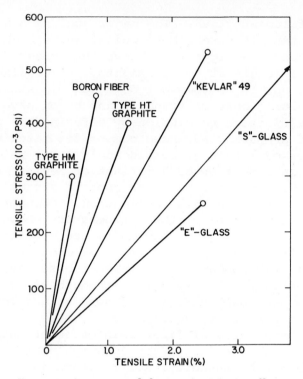

Figure 6. Stress–strain behavior of reinforcing fibers

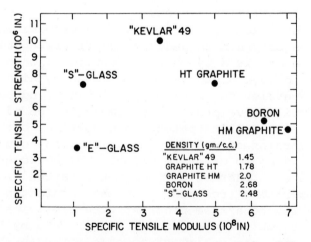

*Figure 7. Specific tensile strength and specific tensile
modulus of reinforcing fibers*

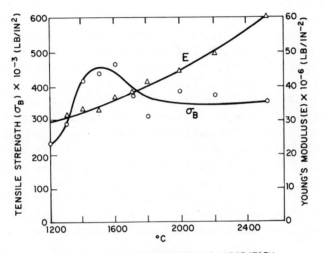

EZEKIEL, H.M., AIR FORCE MATERIALS LABORATORY,
TR−70−100, JANUARY 1971

*Figure 8.   Effect of heat treatment temperature on the mechanical
properties of carbon fibers at room temperature*

correlation between stretching in the pretreatment
stage and tensile strength after carbonization. If the
process incorporates high temperature treatment and
stretching at 2400–2500°C, high modulus fibers
(Graphite HM) are obtained with a somewhat lower
tensile strength. More recently, pitch fibers have
been receiving attention as a potentially economical
route to graphite fibers.

Kevlar® is a fiber from a highly rigid para-
oriented aromatic polyamide prepared by a novel
spinning process which favors alignment of extended
rigid polymer chains, high crystallinity and a high
degree of structural perfection. The fibers have a Tg
(glass transition temperature) above 300°C and can be
heated without decomposition or melting to temperatures
exceeding 500°C. Dimensional stability is outstanding,
with essentially no shrinkage or creep at temperatures
as high as 200°C. Rigid p-oriented aromatic polyamides give liquid crystalline polymer solutions which
upon spinning yield directly highly oriented fibers.
Because of the extended chain and high crystallinity
characteristics of these fibers no further drawing is
needed.

Let us now consider some of the end-uses projected
for Kevlar®. Beyond tire yarns Kevlar® is available
in two types of reinforcing fibers called Kevlar® 29
and Kevlar® 49. The first of these is finding increasing uses in ropes and cables which are as strong
as steel at one-fifth the weight and in protective
garments such as ballistic vests. In recent months
law enforcement officers have reported nine instances
where body armor of Kevlar® 29 has prevented serious
injury or death from gunshot. Kevlar® 49 is now being
used to reinforce resins for aerospace structures,
boat hulls including canoes and kayaks, and sport
equipment such as skis, tennis racquets and golf clubs.

With the attainment of extremely high tensile and
modulus properties with Kevlar®, we are reaching a
range well beyond that achievable heretofore with
organic fibers; and we ask ourselves what are the
limits of strength and stiffness attainable with
organic fibers. The maximum cohesive force in a

polymer such as polyethylene would correspond to rupture of C–C bonds in a polymer where all polyethylene chains are packed parallel to each other. Knowing the C–C dissociation energy and the crystal packing of polyethylene one calculates a maximum strength corresponding to 250 gpd. This maximum value would be realized only if packing of the molecules were completely uniform and regularly arranged without flaws or discontinuities. The highest values reported for highly oriented and crystalline polyethylene filaments is 23 gpd corresponding to a strength smaller than maximum by a factor of 11. This discrepancy has been ascribed to a number of factors: (a) chains are not perfectly parallel and do not break simultaneously over the same cross-section, (b) imperfections in the structure and chain ends lead to stress concentration on a statistically favored few chemical bonds which are then ruptured. This initial crack propagates catastrophically leading to fiber breakage.

Using similar principles on other polymers, maximum tenacity values have been calculated for polymers as shown in Table V.

The subject of ultimate modulus attainable with organic polymers has received considerable study starting with the work of Prof. Mark. Two techniques have been used. One relies on calculations based on force constants of bonds in the polymer chain and the other on crystal lattice extensions observed by x-ray on stressed fibers. In Table VI observed moduli are compared with values calculated by Treloar and Fielding-Russell. The spread between theoretical and actual values is considerably narrower than for ultimate tensile strengths. For p-oriented aromatic polyamides the theoretical limit of stiffness is almost reached.

Future of Man-Made Fibers

Where do we stand today? Man-made fibers have now achieved a status which looked barely possible when nylon was introduced in 1940. Properties of man-made fibers range from low modulus, high elongation fibers like spandex to high modulus, high tenacity

TABLE V

MAXIMUM TENACITY VALUES FOR FIBERS

	THEORETICAL	REF.	ACTUAL	REF.
POLYETHYLENE	250 gpd	(1)	23	(2)
POLYESTER 2G-T	200		10	
POLYAMIDE 66	215		10	
p-ORIENTED AROMATIC POLYAMIDE	165		(~28)	

(1) Tobolsky and Mark (1971).
(2) Black and Preston (1973).

TABLE VI

MAXIMUM MODULUS VALUES FOR FIBERS

(IN/GPD)

	THEORETICAL	REF.	ACTUAL	REF.
POLYETHYLENE	2060	(1)	430	(3)
POLYAMIDE 66	1780	(1)	50	
POLYESTER 2G–T	950	(1)	150	
CELLULOSE	400	(1)	200	
m-ORIENTED AROMATIC POLYAMIDE	950	(2)	175	
p-ORIENTED AROMATIC POLYAMIDE	1500	(2)	1400	

(1) Black, W.B. and Preston, J., "High-Modulus Wholly Aromatic Fibers", Marcel Dekker, Inc., N.Y., 1973, p. 13.
(2) Loc. Cit., p. 21.
(3) Loc. Cit., p. 35.

fibers exemplified by Kevlar®. In between, almost any
combination of properties can be engineered.

The outlook for continued growth and advances in
man-made fibers continues to be highly promising.

Emphasis will be to improve our major polyester,
polyamide, polyacrylic and polyolefin fibers to provide
still better aesthetics, comfort, dye versatility and
ease-of-care performance.

The search for specialty fibers will continue with
the goal of identifying limits of performance attainable with man-made fibers. Developing a new fiber is
a very expensive and lengthy undertaking. Demon-
strating one single outstanding property is not enough;
the fiber to be successful must be cost-competitive,
must have a good balance of properties and be free of
any major negative under end-use conditions.

As fibers with entirely new levels of combinations
of properties are developed, their impact will spread
beyond textiles. We are just beginning to capitalize
on the possibilities opened up by fiber reinforcement.
A breakthrough in fiber strength and stiffness has
been achieved with Kevlar® and graphite fibers. With
the availability of these new fibers a new material
science technology will evolve allowing designers and
engineers new degrees of freedom leading to entirely
new limits of technological feasibility.

Fibers already have been developed for entirely
new end-uses such as optical fibers, hollow fibers as
semipermeable membranes, and low density pneumatic
fibers of the type used in "Pneumacel" cushioning
materials.

The future of man-made fibers will depend in a
great degree on research accomplishments by fiber
producers and the textile industry. Short of unexpected breakthroughs, prospects are for a long period
of evolutionary growth to reach the full potential of
polyesters, polyamides, polyacrylics, and polyolefins.

Dyeing and Finishing

Nonfuming Spin Finishes

WARREN A. SCOTT

ICI United States Inc., Wilmington, DE 19897

The recent impact of OSHA on the textile industry has greatly influenced changes in typical requirements for textile finishes. One of the more dramatic changes has been toward requirement of totally "non-fuming" spin finish systems.

A limited number of critical areas where non-fuming finishes are of particular interest include feeder yarn for texturing applications, bulked yarn such as BCF nylon and acrylic, industrial yarns, and hot drawn nylon. The range of temperatures encountered in these areas is approximately from 280° F (140°C) to 410° F (210° C). As fiber finishes are generally multicomponent mixtures of organic chemicals, it is virtually impossible to design a finish system that is totally nonfuming. So this paper will mainly deal with the optimization of a system to provide the performance properties with a minimum of fuming at the desired processing temperatures.

A typical finish system consists of:
1. Lubricant (40-60%)
2. Emulsifier(s) (15-35%)
3. Antistat (10-25%)

Minor ingredients usually added to provide a more specialized function may include:
1. Friction Modifiers
2. Antioxidants
3. Biocides
4. Viscosity Modifiers

These minor ingredients are used in small quantities when compared to the use of the first three, usually 1-5% and seldom more than 10% of the total

formulation. This paper will deal only with the major
ingredients, beginning with the lubricant, which is u-
sually the largest part of the spin finish.

Note, that as an initial measurement of fuming,
the AOCS smoke point (Cc-940) is used as a guide. Industry experience has indicated that in-plant fuming
will not occur until roughly 35° F - 50° F above the
value obtained by the AOCS smoke point method. 300° F
has been chosen as a minimum temperature for nonfuming
finishes; this correlates well with what is found in
industrial practice. A series of vegetable oil lubricants meeting the smoke point criteria are listed
below:

Lubricant	AOCS Smoke Point, °F
Safflower Oil	475
Peanut Oil	460
Cottonseed Oil	455
Soybean Oil (partially hydrogenated)	440
Coconut Oil (refined)	360
Olive Oil	325
Butyl Stearate	205
Mineral Oil	185

Butyl stearate and mineral oil smoke below 300°F,
obviously, but they are included for comparison because they have excellent friction properties and are
economical, hence they are widely used despite their
fuming properties. The frictional properties of these
lubricants are given in Table I.

The data in this table were obtained with the
ATLAB Friction Tester using ASTM D-3108-32 (for yarn-
to-metal friction) and D-3412-32 (for yarn-to-yarn
friction). The ± figures in the second column are a
measure of yarn-to-yarn cohesion, an important quality
to prevent sluffing of yarns on the package.

Analysis of the data indicates that many vegetable oils will meet the fiber-to-metal frictional properties required for the formulation of nonfuming finishes of the type traditionally built around mineral
oil or butyl stearate. Note also the similar yarn-to-
yarn frictional characteristics existing with most of
the lubricants with high smoke points. The area of
most concern for finish formulation is the amount of
cohesion offered by the vegetable oils. Three of the

TABLE I

Frictional Properties of Various Vegetable Oils As
Compared to Butyl Stearate and Mineral Oil

Product	T_f (grams)[1]			
	Yarn-to-Yarn[2]	Yarn-to-Metal[3]		
		10m/min	50m/min	100m/min
Safflower Oil	28 $\pm$ 0	184	272	232
Soybean Oil	26 $\pm$ 8	56	64	60
Peanut Oil	25 $\pm$ 13	46	60	60
Coconut Oil[4]	22 $\pm$ 16	34	48	44
Coconut Oil[5]	23 $\pm$ 15	34	54	40
Butyl Stearate	27 $\pm$ 23	32	40	42
Mineral Oil	27 $\pm$ 15	48	120	160

[1]$T_f = T_2 - T_1$ where T_1 = 15 grams.
[2]Yarn-to-Yarn contact angle = 180°;   yarn speed =
1 cm/min.
[3]Yarn-to-Metal (stainless steel) contact angle = 180°;
yarn speed = 10, 50, and 100 meters/min.
[4]Refined coconut oil - melting point = 76°.
[5]Refined coconut oil - melting point = 92°.

lubricants will offer cohesion levels bordering those
offered by mineral oil, but none are as high as butyl
stearate.

Many synthetic products also offer nonfuming
properties meeting our smoke point requirements, and
while this list will vary throughout the industry, we
shall consider a few product classes. First we consider a limited series of triesters of trimethylol
ethane and propane.

Product	AOCS Smoke Point, °F
Trimethylol ethane tripelargonate	305
Trimethylol propane triheptonate	310
Trimethylol propane tri Ca 8-10	310
Trimethylol propane trilaurate	310

All of these products have ¨neo¨ structures,
with one carbon having no hydrogen atom but attached
only to other carbons. This probably gives these
products better heat stability, but laboratory studies
have shown that fuming properties are strongly dependent upon purity in terms of residual acid in the final
product. Thus it is extremely important that good
vacuum stripping be employed during production.

Table II gives frictional properties of these, again compared to butyl stearate and mineral oil.

TABLE II
Frictional Properties

Product	Yarn-to-Yarn	Yarn-to-Stainless Steel T_f		
		10m/min	50m/min	100m/min
TME tri pelargonate	34 ± 22	52	72	120
TMP tri laurate	34 ± 14	48	68	112
TMP tri heptanoate	24 ± 10	60	124	160
TMP tri Ca 8-10	34 ± 22	36	90	112
Butyl stearate	27 ± 23	32	40	42
Mineral Oil	27 ± 15	48	120	160

The fiber-to-metal frictional properties of these products are suitable for lubricant bases for use in the formualtion of spin finishes, but as with the vegetable oils, none offers lubricity properties equal to butyl stearate.

Another class of lubricants that also have a secondary usage as emulsifiers are fatty acid esters of polyoxyethylene and polyethylene glycol.

Product	AOCS Smoke Point, °F
POE [7] Pelargonate	270
POE [9] Pelargonate	315
POE [8] Laurate	286
POE [9] Laurate	300
POE [7] Oleate	275
POE [8] Oleate	308
POE [8] Stearate	250
POE [40] Stearate	336

Smoke points and fuming properties of these products will vary extensively depending upon the ethylene oxide or polyethylene glycol chain length. In general, PEG esters with molecular weights of greater than 400 and polyoxyethylene esters with 9 or more moles of ethylene oxide will meet the smoke point requirement. While the relationship is not absolute, a peak appears to be reached at about 15-20 moles of ethylene oxide and PEG molecular weight of 650-750.

Table III shows frictional properties of a few of the more thermally stable products in this class of chemicals.

TABLE III
Frictional Properties
T_f (grams)

Product	Yarn-to-Yarn	Yarn-to-Stainless Steel		
		10m/min	50m/min	100m/min
POE [9]				
Pelargonate	25 + 19	72	168	192
POE [9] Laurate	23 + 7	74	188	108
POE [8] Oleate	19 + 11	152	256	280
Butyl Stearate	27 + 23	32	40	42
Mineral Oil	27 + 15	48	120	160

Many other chemicals can be used to meet the non-fuming lubricant properties necessary for use as a base in formulating spin finishes. Not all can be discussed here because of limitations, but products being used include:

> Tetraesters of pentaerythritol (which also contain neo-carbon structures)
> Mono- and di-esters of glycerol
> Mixed fatty acid esters of propylene and ethylene oxide
> Polyoxyethylene castor oil derivatives

Frictional properties may be modified by blending many of the products mentioned above. For instance, a higher level of yarn cohesion can often be achieved by the addition of POE fatty acid esters; on the other hand, many polyoxyethylene castor oils will serve to effectively reduce the level of yarn-to-yarn friction.

Some of the lubricants mentioned up to this point are not water soluble or dispersible, and since the application of most spin finishes are from an aqueous medium, the selection of proper emulsifiers becomes important. Few emulsifiers are good lubricants, and many do not have low fuming properties. There are so many types of emulsifiers we shall only consider certain ones with wide industry acceptance. Also, it is important to recognize that other lubricants are water soluble and also may serve a dual purpose of emulsification. Examples of these would be found in the class of polyoxyethylene and polyethylene glycol fatty acid esters discussed earlier.

The selection of emulsifiers for spin finish
systems is made easier although still not simple,
through the practical use of the Atlas HLB System.
The letters HLB stand for Hydrophile-Lipophile Balance.
This system has been the subject of many papers, so
let us simply define it as a system that enables you
to assign a number to the ingredient or combination of
ingredients you want to emulsify and then choose an
emulsifier or blend of emulsifiers having this same
number. While the system is not foolproof, it is useful in narrowing the range of emulsifier selections.
Since we have already established a desire to have our
final product exhibit aqueous characteristics, i.e.,
to dilute readily in water, our selection of emulsifiers or combinations of emulsifiers should be made from
oil-in-water emulsifiers, and have an HLB or combined
HLB in the range of 8-18, but more typically 9-13.

Thus, we now have two restrictions when dealing
with emulsifiers, the first, "nonfuming", the second,
"meeting the required HLB".

One of the more popular and long used series of
emulsifiers meeting nonfuming requirements are the
alkyl aryl ethers, more commonly referred to as ethoxylated nonyl phenols. As shown in Table IV, an increase in AOCS smoke point is noted with increases in
the polyoxyethylene chain length which corresponds
with an increase in HLB.

TABLE IV
Ethoxylated Nonyl Phenols

Product	AOCS Smoke Point	HLB
POE [5] nonyl phenol	280	10
POE [6] nonyl phenol	272	10.9
POE [8] nonyl phenol	315	12.3
POE [9] nonyl phenol	332	13
POE [10] nonyl phenol	282	13.3
POE [15] nonyl phenol	335	15
POE [30] nonyl phenol	275	17.1

Several useful products meet the established HLB
and smoke point criteria. The major advantages for
this type of emulsifier are economics and versatility.

One possible drawback is that many do not appear
to be readily biodegradable, although the defini-
tion(s) of biodegradability are still subject to

debate.

A second series of emulsifiers having wide utility are the polyoxyethylene sorbitan fatty acid esters.
Table V reveals that this series of products also
shows variations based on the polyoxyethylene chain
length.

TABLE V
Fatty Acid Esters

Sample		AOCS Smoke Point	HLB
POE [4]	sorbitan monolaurate	265	13.3
POE [20]	sorbitan monolaurate	327	16.7
POE [20]	sorbitan mono-palmitate	335	15.6
POE [4]	sorbitan mono-stearate	230	9.6
POE [20]	sorbitan mono-stearate	330	14.9
POE [20]	sorbitan tristearate	255	10.5
POE [5]	sorbitan monooleate	264	10.0
POE [20]	sorbitan monooleate	366	15.0
POE [20]	sorbitan trioleate	229	11.0

The obvious relationship between fuming properties and ethylene oxide content are again apparent
with the polyoxyethylene sorbitan fatty acid esters.
These products are biodegradable and offer versatility
in a wide range of emulsification areas. The variation in emulsification properties with chemical type,
or more specifically the fatty acid used, allows the
formulator to greatly improve emulsion stability
through optimization of chemical type.

The third and final classification of chemicals
to be introduced as emulsifiers are the polyoxyethylene ethers of alcohols (Table VI). As with the other
compounds having a polyoxyethylene chain length, these
products also show fuming properties correlating to
the ethylene oxide chain length.

Another notable feature of the polyoxyethylene
ethers is the good lubricant properties, coupled with
adequate emulsification properties in a wide range of
areas, and this suggests use of these products in
applications where low frictional properties are desired. This series of products are biodegradable.

The area presenting the greatest problem to the
formulator of nonfuming finishes is the selection of

TABLE VI
Polyoxyethylene Ethers

Product			HLB	Smoke Point AOCS, °F
POE	[4]	lauryl ether	9.7	185
POE	[23]	lauryl ether	16.9	345
POE	[2]	cetyl ether	5.3	185
POE	[10]	cetyl ether	12.9	258
POE	[20]	cetyl ether	15.7	306
POE	[2]	stearyl ether	4.9	203
POE	[10]	stearyl ether	12.4	284
POE	[20]	stearyl ether	15.3	300
POE	[2]	oleyl ether	4.9	193
POE	[10]	oleyl ether	12.4	273
POE	[20]	oleyl ether	15.3	309

proper antistatic agents. Basically, antistats work via either of two routes. Most ionic types dissipate the static charge, while moisture is retained by most nonionic agents, although there are exceptions to that method of classification. The most effective antistats are normally found among the two ionic types, but many of these compounds present fuming problems. Some notable exceptions may be found with the heterocyclic amine quaternaries with diethyl or dimethyl sulfate which have smoke points above 320° F. Another class is the polyoxyethylene diethyl sulfate quaternary fatty amines.

While not as effective on a weight basis, a wider selection of nonfuming components is found with nonionic antistatic components. Many of the components already discussed such as the series of polyoxyethylene sorbitan fatty acid esters, or the polyoxyethylene fatty acid esters will offer a reasonable level of static protection. Thus the use of these components as emulsifiers and/or lubricants may eliminate or reduce the amount of additional antistat required.

Perhaps a more widely accepted class of nonionic antistats would be the polyoxyethylene fatty amines. Many products in this category meet the smoke point criteria, especially those in the range of 12-20 moles of ethylene oxide.

We have now discussed all of the major components necessary in the design of a "nonfuming finish". The selection of components will depend on the final properties one is attempting to achieve as well as any other ecological or asthetic requirements to be met.

There are many other tests that may and should be used during prescreening of nonfuming spin finish systems. Two of the more commonly used are:

> <u>Fuming Test</u> -- Usually 15 minutes at 265° C using a 5 gram specimen. 10% or less finish loss with a minimum of color degradation is desirable.

> <u>Varnish or Residue</u> -- Normally 16-24 hours using a 1 gram specimen. Maximum of 10% remaining residue is desirable.

While laboratory testing is of extreme importance, we must keep in mind that the real test is in how well the finish runs in the plant, enabling the mill to process yarn without difficulty.

In summary, we have discussed a large number of chemicals useful in the formulation of nonfuming spin finish systems. By proper selection, it is possible to achieve many varied finish properties and design systems meeting OSHA requirements in terms of fuming while achieving finish properties similar to those of more traditionally used components.

10

Reactions of a Difluorochloropyrimidine Dyestuff with Wool Peptide Models

ULRICH ALTENHOFEN (1) and HELMUT ZAHN

Deutsches Wollforschungsinstitut an der Technischen Hochschule Aachen, Bundesrepublik Deutschland

1. The present state of our knowlege of reaction rates in reactive dyeing of wool

W. F. Beech (2) has given a clear account on the mechanism of reaction of proteins with reactive dyes and quotes Shore (3) in summarizing the position: "It appears that the main groups in protein fibres which participate in the reaction with reactive dyes are the primary amino groups of lysine, the N-terminal residues, the imidazole group of histidine, followed by the cysteine thiol group and the tyrosine phenolic group." Beech is correct in stating that the distribution of the dye molecules between the different groups will vary for different proteins, for different reactive systems and for different experimental conditions. The behaviour of chloroacetyl, omega-chloroalkylsulfonamide, vinyl sulfone , chlorotriazinyl, chloropyrimidyl dyes as well as of dyes containing acrylamido groups with wool has been studied (2),(4). By detailed examination of rate fixation curves, the variation of reactivity of acryloylamino dyes with pH at 100°C was obtained by Derbyshire and Tristram (5), while Hildebrand and Meier (6) have investigated the reaction of Verofixorange GL, a difluorochloropyrimidine dyestuff with histidine, thioglycolic acid and glycine at pH 4.5 and 80°C and have presented data for the reaction rates. We were stimulated by this paper as well as by our standing interest in compounds with two reactive fluorines (7). Dr. Bien from Bayer, Leverkusen synthesized the blue anthraquinone dyestuff (I) according to example 400 of Bayer's patent application (Offenlegungsschrift Nr. 1,644,171) and Dr. Siegel provided us with a sample of this wool blue dyestuff. Dr. Hildebrand (8) proposed to study not only the site of reaction in wool but also the reaction velocities in a more sophisticated manner than he reported in his paper quoted above. We decided to dye the N_α-acetyl-methylamides of amino acids as a result of results obtained from earlier experiments with N_α-acetyl-lysine-methylamide (9). The following is a description of our experiments with the dyestuff (I) and the wool peptide models mentioned above. We succeeded in isolating the single reaction products and in calculating reaction rates from colorimetric data with the aid of a FORTRAN computer program.

2. Material and methods

The dyestuff (I) was kindly provided by Dr. Siegel, Bayer AG, Leverkusen and was used without further purification. N_α-acetyl-methylamides of lysine, histidine and tyrosine were prepared according to published procedures (9) with some minor modifications (10). Acetyl-cysteinemethylamide was obtained from bisacetyl-cystinemethylamide (11) by reduction with zinc in acetic acid: 0.5 g cystine derivative were dissolved in 20 ml acetic acid. 0.5 g zinc were added. After stirring for 3 hours at room temperature the excess of zinc was removed by filtration and the filtrate was evaporated in vacuo. The product gave a thiol content 70-80% of theory as determined with Ellman's reagent (12).

Reactions of dyestuff (I) with the wool peptide models were carried out in a double chamber vessel provided with Ingold high temperature electrodes type 202 and 262, nitrogen inlet, reflux condenser, and thermometer. pH values were kept constant by connection with an Autotitrator (Radiometer Copenhagen). At various times samples 0.5 ml each were withdrawn kept at $0°C$ and 50 µl 1N hydrochloric acid was added.

Samples (10 µl) were applied to thin layer plates (F 254, Merck, Darmstadt) which were developed with a mixture of n-butanol, ethanol and water (4:3:3). After elution to 2 and 5 cm, the plates were dried and again chromatographed in the same solvent mixture to a distance of at least 12-15 cm. The plates were again dried and immediately measured in a Zeiss PMQ II plate photometer. With the photocell closed transmission was calibrated at 0% and at a substance free spot of the thin layer plate at 100%. The plate was scanned in the direction of running by a slit diaphragm. The photometer data were evaluated by a FORTRAN computer program on the basis of an empirical calibration function.

3. The various possibilities for reaction of (I) with functional groups and water

Fig. 1 shows some of the possible reactions in aqueous solutions of the difluorochloropyrimidine dyestuff (I) with four wool peptide models (R-H) containing the functional side chain groups of lysine, cysteine, histidine and the functional main chain group of N-terminal glycine. The first reaction shows the substitution reaction on the first fluorine, the second reaction the substitution of the monosubstituted product with a further wool peptide model. The last reaction represents the hydrolysis of the first fluorine, leading to a monohydroxylderivative of dyestuff (I). By titration of the hydrogenfluoride formed in the three reactions depicted in fig.1 only the sum of the reactions can be measured.This was done by one of us (10) and has provided very useful data on the reactivities of the functional groups at pH values 4.5 - 8.5 at various temperatures as well as on the dyestuff hydrolysis. These data served as essential facts for planning the experiments described in this communication. In order to study the three reactions outlined in fig. 1 separately, the mono-and disubstituted and the hydrolysed products were separated by thin layer chromatography following procedures already described by Mäusezahl (13) and G. Reinert (14).

   We have found that the photometric assessment of our silica gel thin layer plates by combination of remission and transmission measurement can be improved if a white paper is put under the thin layer plate (see fig. 2).

   Fig. 3 shows an example of the data obtained by the photometric assessment of dyestuff-derivatives separated on thin layer plates for the reaction of dyestuff (I) with glycine methylamide at 80°C and pH 5. Only mono- and disubstituted reaction products were found and identified. The bifunctional reaction of (I) is very slow. Dyestuff hydrolysis can be neglected. In this simple case titration of HF formed can be used to calculate approximate values for the reaction velocity k_1. We found 0.262 l/mol.min. Later, a value of 0.226 l/mol.min was calculated on the basis of the separated monosubstituted dye derivative.

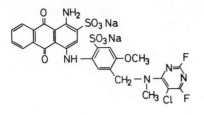

Dyestuff (I), German Offenlegung-schrift 1,644,171; example 400

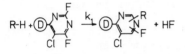

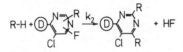

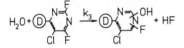

R = -NH-(CH₂)₄-X   -S-CH₂-X

-NH-CH₂-CO-NH-CH₃

X = CH₃-CO-NH-CH-CO-NH-CH₃

Figure 1.   Mono- and disubstitution of the dyestuff (I) by peptide models and hydrolysis of (I)

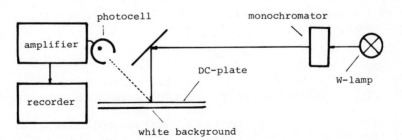

Figure 2.   Scheme showing the photometric assessment of thin layer plates with the Zeiss PMQ II

4. Calculation of reaction rates

The substance within a spot in the thin layer chromato-
gram shows a normal distribution (15). Constant spot
widths allow the mathematical description of a spot by
peak height and peak width at half height. It was found
that the logarithm of the amount of the dyestuff derivative in a spot is not linearly related to the values
of height and width even after logarithmization. One
must add the quadratic terms. We can not deal with the
detailed description of the mathematics applied within
this communication but it can be found in the thesis
of one of us (1). The final formula for the calculation
of amounts of dyestuff derivatives contained as many
as 6 terms and was applied to assess quantitatively
thin layer spots containing 0.14 - 7.5 nmol substance
per spot. The evaluation had to be done by means of a
computer program.
      Coloured substances such as the dyestuff itself,
its reaction products with the peptide models as well
as hydrolysed dye can now be assessed quantitatively
after having established the calibration curve for the
dyestuff. The reaction mixture can be expressed as
follows:

$$F_o = F_t + M_t + B_t + H_t$$

where F_o = molar amount of dyestuff at the start
      F_t = molar amount of dyestuff at time t
      M_t = molar amount of monosubstituted dyestuff at
            time t
      B_t = molar amount of disubstituted dyestuff at
            time t
      H_t = molar amount of hydrolysed dyestuff at time t

The peptide models are colourless and therefore cannot
be estimated by colorimetry of the spots on the thin
layer chromatograms. The concentration of the peptide
model however was calculated from the following
equation:

$$P_t = P_o - M_t - 2 \cdot B_t$$

P_t = molar amount of peptide model at time t
P_o = molar amount of peptide model at the start

In order to calculate the concentration of dyestuff
and its derivatives all values had to be divided by the
sample volumes. The following kinetic equations
were used:

Hydrolysis: $\dfrac{dH(t)}{dt} = k_3 \cdot F(t)$

Monosub-
stitution: $\dfrac{dM(t)}{dt} = k_1 \cdot F(t) \cdot P(t) - k_2 \cdot M(t) \cdot P(t)$

Consumption of
the peptide $\dfrac{dP(t)}{dt} = -k_1 \cdot F(t) \cdot P(t) - k_2 \cdot M(t) \cdot P(t)$
model:

Simultaneous and consecutive reactions of this kind
have not been described in literature (16). The above
equations were transformed in order to make integration
possible.

Reaction rate
of hydrolysis: $k_3 = \dfrac{H(t)}{\displaystyle\int_{\tau=0}^{t} F(\tau) \cdot d\tau}$

Reaction rate of
monosubstitution: $k_1 = \dfrac{P_0 - P(t) + M(t)}{\displaystyle\int_{\tau=0}^{t} F(\tau) \cdot P(\tau) \cdot d\tau}$

Reaction rate of
the second sub-
stitution: $k_2 = \dfrac{P_0 - P(t) - M(t)}{\displaystyle\int_{\tau=0}^{t} M(\tau) \cdot P(\tau) \cdot d\tau}$

The equations were solved using the current methods of
numerical mathematics such as trapezoid formula,
Simpsons's formula and a polynom approximation, the
latter offers the advantage that random errors of
measurement can be compensated. Fig. 4 gives an example
of the kind of results which were obtained using the
equation for the calculation of the reaction rate k_1
for monosubstitution of dyestuff by acetyl-cysteinemethylamide at pH values between 4.5 and 6 at temperatures between 80°C and 95°C.
    Fig.5 shows the results for the reaction of
dyestuff (I) with N_{ξ}-acetyl-lysine-methylamide. It can
be seen that the reaction rates differ not only if
compared at the same pH but also in their pH-dependence.
The next chapter will show how absolute reactivities
of wool peptide models can be obtained.

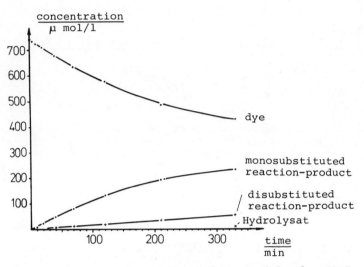

Figure 3.   *Reaction of dyestuff (I) with glycine–methylamide at 80°C,*
pH 5

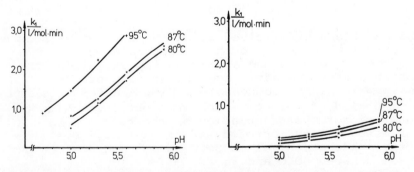

Figures 4 and 5.   Reaction of dyestuff (I) with N-acetyl–cysteine–methylamide
(left) and N α -acetyl–lysine–methylamide (right).   Variation in velocities of the
monosubstitution reaction with pH and temperature.

5. pH-Dependence of reaction velocities

It is known that amino groups in proteins, peptides or
amino acids do react by substitution or addition in
their unprotonated nucleophilic form (17),(18). In the
case of our reaction with dyestuff (I) (F-D) the
following equations hold true:

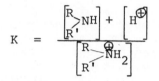

k_d is the rate constant for the reaction of dissociated
form of the amino acid. Therefore the concentration of
R(R')NH can be derived from the dissociation equilibrium
where the dissociation constant is:

$$K = \frac{\left[\begin{smallmatrix}R\\ >NH\\ R'\end{smallmatrix}\right] + \left[H^{\oplus}\right]}{\left[\begin{smallmatrix}R\\ >\overset{\oplus}{N}H_2\\ R'\end{smallmatrix}\right]}$$

Lindley (18) first calculated linear regression
equations describing the relation between reaction
rates and pH-values. His method was the basis for our
FORTRAN program and provided the pH independent rate
constants k_d. In addition the dissociation constants
K were calculated. We can not deal in this communication
used and refer to the formula of Gorin, Martin and
Doughty (20) which was used for evaluating reactions
of thiol compounds. pK-values of our peptide models
were, in addition, directly measured by potentiometric
titration up to temperatures of 95°C. Dyeing is
normally effected at 100°C but potentiometric measurements at this temperature were not possible. The
pK-values were therefore obtained by extrapolation.
Fig. 6 shows the temperature dependence of pK-values
for the five peptide models studied. From these plots
dissociation enthalpies were calculated. Values are
given in J/mol in the legend of fig. 6.
    Fig. 6 shows clearly the influence of the enthalpy
of dissociation. Whereas the values for the $\mathcal{E}$-amino
group of the lysine derivative, for the imidazole of
the histidine derivative as well as for the amino
group of glycine methylamide are closely related,
the enthalpy of dissociation for the phenolic hydroxyl
group of the tyrosine derivative is only about half.
This means that increased temperatures favour the
dissociation of the protonated amino groups more than

that of the phenolic hydroxyl. This clearly explains
an earlier observation (10) namely that the tyrosine
peptide model reacts with dyestuff (I) with normal
rates at alkaline pH-values only.

    The estimation of pK-values by titration was not
possible with the cysteine derivative because thiolate
anions are extremely sensitive to oxidation at higher
temperatures. Hence we had to calculate the pK-values
from the reaction rates at higher temperatures. The
most significant results of these calculations are
the very small reaction rates of the SH form of the
cysteine derivative. We therefore believe that only
the thiolate anion -S$^\circ$ is able to react with the
dyestuff (I).

6. Nucleophilicity of reactive groups of peptide models

If one plots the reaction rates of the peptide models
in their reactive dissociated form against the pK-
values, curves such as those in fig. 7 are obtained. It
can be seen that the pH independent reaction rate
increases with the pK-value. Peptide models whose
functional group is an amino or imino group show a
linear function in the logarithmic scale, whereas the
cysteine derivative shows an higher reactivity than
predicted on the basis of the pK-value. This corresponds to the known greater nucleophilicity of -S$^\circ$
groups compared to that of amino groups.

7. Reaction rates at different temperatures

Fig. 8 shows an Arrhenius plot of the influence of
temperature on the rate of substitution of the first
fluorine by various peptide models at pH 5. It can
be seen that the slope and hence the energies of
activation do not differ greatly between the peptide
models studied. The reaction rates at the dyeing
temperature of 100°C were obtained by extrapolation
and are given in table 1.

Table 1: Reaction rates at 100°C obtained by extra-
         polation of the curves in fig. 8

Peptide model	Reaction rate at 100°C 1/mol.min
Ac-Lys-NH-Me	0.4
Gly-NH-Me	1.1
Ac-His-NH-Me	1.2
Ac-Cys-NH-Me	2.1

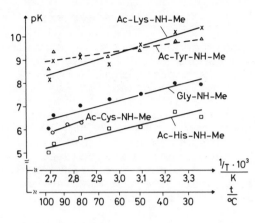

Figure 6. Temperature dependence of pK values of peptide models. Enthalpy values of dissociation in parentheses in J/mol. Ac–Lys–NH–Me (54.8 ± 15.6) Ac–Tyr–NH–Me (25.6 ± 8.5), Gly–NH–Me (52.7 ± 13.6) Ac–His–NH–Me (50.6 ± 9.5)

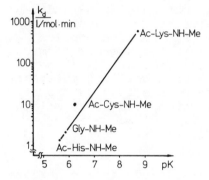

Figure 7. pH independent reaction rates vs. pK values based on measurements at 80°C

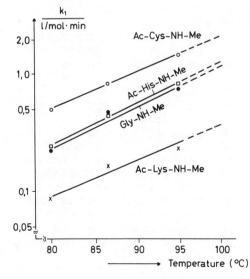

Figure 8. Arrhenius plot of the rate of reactions of four peptide models with dyestuff (I) at pH 5.0

8. Reactions of the second fluorine of dyestuff (I)

We investigated the pH dependence of the second substitution reaction in the same manner as it has been done
for the first substitution. The experimental errors
however were greater because we terminated the reactions
at times where the amount of the bifunctional reaction
product was relatively small. For this we have not
provided values for the ratio k_2/k_1. We will simply
state that the second reaction occurs at approximately
the same rate as the first substitution in the case
of the lysine peptide model. The second substitution of
the derivatives of cysteine, histidine and glycine on
the other hand, seem to proceed much slower.

9. Hydrolysis of dyestuff (I)

It can be seen from fig.1 that not only mono- and
disubstituted reaction products but also hydrolysed
dyestuff is formed if (I) is reacted with peptide
models. In view of the fact that the amounts formed
were very small, the hydrolysis rate k_3 cannot be
measured very accurately. The only point of interest
here is the fact that the hydrolysis is significantly
greater if the dyestuff is reacted with the histidine
derivative at $95^{\circ}C$ and pH 5.6.

10. Conclusions

Evidence is presented that a detailed kinetic analysis
of complicated simultaneous and consecutive reactions
such as reactions of various peptide models and water
with a bifunctional compound can be executed. The
single steps of the procedure are: separation of the
coloured spots by thin layer chromatography, scanning
photometry, and numerical evaluation of the photometer
data by a FORTRAN computer program based on an empirical calibration function. The kinetic data presented
differ greatly from published data for reactions of
similar dyestuffs with wool or amino acids (6).
Nevertheless one cannot discuss possible explanations
considering the fact that experimental conditions such
as pH , temperature and reactants cannot be compared.
Experimental errors cannot be excluded from the present
work and only through further progress in this field
these data can be verified. In any case one can conclude
that the difluorochloropyrimidine dyestuff reacts under
mildly acidic dyeing conditions at 80 - $95^{\circ}C$ with the
amino and imino groups of lysine and histidine and the
$-S^{\ominus}$ group of cysteine predominantly whereas the reactions

with the phenolic hydroxyl groups of tyrosine can be neglected under the conditions chosen. The fact that Verofix [R] dyes react with wool from acidic dye bath liquors (6) can now be explained by our finding that the dissociation constant of the protonated amino group of lysine increases unexpectedly rapidly as the temperature approaches $100^{\circ}C$. To our knowledge no data on pK-values of functional groups of proteins near $100^{\circ}C$ have been published. The twofold estimation of pK-values at different temperatures, one by evaluation of the pH-dependence of reaction rates, and the other by direct titration of the peptide functional groups seems to be a sound basis for further refinement and application in other fields of protein chemistry.

　　We are uncertain as far as our values for the second substitution and the hydrolysis are concerned. How can one understand the fast second reaction of the $\mathcal{E}$-amino group of lysine and the slow reaction of the α-amino group of glycine? Steric reasons offer no explanation. Further work is needed to clear this point. The increased rate of dyestuff hydrolysis during the reaction with the histidine peptide model is not unexpected if one considers the catalytic role of the imidazole moiety (21). One should carry out more experiments on the possible role of dyebath constituents on the hydrolysis of reactive dyes. The method presented in this short communication can be applied for comparing various reactive dyestuff systems in their reactivity towards the more important functional groups in fibrous proteins. Altenhofen et al. (22) have already compared the reactivities of a vinylsulfone dye with the difluorochloropyrimidine dye of the present investigation. Although many papers have been published from our own laboratory on reactions of 1.5-difluoro-2.4-dinitrobenzene (23) and p.p'-difluoro-m.m'-dinitrodiphenylsulfon (24) with amino groups and proteins, the main emphasis was the separation of bridged amino acids and their isolation. Kinetic data are missing. It would be worthwile to apply the thin layer chromatography-, scanning-and computerizing technique described to solve some of the unanswered kinetic questions.

Acknowledgements

Thanks are due to Dr. Siegel and Dr. Bien (Bayer AG) for providing us with samples of reactive dyestuffs. We are indebted to the Rechenzentrum of Technische Hochschule Aachen for help during the working out of FORTRAN computer programs and evaluating the data.

Abstract

The $N_{\mathcal{C}}$-acetyl-methylamides of cysteine, histidine, lysine tyrosine as well as glycine-methylamide were reacted as peptide models with the difluorochloro-pyrimidine dyestuff (I) at pH 5 to 9 at temperatures between $80^{\circ}C$ and $95^{\circ}C$. Either one or both fluorines of (I) were replaced by the amino-, hydroxy- or thiol groups of the peptide models (as well as by hydroxylic groups through hydrolysis). The amino acid derivatives of (I) and the hydrolysed product of (I) were separated by thin layer chromatography and assessed by photometry. Average reaction rates for the substitution of the first and second fluorine as well as for the hydrolysis have been calculated from the colorimetric data by a computer program.

Literature cited

1. Altenhofen,U.; Thesis Technische Hochschule Aachen 1975
2. Beech,W.F.; "Fibre-Reactive Dyes", Logos Press London 1970
3. Shore,J.; J.Soc.Dyers Colour. (1968),84,408
4. Hildebrand,D.; "The Chemistry of Synthetic Dyes" Vol. VI, ed. by K. Venkataraman, Academic Press, New York and London (1972) p.327
5. Derbyshire,A.N.;Tristram,G.R.; J.Soc.Dyers Colour. (1965),81,584
6. Hildebrand,D.; Meier,G.; Textil-Praxis (1971),26,499 557
7. Zahn,H.; Angew. Chem. (1955),67,561
8. Hildebrand,D., private discussion 3.5.1972
9. Zahn,H.; Mella,K.; Hoppe-Seyler's Z. Physiol. Chem. (1966),344, 75
10. Altenhofen,U.; Diploma thesis, Fachabteilung für Chemie und Biologie der Technischen Hochschule Aachen, 1972
11. Zahn,H.; Sroka,W.; Monatsh. Chemie (1967),98,745
12. Meichelbeck,H.;Hack,A.G.; Sentler,Chr.; Z.ges. Textilind., (1968),70, 242
13. Mäusezahl,D.; Textilveredlung (1970),5, 839
14. Zahn,H.; Reinert,G.; Kolloid-Z. (1968),226, 141
15. Stahl,E.; "Dünnschichtchromatographie, ein Laboratoriumsbuch" 1. Auflage, Springer Verlag, Heidelberg 1962
16. Frost,A.A.;Pearson,R.; "Kinetics and Mechanism" 2nd edition, John Wiley & Sons, Inc., New York-London 1961

17. Kemp,D.S.; Bernstein,W.; McNeil,G.N.; J. Org.
    Chem. (1974),39, 2831
18. Leon,N.H.; Textile Progress (1975),7, 1
19. Lindley,H.; Biochem. J. (1960),74, 577
    Lindley,H.; Biochem. J. (1962),82, 418
    Voigt,R.;Wenck,H.;Scheider,F.;Z. Naturf. (1971),26b, 1010
20. Gorin,G.; Martic,P.A.; Doughty,G.; Arch. Biochem.
    Biophys. (1966),115, 593
21. Overberger,C.G.; Chah-Moh Shen; J.Am. Chem. Soc.
    (1971),93, 6992
22. Altenhofen,U.;Baumann,H.;Zahn,H.; Proc. 5. Internat.
    Wool Textile Res. Conf. Aachen (1975), Vol III,529
23. Zahn,H.; Siepmann,E.; Kolloid. Z. & Z. Polymere
    (1972),250, 849
24. Zahn,H.; Hammoudeh,M.M.; Kolloid Z. & Z. Polymere
    (1973),252, 289

11

Shrink-Resist Polymers for Wool: A Comparative Study of Reactive Poly(Alkylene Oxides) for Pad Application

DAVID J. KILPATRICK, JOHN A. RIPPON, MICHAEL A. RUSHFORTH, and TREVOR SHAW

IWS Technical Centre, Valley Drive, Ilkley, West Yorkshire, LS29 8PB, England

In recent years the commercial importance of polymer shrink-resist processes for wool has increased considerably, until, at the time of writing, approximately half the world production of SR wool is polymer treated, the remainder being treated by the older and less effective oxidative processes.

Shrink-resist polymers may be applied to wool at any stage of manufacture, from loose stock to garments, but treatment of tops or slivers, fabrics and garments are of most commercial significance.

The polymer treatments which are in industrial use may be divided into two types - those in which prechlorination of the wool is a necessary part of the process (1) and those in which prechlorination is not required (2-7). There are fundamental differences between these two types of process with regard to the polymers used and the mechanism by which shrink-resistance is conferred on the treated goods. From the practical point of view, the chlorination/resin processes have the disadvantages mainly associated with the chlorination step, which degrades and therefore weakens the wool fibre and makes dyeing to high standards of wet-fastness more difficult. But the overriding advantage of these processes is that they are applicable to a wider range of substrates by convenient processing techniques. Thus chlorination/resin processes are effective on tops or slivers, but no polymer has yet been discovered which gives shrink-resistance when applied to unchlorinated tops. Again, long-liquor batch-exhaust processes of the chlorination/resin type have been in commercial use for the treatment of knitted garments for some years (1), whilst the development of a technology by which polymers may be exhausted from long liquor on to unchlorinated wool is still in its infancy (8).

For these reasons chlorination/resin processes have been more successful in terms of weight of wool treated than the alternative processes by which polymers can be applied by padding techniques to unchlorinated woven or knitted fabrics, or to knitted garments in modified dry cleaning machines by dip-

extract-dry methods. However, significant developments have
occurred in recent years in the technology of the application of
prepolymers to unchlorinated wool substrates and in the design
and synthesis of polymers for this purpose. Typically, these
prepolymers consist of a polymeric backbone with terminal
reactive groups. After application to the wool the products can
be polymerised through these groups. It is the object of this
paper to discuss these developments, and to attempt to demonstrate
how the properties of the treated wool, the stability of
application baths, the curing conditions required and the shelf-
life of the polymer depend on its functional groups and other
aspects of its chemical structure.

Experimental Materials

Wool Fabrics. The knitted fabric used was single jersey,
knitted from R74/2 tex 100% wool yarn to a tightness factor of
13. The fabric was scoured in an aqueous solution of Lissapol N
(ICI, 1 g/l) and sodium bicarbonate (1 g/l), at a liquor:goods
ratio of 40:1 for 20 min at 40°C, followed by thorough rinsing
with water. The fabric pH was 8. The woven fabric was undyed,
all-worsted, 2 X 2 twill of weight 192 g m^{-2} (Salts of Saltaire
Ltd., UK). The fabric pH was 7.5.

Polymers. These were synthesised in the laboratory, with
the exception of the polyacrylate, Acramin SLN (Bayer), and
Hercosett 57 (Hercules Powder Co). The synthetic methods can be
found in the literature, as follows: polythiomalate (2),
polycarbamoyl sulphonate (3), polyisocyanate (4), polythiosulphate
(5), polythioglycollate (6) and polysulphonium bromide (7).

Other Reagents. The wetting agent used was Tinovetin LB
(Ciba-Geigy) and the emulsifying agent was Lissapol NX (ICI); all
other reagents were laboratory grade.

Experimental Methods

Application of Prepolymers to Fabric. Polymers IV and VI
were emulsified with Lissapol N (20% on weight of polymer), and
stock emulsions used to make up padding-strength emulsions with
other additions (Table II) as required. The remaining polymers
were soluble in the padding liquor, and solutions were prepared
immediately prior to padding.
   Solutions or emulsions were padded onto weighed pieces of
fabric, using a laboratory padmangle, and the pieces were
subsequently reweighed to enable calculation of the wet pick-up.
They were then dried in a forced-air oven and steamed where
necessary (see Table II). Half of each treated sample was
subjected to a simulated afterwash process consisting of 2 X 10
min cycles in 25 l of water in an International Cubex wash

testing machine. The fabrics were redried at 100°C and finally
semi-decated (5 min steam).

Test Methods. The fabrics were wash tested 7 days after
treatment.

The felting shrinkage test consisted of 180 min agitation
in the Cubex washing machine in 15 litres of pH 7 phosphate
buffer at 40°C with a 1 kg load. After washing, samples were
spin dried, then line dried. Area shrinkage was determined by
measuring previously applied bench marks. Durable Press rating
was assessed by comparison of the fabrics with the AATCC replicas
(9) (D.P. ratings 1-5). Flexural rigidity was measured by the
cantilever bending length method according to British Standard
3356:1961.

Results and Discussion

Properties Required in Shrink-Resist Polymers. It is not
difficult to list the criteria which an ideal shrink-resist
polymer should satisfy. This list consists of two sets of
attributes: one concerned with the ease of application of the
polymer and the other with the performance and properties of the
treated fabric. Since it is intended to discuss the polymers
examined in this paper in terms of how nearly they satisfy these
criteria, it is as well, at this stage, to consider in full the
points in this list.

Application criteria:

(i) The shelf life of the prepolymer concentrate, stored under
normal conditions, should exceed a certain minimum, and six
months is probably the minimum acceptable.

(ii) Preparation of the padding liquor should be simple and
should not require special equipment. For example, a prepolymer
which is insoluble in water may be applied to wool fabric from
an aqueous emulsion, but the chemistry of the polymer should be
such that it is possible for a stable emulsion to be prepared by
the chemical manufacturer since this requires special equipment
not normally found in textile finishing plants.

(iii) The prepared padding liquor should be stable and usable for
at least 8 h (a full shift) after preparation, and preferably
for longer than this. Of course, the padding liquor must contain
any curing catalysts which are used and this tends to make it
less chemically stable than a liquor containing the prepolymer
alone. Additionally, dilute emulsions may have a greater
tendency to separate or "cream" than concentrates.

(iv) After application to the fabric, the prepolymer must cure
readily, and under relatively mild conditions. Ideally, drying
the treated fabric in the conditions normally used for drying
wool should be sufficient. Any necessity for heat curing at
elevated temperatures is a distinct disadvantage because wool
finishers often do not have facilities for this type of treatment,

and in any case, it may damage the wool or cause it to yellow, particularly if the cloth is in an alkaline condition.

(v) In the ideal system, afterwashing, either to improve the fabric hand or to remove excess catalysts or wetting agents etc. should not be necessary.

(vi) The cross-linked polymer should have minimal effects on the dyeing properties of treated wool, so that unlevel polymer application will not lead to unlevel dyeing when dyeing succeeds the shrink-resist treatment.

Performance criteria:

(vii) The felting resistance of treated fabrics should enable them to survive a severe wash test, at least equivalent to the maximum amount of washing a garment will receive during its anticipated wear life.

(viii) The treated fabric should have good wash and wear (minimum iron) properties, equivalent at least to a DP3 rating after severe machine washing. Knitted fabrics should retain good stitch clarity through the machine wash.

(ix) The cost of the polymer and the required add-on must be such that criteria (vii) and (viii) can be satisfied at reasonable cost.

(x) The aesthetic properties of the finished fabric must be virtually indistinguishable from untreated wool. In particular the process must not noticeably increase the stiffness or harshness of the fabric, nor cause its hand to become greasy or tacky.

With such a list of criteria to satisfy, it is hardly surprising that the ideal shrink-resist polymer finish has yet to be found. It is particularly difficult to find polymers which have good shelf life and application-bath stability, and yet cure under mild conditions after application to the fabric; the reasons for this conflict in properties are quite obvious. It is also very difficult to produce a high level of shrink-resistance combined with good fabric aesthetics without washing-off after polymer application to improve the fabric's hand.

Polymer Structure. (Table I). The polymers discussed in this paper are more accurately described as reactive, self-crosslinking oligomers. Typically, they consisted of a soft backbone structure, often a poly(alkylene oxide) of molecular weight ~3000, to which were attached two or more self-crosslinking reactive groups. After application to the wool fabric, crosslinking or chain extension reactions were caused to occur until the polymer molecular weight became infinite, and the polymer was thus rendered insoluble on the fibre surface.

It is intended, in this paper, to show how polymer structure, particularly reactive group type, affects performance as judged by the criteria set out above.

Polymer IV (Table I) will be described first, since two of the other polymers were obtained from polymer IV by modifying its

TABLE I

THE STRUCTURES OF THE POLYMER SYSTEMS STUDIED

	Polymer system	Backbone *	Functional group	Nominal functionality
I	Polythiomalate	PTMO	$-OOC.\underset{\underset{SH}{\mid}}{CH}.CH_2.COO-$	4
II	Polycarbamoyl sulphonate	PPO	$-NH.CO.SO_3^-Na^+$	3
III	Polycarbamoyl sulphonate -polyacrylate	PPO/PACR	$-NH.CO.SO_3^-Na^+$	3
IV	Polyisocyanate	PPO	$-NCO(aliphatic)$	3
V	Polythiosulphate	PPO	$-S_2O_3^-Na^+$	3
VI	Polythioglycollate	PPO	$-OOC.CH_2SH$	3
VII	Polysulphonium bromide	PPO	$-NH.CO.CH_2\overset{+}{S}R_2\overset{-}{Br}$	3

* PTMO: poly(tetramethylene oxide)diol, MW$\sim$1000

   PPO: poly(propylene oxide)triol, MW$\sim$3000

   PACR: "soft" polyacrylate

functional groups. This polymer was a polyisocyanate obtained by the reaction of one mole of a poly(propylene oxide)triol of molecular weight ~3000 with three moles of hexamethylene diisocyanate, thus giving an oligomer with a nominal isocyanate functionality of 3 <u>(4)</u>.

$$R(OH)_3 + OCN(CH_2)_6NCO \longrightarrow R\left\{OOC.NH(CH_2)_6NCO\right\}_3 \qquad (1)$$
$$\text{polymer IV}$$

Although the aliphatic isocyanate groups in polymer IV are reactive towards water, a technique which allows the polymer to be applied from aqueous emulsion has been described <u>(13)</u>.

Polymers II and VII were derivatives of polymer IV. Polymer II was formed by the reaction of the free isocyanate groups of polymer IV with sodium bisulphite in aqueous alcohol solution <u>(3)</u>.

$$R'(NCO)_3 + 3NaHSO_3 \longrightarrow R'(NH.CO.SO_3^-Na^+)_3 \qquad (2)$$
$$\text{polymer IV} \qquad\qquad \text{polymer II}$$

The sodium salt of the polycarbamoyl sulphonate (polymer II) was water soluble.

Polymer VII was obtained by reaction of polymer IV with bromoacetic acid, followed by thiodiglycol, to give a water soluble sulphonium derivative <u>(7)</u>.

$$R'(NCO)_3 + 3HOOC.CH_2Br \longrightarrow R'(NH.CO.CH_2Br)_3 + 3CO_2 \qquad (3)$$
$$\text{polymer IV}$$

$$R'(NH.CO.CH_2Br)_3 + 3S(C_2H_4OH)_2 \longrightarrow R'\left\{NH.CO.CH_2\overset{+C_2H_4OH}{\underset{C_2H_4OH}{S}}\right\}_3 3Br^- \qquad (4)$$
$$\text{polymer VII}$$

Polymers V and VI also used poly(propylene oxide)triol backbones, but their functional groups were attached through ester linkages, rather than the urethane groups used in the three polymers described above.

Polymer V, a water soluble poly(thiosulphate), was obtained by esterification of the triol with chloroacetic acid, followed by reaction of the tris-chloroacetate with sodium thiosulphate <u>(5)</u>.

$$R(OH)_3 + 3HOOC.CH_2Cl \longrightarrow R(OOC.CH_2Cl)_3 + 3H_2O \qquad (5)$$

$$R(OOC.CH_2Cl)_3 + 3S_2O_3^= \longrightarrow R(OOC.CH_2.S_2O_3^-)_3 + 3Cl^- \qquad (6)$$
$$\text{polymer V}$$

Polymer VI was the tris-thioglycollate of the poly(propylene oxide)triol <u>(6)</u>.

$$R(OH)_3 + 3HOOC.CH_2SH \longrightarrow R(OOC.CH_2SH)_3 + 3H_2O \qquad (7)$$
$$\text{polymer VI}$$

This polymer was not water soluble, and was applied as an aqueous emulsion.

Polymer I also had thiol reactive groups but was obtained by the esterification of three moles of poly(tetramethylene oxide) of MW $\sim$1000 (HO.R''OH) with four moles of thiomalic acid <u>(2)</u>.

$$3HO.R.''OH + 4\ HOOC.CH(SH)CH_2.COOH \longrightarrow$$

$$HO\left\{OC.CH(SH)CH_2.COOR''O\right\}_3 OC.CH(SH)CH_2.COOH \qquad (8)$$
$$\text{polymer I}$$

The resulting polymer contained (nominally) four thiol groups and two free carboxyl groups and was soluble in the dilute alkali used as a curing catalyst <u>(2)</u>.

Finally, polymer system III, was a mixture of the poly-carbamoyl sulphonate (polymer II) with a polyacrylate emulsion in the ratio 1 part polymer II: 2 parts polyacrylate (resin solids w/w). This mixture has been claimed to have advantages over the polycarbamoyl sulphonate used alone <u>(10)</u>.

<u>Application.</u> All the polymers described were applied by immersion of the fabric to be treated in the polymer solution or emulsion, followed by removal of excess in a pad mangle. The conditions required for curing the polymers on the fabrics - curing catalyst, curing temperature etc. - were obviously dependent on the chemistry of the reactive groups of the polymers, and in each case, the application methods used were those claimed in the literature to be optimum, or known to be optimum from previous work in these laboratories. The conditions used are listed in Table II, together with their sources.

Most of the polymers required mildly alkaline or neutral conditions for optimum cure, and alkaline salts were added to the pad liquors in all cases except the polyisocyanate (polymer IV). In addition, the polythioglycollate pad-liquor (polymer VI) contained a small amount of a polyamide epichlorhydrin resin (Hercosett 57) which has been claimed to improve the performance of this polymer <u>(6)</u>.

Curing conditions again varied from one polymer to another. The polythiomalate cured by drying at 80°C <u>(2)</u>, and the poly-thioglycollate cured if it was stored at ambient conditions for one day after drying <u>(6)</u>.

Steaming brought about full cure in the case of the poly-isocyanate and its two derivatives <u>(3,11,12,13)</u> and to cure the

TABLE II

APPLICATION CONDITIONS USED FOR SHRINK-RESIST

Polymer	pad liquor additions		Application Sequence	Reference
	Catalysts	Wetting agent		
I Polythiomalate	20 g/l Na_2CO_3	5 g/l	pad - dry (10 min/120°C)	(2)
II Polycarbamoyl sulphonate	5 g/l $NaHCO_3$	1 g/l	pad - dry (15 min/100°C) - steam (2 min)	(3)
III Polycarbamoyl sulphonate -polyacrylate (1:2)	5 g/l $NaHCO_3$	1 g/l	pad - dry (15 min/100°C) - steam (2 min)	(10)
IV Polyisocyanate	-	*	pad - dry (15 min/100°C) - steam (2 min)	(13)
V Polythiosulphate	10 g/l Na_2CO_3 + 10 g/l Na_2SO_3	1 g/l	pad - dry (10 min/130°C)	(5)
VI Polythioglycollate	10 g/l $NaHCO_3$ + H57**	*	pad- dry (10 min/120°C) - store	(6)
VIII Polysulphonium bromide	5 g/l urea +5 g/l Na acetate	1 g/l	pad - dry (10 min/100°C) - steam (2 min)	(13)

* Emulsifying agent present
** H57 = 10% Hercosett 57 (resin solids) on weight of polythioglycollate.

polythiosulphate, it was necessary to dry at a rather higher
temperature than is normal for wool fabrics (5).

Pad-Liquor Stability. Pad liquor stability was assessed
by treating fabrics in fresh pad-baths and also in baths which
had been prepared and stored for periods of up to 5 days. The
liquors were stored in the laboratory in open vessels.
    Table III contains the results of this experiment, and shows
that the prepared pad liquors were widely different in stability.
The polyisocyanate emulsion lost its ability to shrink-resist the
fabric after storage for one day. Although the appearance of the
liquor was not markedly changed, titration of the one day old
emulsion (11) showed its isocyanate content to be zero, indicating
that premature reaction with water had occurred. The polythiosulphate solution was also unstable and after about 6h storage,
gelation occurred so that it was impossible to pad the fabric
through the bath.
    All the other polymers could be used successfully after 5
days. The polythioglycollate emulsion tended to separate but
there was no apparent chemical instability, and stirring the
liquor restored its usefulness.

Shrink-Resist Effectiveness. Shrink-resist effectiveness
has been defined in terms of the threshold treatment level (TTL)
i.e. the minimum add-on of polymer which will give a specified
level of washability when applied to a particular fabric (14).
Here, the treated fabrics were required to have less than 5% area
felting shrinkage when washed according to IWS Test Method 185,
that is 3h agitation in 15 l of pH 7 buffer at 40 C in an
International Cubex washtesting machine. TTL was determined by
interpolation from plots of area shrinkage against polymer add-on.
Plots for three of the polymers investigated, when applied to a
woven worsted fabric are shown as examples in Fig. 1. TTL
values for all the polymers on this fabric and a knitted botany
fabric are given in Table IV. In a similar manner, the add-on
required to give a DP rating of 3 on the woven fabric was
determined for each polymer.
    Two factors are immediately apparent from Table IV. The
first is the wide variation in the amounts of different polymers
required to achieve similar effects, and the second is the fact
that the knitted fabric required a much higher add-on of all the
polymers than the woven fabric.
    To obtain the desired level of washability, it was necessary
to apply 5-7 times as much of the least effective polymer (VII)
as of the two most effective polymers (I and II). The other
polymers had intermediate performance, but even the most effective
of these, the polyisocyanate (IV), was only half as effective as
polymers I and II.
    It is of interest to consider the curing reactions of the
various polymers in greater detail, and to examine more closely

TABLE III

THE EFFECT OF AGE OF PAD-LIQUOR ON THE SHRINKAGE

OF TREATED FABRIC

Polymer system	Add on (% oww)	Area shrinkage (%) of fabrics treated with pad-liquors aged			
		0 days	1 day	2 days	5 days
I Polythiomalate	1.6	1	2	4	3
II Polycarbamoyl sulphonate	1.6	2	0	1	2
III Polycarbamoyl sulphonate -polyacrylate	3.0	1	0	2	2
IV Polyisocyanate	2.0	0	43	45	45
V Polythiosulphate	2.5	0	pad-liquor gelled after approx. 6 hours		
VI Polythioglycollate	3.0	2	2	1	2
VII Polysulphonium bromide	4.0	2	0	0	2
Untreated fabric	-	58	-	-	-

Woven worsted fabric
See text for details of application
Wash test: 3h, 15 l Cubex

TABLE IV

THE EFFECTIVENESS OF POLYMERS IN CONFERRING

SHRINK-RESISTANCE AND SMOOTH DRYING

CHARACTERISTICS ON WOVEN AND KNITTED FABRICS

| Polymer system | Threshold treatment level (%) | | |
| | Woven fabric | | Knitted fabric |
	AS < 5%	DP > 3	AS < 5%
I Polythiomalate	0.6	1.2	1.1
II Polycarbamoyl sulphonate	0.6	0.8	0.8
III Polycarbamoyl sulphonate -polyacrylate (1:2)	1.5	1.8	2.3
IV Polyisocyanate	1.3	2.2	2.6
V Polythiosulphate	1.5	3.2	4.0
VI Polythioglycollate	1.7	3.2	3.5
VII Polysulphonium bromide	3.2	6.0	7.0

AS = area felting shrinkage after 3h 15 1 Cubex wash test

DP = durable press rating

the type of cured structure to be expected in each case, in order to find an explanation for the very different performance of these apparently similar polymers.

Polymers V and VI, which have thiosulphate and thioglycollate reactive groups respectively, are both believed to form poly-disulphides when cured on the wool. The thioglycollate cures by alkaline-catalysed aerial oxidation of its thiol groups (6),

$$RSH + [O] \longrightarrow R.SS.R + H_2O \qquad (9)$$

and the thiosulphate by alkaline hydrolysis of its reactive groups, followed by reaction of the thiol so formed with a second thio-sulphate group.

$$R.SSO_3^- + OH^- \longrightarrow R.SH + SO_4^= \qquad (10)$$

$$R.SSO_3^- + R.SH \longrightarrow R.SS.R + HSO_3^- \qquad (11)$$

Thus, virtually identical cured structures would be expected from these two polymers, and indeed, their levels of performance on both knitted and woven fabric were closely similar.

The polythiomalate, however, was three times as effective as either the polythioglycollate or the polythiosulphate and this may be due to one or a number of the following differences in the chemical reactivity and structure of the polymers.

(i)   The polythiomalate was soluble in the alkaline pad liquor which was used for its application, in contrast to the thiogly-collate which was applied as an emulsion. Thus there was more intimate contact between the polythiomalate and the catalysing medium, which may well have led to more efficient curing. In fact, it is possible to cure the thiomalate under milder conditions than those required for the thioglycollate (2).

(ii) In the thiomalate, two of the four thiol groups are much more highly acidic than normal thiol groups because they are activated by two neighbouring carbonyl groups (structure A below). By contrast, the thiol groups of the thioglycollate are activated by only one carbonyl group (structure B below).

A: thiomalate   B: thioglycollate

Since the thiol anion is believed to be the reactive species in the oxidation reaction to form the disulphide crosslinks (hence the need for alkaline catalysis) it is to be expected that the polythiomalate would cure more readily, and possibly more completely than the polythioglycollate.

(iii) The polythiomalate has a nominal functionality of 4, compared with three for the other polymers. This increased

functionality will lead to the more rapid formation of a high
molecular weight product on the fibre surface, by facilitating
branching reactions (15).

(iv) The properties of the different poly(alkylene oxide) backbones used in the two polymers were different. The thioglycollate was based on poly(propylene oxide) whilst the thiomalate
was obtained by esterification of poly(tetramethylene oxide)
(polytetrahydrofuran). PTMO is a much harder polymer than PPO
because of the greater level of non-covalent interactions between
its chains. Thus a PTMO of MW~1000 is solid at room temperature
whilst PPO of similar MW is a liquid. These non-covalent bonds
in PTMO are believed to act as extra, reinforcing crosslinks in
the cured polythiomalate, thus increasing its efficiency as a
shrink-resist polymer. Experiments reported elsewhere (2),
which compared the shrink-resist effectiveness of a series of
polythioglycollates and polythiomalates on both PTMO and PPO
backbones of various molecular weight and functionality, support
this theory.

The three remaining polymers (ignoring the mixed PCS-
polyacrylate system for the moment) are all based on poly(propylene oxide)triols. Indeed polymers II and VII are derivatives
of polymer IV.

The primary curing reaction of the polyisocyanate (polymer
IV) is hydrolysis, followed by reaction of the amine formed with
a second isocyanate group to give a polyurea (16).

$$R.NCO + H_2O \xrightarrow{\text{slow}} R.NH_2 + CO_2 \tag{12}$$

$$R.NCO + R.NH_2 \xrightarrow{\text{fast}} R.NHCONH.R \tag{13}$$

The polycarbamoyl sulphonate (polymer II) which was the
bisulphite adduct of polymer IV, may be regarded as a blocked
isocyanate capable of unblocking to give a free isocyanate which
then cures as shown above. Alternatively it may be considered
as a reactive polymer in its own right, which does not
necessarily cure via a reaction sequence involving the
intermediate formation of free isocyanate:

$$R.NH.CO.SO_3^- \rightleftharpoons R.NCO + HSO_3^- \tag{14}$$

$$\xrightarrow[+H_2O]{} \downarrow{+H_2O} \quad R.NH_2 + HSO_3^- \tag{15}$$

$$R.NH.CO.SO_3^- + R.NH_2 \longrightarrow R.NHCONH.R + HSO_3^- \tag{16}$$

The polycarbamoyl sulphonate is known to cure more rapidly
than the polyisocyanate when treated wool fabrics are steamed
(12) and this can only be caused by an increased rate of formation
of the amine, since the subsequent reaction between the amine and
the isocyanate is fast and therefore not rate-determining. There

are two possible explanations for the increased rate of amine formation: either the polycarbamoyl sulphonate behaves as an activated isocyanate, i.e. reaction (15) is faster than reaction (12), or the increased hydrophilicity of the polycarbamoyl sulphonate over the polyisocyanate allows easier access of water to the sites of reaction.

The polyisocyanate (polymer IV) was more effective as a shrink-resist agent than either the polythiosulphate (V) or the polythioglycollate (VI) despite the fact that all three polymers had closely similar backbones. This has been ascribed to the possibility of hydrogen bond formation between the urethane and urea groups of the cured polyisocyanate which contribute to the cohesive properties of the polymer (17). No such possibility is available in the cured polydisulphides formed from the two sulphur-containing polymers.

It is difficult to explain the increase in shrink-resist efficiency obtained by converting the polyisocyanate to the polycarbamoyl sulphonate. After polymerisation these two pre-polymers should give closely similar networks, although certainly there is the possibility of more efficient curing in the polycarbamoyl sulphonate. In terms of overall washing performance of treated fabrics, this polymer was the most effective of the seven systems studied.

The polysulphonium bromide, although it is prepared from the polyisocyanate cannot revert to the polyisocyanate by unblocking reactions because a carbon atom is lost (as CO_2) in the reaction of the bromoacetic acid with the polyisocyanate (reaction 3). The product of this reaction is a substituted amide. The curing reactions of the sulphonium group are rather obscure, and judging by its shrink-resist effectiveness, these reactions are not very efficient. There are two possibilities. Firstly, the sulphonium group may act as a leaving group, allowing reaction of the polysulphonium bromide with active hydrogen in amine, thiol or hydroxyl groups in the wool surface:

$$R.NH.CO.CH_2\overset{+}{S}(C_2H_4OH)_2 + NH_2\!\!-\!\!Wool \longrightarrow$$

$$R.NH.CO.CH_2.NH\!\!-\!\!Wool + S(C_2H_4OH)_2 + H^+ \qquad (17)$$

Reactive dyes based on this principle have been described (18), but dyestuffs are able to penetrate the fibre under normal dyeing conditions, whereas it is unlikely that a polymer of $\sim$3000 MW would be able to do so when applied by padding. Thus reaction of the polysulphonium bromide with the fibre, if it occurs at all, must be confined to the surface, and would be expected to be inefficient.

The second possibility is that the polysulphonium bromide undergoes crosslinking reactions with the urea which was included in the padding liquor:

$$2 \ RNH.CO.CH_2\overset{+}{S}(C_2H_4OH)_2 + NH_2CONH_2 \longrightarrow$$

$$R.NH.CO.CH_2NH.CO.NH.CH_2.CONH.R + 2S(C_2H_4OH)_2\overset{+}{+}2H \qquad (18)$$

There is limited experimental evidence to support both these possible curing mechanisms. The sulphonium polymer is known to be more effective when applied with bisulphite (19). The bisulphite would react with the wool to produce thiol groups which could then react with the polymer as in the first mechanism described. On the other hand, omission of urea from the pad-liquor decreases the shrink-resist effectiveness of the polymer, which supports the second mechanism. It is unlikely that the relatively small amount of urea used would be sufficient to open up the fibre structure by breaking hydrogen bonds, thus making the fibre interior more accessible to the polymer and promoting its reaction with the wool.

The mixed polymer system, the polycarbamoyl sulphonate-polyacrylate mixture (III) was of approximately the same effectiveness, in terms of total polymer add-on, as the polyisocyanate (IV). However, comparison of the results obtained for this mixed system with those for the polycarbamoyl sulphonate (II) alone, show that the inclusion of the polyacrylate contributed very little to the washing performance of treated fabrics. As will be shown later, the polycarbamoyl sulphonate alone also had advantages over the polyacrylate mixture in terms of hand at a given level of shrink-resistance. However, use of the poly-acrylate-polycarbamoyl sulphonate system may have advantages in improving properties which were not measured in this study.

Most of the polymers investigated gave adequate smooth drying (DP rating greater than 3) on the woven worsted at approximately twice the minimum add-on required for the elimination of felting shrinkage. A rather greater add-on than this was usually required to stabilise the single jersey fabric. The two systems containing polycarbamoyl sulphonate (II and III) were exceptional in giving good smooth drying of the woven fabric and stabilisation of the knitted fabric at only 1.3-1.5 times the add-on required to give a non-felting finish on the woven worsted.

The performance of the polymer finishes has only been studied on two fabrics, and these fabrics were found to require quite different amounts of polymer for the achievement of the same level of antifelting behaviour. However, the ranking of the polymers in terms of shrink-resist effectiveness was only slightly different on the two fabrics, so although it is not possible to extrapolate these results to other fabrics with absolute confidence, it is probably true to say that the ranking of the polymers would not change greatly if the experiments were to be repeated on other fabrics. In fact, the two fabrics used were chosen specifically because the woven worsted was known from past experience to be quite easy to shrink-resist, whilst the single jersey was known to be exceptionally difficult.

Hand of Treated Fabrics. The hand of textile fabrics is
notoriously difficult to measure quantitatively, but in the case
of polymer-treated woven wool fabrics, experience has shown that
flexural rigidity measurements correlate quite well with
subjective hand ratings, provided that the polymer treatment does
not render the surface of the fabric greasy, tacky or harsh.
Accordingly, flexural rigidity measurements were used in this
study for the objective assessment of changes in hand brought
about by polymer treatment of the woven worsted fabric.

The increase in stiffness which occurs when a wool fabric is
treated with a shrink-resist polymer is only of interest in
relation to the fabric's level of washability, and in view of the
very different TTL values of the polymers described, it would be
meaningless to consider the flexural rigidity of the fabrics as
a function of polymer add-on. In Fig. 2, therefore, flexural
rigidity has been plotted against area felting shrinkage, so that
direct comparison can be made between stiffness and washing
performance. In addition, Table V gives the flexural rigidity
values of samples of the woven worsted treated with the minimum
add-on of polymer required to give less than 5% area felting
shrinkage. The results in Table V and the curves in Fig. 2
were obtained by interpolations from plots of flexural rigidity
and area felting shrinkage against polymer add-on, as shown in
Fig. 1.

Fig. 2 shows that with all the polymer treatments, flexural
rigidity increased as area felting shrinkage decreased, up to the
point where shrinkage was eliminated. Flexural rigidity then
continued to increase as polymer add-on was increased further.
Polymers I and II, which were the most effective polymers in
terms of add-on required to give machine washability, were also
the best with regard to fabric hand at this level of washability.
However, there was no general relationship between the shrink-
resist effectiveness of a polymer and the hand of treated
fabrics at the polymer add-on corresponding to TTL. The addition
of polyacrylate to the polycarbamoyl sulphonate (II) had the
effect of increasing the flexural rigidity of the treated fabrics
without a commensurate decrease in their felting shrinkage values.

An interesting aspect of Fig. 2 is the different shapes of
the curves, especially at low shrinkage values. Fabrics treated
with the three polymers (I, V and VI) which cure via formation of
polydisulphide crosslinks increased markedly in stiffness as polymer add-on was increased sufficiently to reduce shrinkage from
5% to zero, whilst the four polyisocyanate-based polymers did not
show this trend. This difference was due partly to the greater
amount of polydisulphide-forming polymer which was necessary to
bring about this final reduction in shrinkage, and partly to the
shape of the flexural rigidity versus add-on curves for these
polymers which were steeper than the curves for the polyisocyanate-

TABLE V

THE FLEXURAL RIGIDITY OF POLYMER TREATED WOVEN

WORSTED FABRIC AT THRESHOLD TREATMENT LEVEL

	Polymer system	Add-on* (% oww)	Flexural Rigidity (mg. cm.)	
			after treatment	after gentle washing**
I	Polythiomalate	0.6	195	150
II	Polycarbamoyl sulphonate	0.6	200	155
III	Polycarbamoyl sulphonate -polyacrylate	1.5	245	175
IV	Polyisocyanate	1.3	285	185
V	Polythiosulphate	1.5	310	175
VI	Polythioglycollate	1.7	240	195
VII	Polysulphonium bromide	3.2	260	185
	Untreated control	-	110	-

*   Minimum add-on required to give <5% area felting
      after 3h 15 l Cubex wash test.

**   2 X 10 min agitation in 25 l water in International Cubex
      wash tester.

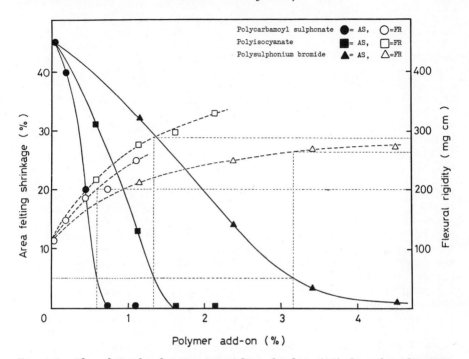

Figure 1. The relationship between area felting shrinkage (AS), flexural rigidity (FR), and polymer add-on for wool worsted fabric treated with three reactive polypropylene oxide derivatives

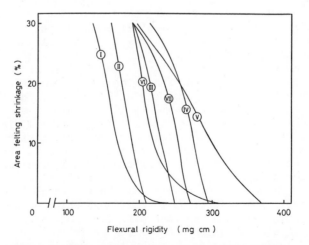

Figure 2. The relationship between area felting shrinkage and flexural rigidity of wool worsted fabric treated with seven reactive prepolymers. For key, see Table I.

based polymers. There may be some connection between this
phenomenon and the fact that the ratio between the add-on levels
required to achieve shrink-resistance in the knitted fabric and
the woven worsted fabric was greater in the case of the polydisulphide polymers, as was the ratio between the polymer levels
required for the attainment of smooth drying and shrink-resistance
on the woven fabric. Shrink-resistance of the knitted fabric and
smooth drying in the woven were obviously more difficult to
achieve, and the polymer add-on required probably corresponds
to rather more than that required for the total elimination of
felting shrinkage in the woven worsted.

    All the polymers discussed here are believed to give shrink-
resistance by a mechanism involving the formation of fibre-fibre
bonds or spot-welds in the structure of treated fabrics. These
fibre-fibre bonds prevent the relative movement of fibres which
occurs when wool fabrics felt, provided they are strong enough
to withstand the forces of agitation in washing. Breakdown of
the bonds can occur either by adhesive failure between the
polymer and the wool, or by cohesive failure of the polymer.
Scanning electron microscopic evidence (11) indicates that
increasing the polymer add-on does not normally lead to an
increased number of fibre-fibre bonds; rather, it results in the
formation of thicker bonds and in the coalescence of the thinner
bonds formed at lower add-on. The stiffness of polymer treated
fabrics will be increased by the formation of fibre-fibre bonds
to an degree which depends on the extensibility and other physical
properties of the polymer, and on the number and thickness of
the bonds. The results presented here show that on balance, the
achievement of shrink-resistance by means of the thinner and
stronger fibre-fibre bonds provided at lower add-on by the more
effective polymers leads to better hand than when shrink-
resistance is obtained by treatment at a higher polymer add-on
with a weaker polymer, or a polymer which does not adhere
efficiently to the fibre.

    The hand of polymer treated wool fabrics can be improved
by using a pad-cure-afterwash finishing route and the effects
of using this route on flexural rigidity are shown in Table V.
Afterwashing was simulated by a very gentle wash in an
International Cubex machine. In all cases, flexural rigidity
was reduced by the afterwash procedure, and this must correspond
to the breakdown of the weakest interfibre bonds, which
presumably do not contribute significantly to shrink-resistance,
since the forces applied to the fabric during the simulated
afterwash process were not as high as the forces applied during
the wash test. The reductions in stiffness which occurred in
the fabrics treated with the less effective polymers were, on
the whole, greater than those occurring in fabrics treated with
the more effective polymers, but the latter still had lower
flexural rigidity after the afterwashing process. This indicates
that the less effective polymers formed a relatively larger

number of weak fibre-fibre bonds, which has an adverse effect on
fabric hand before washing, yet were so easily broken that
they did not contribute to the shrink-resistance of the fabric.
Furthermore, since the fabrics treated with the more effective
polymers were less stiff after a mild washing treatment than
the fabrics treated with the less effective polymers, it appears
that the fibre-fibre bonds which do contribute to shrink-resistance are stronger in the case of the more effective polymers, and
that fewer bonds, or bonds of smaller dimension, are required to
give a specified level of shrinkage control.

Conclusions

(i)   Of the seven polymer systems examined, in aqueous pad-cure
shrink-resist processes, the poly(tetramethylene oxide)-poly-
thiomalate (polymer I) and the poly(propylene oxide)-polycarbamoyl
sulphonate (polymer II) gave the best results in terms of the
stability of the pad-liquor, the shrink-resist effectiveness,
and the hand of treated fabrics for a given level of shrink-
resistance.
      The greater effectiveness of these two polymers is ascribed
to the presence of non-covalent crosslinking in the cured polymer
networks in addition to the covalent crosslinks formed by their
curing reactions.
(ii)   The add-on of the various polymers required for shrink-
resist treatment of a single jersey knitted fabric was always
higher than the add-on required to shrink-resist a woven worsted
fabric, but the ratio between the two add-on levels was
different for different polymers.
(iii) The polymer add-on required to give good smooth drying
characteristics to treated fabrics was greater than that required
for shrink-resist treatments. The ratio between these two add-on
levels again varied with polymer composition, and polymers which
required relatively higher add-on to prevent shrinkage in the
knitted fabric also required higher add-on to give good DP ratings
in the woven fabric.
(iv)   Measurements of fabric stiffness immediately after polymer
treatment and after gentle washing indicated that the less
effective polymers (in terms of the add-on required to produce
a given level of shrink-resistance) formed a relatively large
number of weak fibre-fibre bonds which increased the stiffness
of the treated fabric, but were broken by gentle washing and
therefore could not contribute significantly to shrink-resistance.

Summary

      Seven shrink-resist polymer systems for application to wool
fabrics by aqueous padding procedures have been compared. All
the polymers were poly(alkylene oxide)-based, and five different
reactive or self-crosslinking groups were used. It has been

shown that properties such as threshold treatment level (i.e. minimum add-on of polymer required to give a specified level of shrinkage control), the hand of treated fabrics, the shelf-life of the polymer, and the stability of the formulated pad-liquor are all dependent upon polymer structure.

Those polymers which cured to form networks which were reinforced by non-covalent bonding (e.g. hydrogen bonding in polyurethane/polyureas, or hydrophobic interactions between backbone chains) were found to give optimum results in terms of shrink-resist effectiveness and the hand of treated fabrics.

Acknowledgements

The authors wish to thank Messrs. David Allanach, Peter Greenhill and David Westmoreland and Miss Wendy Halfpenny for valuable technical assistance.

Literature Cited

1. Mills, J.H. and Smith, P., Chem Tech, (1973), 3, 748.
2. Kilpatrick, D.J. and Shaw, T., Proc. 5th Intern. Wool Text. Res. Conf., (1975), V, 19.
3. Guise, G.B. and Jackson, M.A., J. Text. Inst., (1973), 64, 665.
4. U.S. Patent, 3, 558, 264 (1963).
5. Bell, V.A. and Lewis, D.M., Proc. 5th Intern. Wool Text. Res. Conf. (1975), III, 595.
6. Brown, T.D., Rushforth, M.A., Shaw, T., Dobinson, B., Massy, D.J.R., Wilson, W. and Winterbottom, K., Text. Res. J., (1976), 46, 170.
7. British Patent, 1, 259, 048 (1972).
8. Rippon, J.A., J. Soc. Dyers Col., (1975), 91, 405.
9. AATCC Test Method 124-1975.
10. Anon., Internat. Dyer, (1976), 155, 204.
11. Rushforth, M.A. and Rippon, J.A., in preparation.
12. Rippon, J.A. and Rushforth, M.A., Textilveredlung, (1976), 11, 224.
13. Reich, F., Bayer Farben Rev., (1969), 15, 53.
14. Guise, G.B., and Rushforth, M.A., J. Soc. Dyers Col., (1975), 91, 305.
15. Guise, G.B., and Rushforth, M.A., J. Soc. Dyers Col., (1975), 91, 389.
16. Saunders, J.H. and Frisch, K.C., in "High Polymers", Vol. XVI, 457, Interscience, New York, (1964).
17. Rippon, J.A. and Rushforth, M.A. Textilveredlung, (1976), 11, 229.
18. Beech, W.F., "Fibre Reactive Dyes", 210, 233, Logos Press, London (1970).
19. British Patent, 1, 403, 297 (1973).

Recent Developments in Grafting of Monomers to Wool Keratin Using UV and γ-Radiation

JOHN L. GARNETT

The University of New South Wales, Kensington, NSW, Australia 2033

JOHN D. LEEDER

C.S.I.R.O. Division of Textile Industry, Belmont, Victoria, Australia 3216

The application of synthetic polymers to wool is potentially of great importance for modifying a large number of end-use properties of the fibre (1-6). For graft copolymerization of vinyl monomers, radiation-induced techniques utilizing ionizing radiation and, more recently, UV have attracted considerable research attention because of their potential to reduce effluent problems and lower costs of chemicals and energy.

Ionizing radiation copolymerization has been studied by a number of workers (1, 6-10). However, radiation doses to achieve satisfactory grafting have generally been relatively high, thus reducing the possibility of a practical treatment. Recently the radiation-induced grafting of acrylonitrile to wool in the presence of vinyl sulfonyl dyes was reported (11). Photochemical initiation for copolymerization to wool has also been studied, both in the vapour phase (12) and in solution, essentially by the mutual irradiation method (10,13,14). In the ionizing radiation procedure it is advantageous to increase the degree of conversion of monomer to (grafted) polymer, and to reduce significantly the irradiation time, the total dose received by the trunk polymer, and the formation of homopolymer, if the mutual irradiation procedure (the most versatile method) is to be commercially viable. In addition it is important to consider grafting systems where the organic solvent has been replaced by an aqueous medium.

It is the purpose of this paper to discuss recent advances in this field, with particular regard to practical development of UV and ionizing radiation processes for grafting vinyl monomers to wool.

Experimental Grafting Procedures

The ionizing and photochemical-radiation equipment and procedures used for the wool work were essentially similar to those described at this Conference for grafting to cellulose (15). The wool used was either a light-weight (150 gm m^{-2}) plain weave fabric made from 21μ diameter Merino wool fibres, or loose wool (in "top" form) from the same source. Small squares of fibre

197

bundles of 0.4-0.5 g were weighed after equilibration at 23°C, 65% RH for at least 24 hours. For the emulsion experiments, emulsions of ethyl acrylate were prepared by vigorously shaking monomer, water and emulsifying agent until a stable emulsion was formed. For a 50% emulsion, this required about 30 seconds shaking. For lower concentrations of monomer, it was preferable to dilute the 50% emulsion. For the UV work, two sources were used, namely a Philips 90W high-pressure lamp (15) and a 6-inch (200W/inch) Hanovia high pressure lamp. For the padding technique wool samples were squeezed with an equal weight of liquor in a device designed to simulate a pad mangle. After all treatments, samples were washed in hot methanol to remove unreacted monomer, then exhaustively extracted to remove homopolymer (1).

Acid Catalyzed Grafting

Recent work has shown that mineral acids are capable of catalyzing grafting of monomers to wool (16). Further data on acid catalysis are presented here as a prelude to results for radiation grafting. These results actually represent control experiments for the acid enhancement of radiation grafting to be discussed in one of the following sections.

The rate of acid-catalyzed copolymerization in wool (Table 1) is very much faster and more uniform than in other common polymers

TABLE 1.   Grafting of Styrene to Wool in Acidified Methanol Solution at 43°C a

Time (hours)	50% Styrene % Graft	75% Styrene % Graft
1.0	4	6
2.0	8	12
3.0	12	20
5.0	26	35
7.0	46	45
14.0	44	242
32.5	58	4850
72	68	-

a 0.2N methanolic HNO_3 solution in air and "infinite" liquor to wool ratio used.

such as cellulose and the polyolefins (16,17). In Table 1, typical results are shown for the grafting of styrene to wool in the presence of dilute nitric acid and a typical swelling solvent such as methanol. The grafting rate is increased remarkably by increasing the monomer concentration (1,16,17) or the temperature (16,17). No induction period is observed but grafting becomes extremely rapid after a certain level of copolymerization has been attained. Air exerts negligible effect on the reaction. The physical form of the wool affects the grafting rate; loose wool fibres and wool powder graft more rapidly than wool fabric. Very highly grafted fibres increase their physical dimensions several times, and eventually burst at around 5000% graft. Extremely slow grafting is observed over long periods in the absence of acid. Homopolymer formation, as evidenced by an increase in viscosity, is only significant at 80% styrene concentrations; at lower monomer concentrations, even at 2500% graft, the viscosity of the supernatant liquid does not change significantly (17).

Changing the acid used for catalysis has a profound effect on the grafting reaction, nitric acid being the most active, followed by sulfuric acid (Table II).   A maximum in graft is reached at the highest styrene concentration.   Increase in temperature has a dramatic effect on the grafting, as shown by the behaviour with sulfuric acid at 50°C (Table II).

TABLE II.   Effect of Acid Structure in Catalyzed Grafting of Styrene to Wool [a]

% Styrene	% Graft in Acid						
	H_2SO_4		HCl	HNO_3	$HClO_4$	HCOOH	CH_3COOH
20	7	14[b]	6	28	7	2	1
40	8	57[b]	6	121	8	1	1
60	15	150[b]	7	1750	12	0	1
80	26	900[b]	7[c]	2630	20[c]	3	1
90	32[c]	2210[b]	7	3050	19[c]	44	1

[a] 0.2N methanolic acid solutions; 10 days reaction in air at 23°C except for formic and acetic acids (0.1N for 4 days) and [b].

[b] 0.2N methanolic H_2SO_4; reaction time 45 hours at 50°C.

[c] Phase separation.

Even at 23°C, if the reaction is allowed to proceed for very long (*e.g.* 400 hrs), 80% styrene in methanolic H_2SO_4 can yield grafts of the order of 2000%.   When methanol is replaced by other polar solvents such as ethanol, dimethyl sulfoxide and dimethyl formamide, similar results to those shown in Tables I and II are obtained (17), accentuating the role of swelling solvents in this copolymerization.

When the acid catalyzed process is applied to the copolymerization of monomers other than styrene, there is either little grafting, or severe homopolymer formation.   Thus, with ethyl acrylate, although some grafting is achieved the supernatant is virtually completely gelled after 24 hours at 43°C, while acrylonitrile gave neither grafting nor homopolymer formation.   Methyl

methacrylate exhibits both properties shown by these two
monomers in that, at 20% concentration there is little grafting
and very little homopolymer formation (17), whereas at higher
monomer concentrations appreciable copolymer and homopolymer formation is observed (Table III).   This general pattern of

TABLE III.   Acid Catalyzed Grafting of Various Monomers to Wool[a]

Monomer	Graft (%)	Homopolymer
Styrene	66	No
Divinyl benzene	50	No
α-Methyl styrene	10	Yes
4-t-butyl styrene	23	Yes
Acrylic acid	12	No
Ethyl acrylate	8	Yes
Allyl acrylate	9	Yes
Acrylamide	8	No
Ethylene dimethacrylate	25	Yes
Vinyl acetate	13	No
Isoprene	17	No
Vinyl ethyl ether	8	No
Methyl methacrylate[b]	90	Yes

[a] 50% monomer in 0.2N methanolic HNO_3;   reacted at 43°C for
   62 hrs in air;   liquor to wool ratio 50:1;   wool fabric
   used except in b.

[b] 0.1N methanolic HNO_3;   43°C for 18.5 hrs in air;   loose wool.

behaviour occurs with acid catalyzed grafting of a range of
unsaturated monomers (Table III).   Considering the excellent
specificity of styrene for copolymer formation without accompanying homopolymerization, it is perhaps surprising that some styrene
derivatives tend towards homopolymerization.   However, it must be
stressed that the results in Table III were obtained under a
standard set of conditions.   Thus, although these results give an
indication of the comparative reactivities and specificities of
the monomers studied, it is possible that further work on any of
these systems could yield conditions where there is less
homopolymerization and/or increased grafting.

   Mechanism of Acid Catalyzed Grafting.   The preceding observations on copolymer/homopolymer formation, plus studies using
electron microscopy (17) indicate that acid catalyzed polymerization can specifically occur within the wool structure,
particularly with styrene.   Free radical scavengers have been
found to inhibit copolymerization (17).   Grafting was only effective in polar solvents capable of swelling the trunk polymer.
   It has recently been shown (18) that ethyl acrylate grafts
"spontaneously" to wool from aqueous emulsion, but a long

induction period is associated with the reaction. In the present
acid system, no induction period is observed even with ethyl
acrylate, but the grafting reaction becomes extremely rapid after
a certain level of copolymerization has occurred. This change in
rate probably coincides with a change from a diffusion-controlled
reaction to one that is essentially a bulk reaction and may
correlate with rupture of histological or macromolecular regions
within the wool fibres. This type of breakdown would be consistent with the mechanochemical theory of grafting discussed by
Stannett and coworkers (18).

Styrene Comonomer Studies Utilizing Acid-Catalyzed Grafting.
The foregoing results have shown that styrene grafts to wool with
little tendency to homopolymerize. A large number of studies of
wool/polymer systems have been made since the early work of
Lipson and Speakman (19), although extensive commercial use has
not yet been found for such copolymers. For maximum utilization
of such a copolymerization technique, it should preferably be
applicable to monomers other than styrene; thus the technique
must overcome problems of homopolymer formation and/or failure to
graft to the trunk polymer. The use of comonomers, in which one
of the monomers is styrene, has been found, during the present
work, to decrease the tendency of other monomers to homopolymerize
and at the same time to increase grafting efficiency. When
methyl methacrylate is grafted to wool using the combined acid
catalyzed/styrene comonomer technique (Table IV), virtually no

TABLE IV. Acid-Catalyzed Grafting of Methyl Methacrylate and
Acrylonitrile to Wool Using Styrene Comonomer
Technique [a]

Styrene (%)	Comonomer (%)[b]	Graft (%)[c]	Solution Viscosity
10	10 MMA	20 (2)	No change
20	20 MMA	116 (50)	No change
20	-	12 -	-
30	30 MMA	800 (120)	70-100
40	40 MMA	1685 (80)	700-800
40	-	154 -	-
10	10 AC	3 (2)	No change
20	20 AC	4 (0)	No change
30	30 AC	10 (3)	No change
40	40 AC	4400 (4)	No change

[a] 0.1N methanolic HNO_3, reacted at 43°C for 18.5 hrs in air;
liquor to wool ratio 50:1; loose wool used.
[b] MMA = methyl methacrylate; AC = acrylonitrile.
[c] Figures in brackets are grafts obtained for MMA or AC alone.

homopolymer is observed at low styrene/methyl methacrylate
monomer concentrations, and grafting is significant. As the mixed
monomer concentration is increased, considerable grafting occurs
(800%) accompanied by some homopolymer formation.
    The results of acid catalyzed grafting of acrylonitrile
using the styrene comonomer technique (Table IV) are even more
significant, since grafting (4400%) is now achieved with virtually
no homopolymer formation. A similar reduction in homopolymerization is observed with the grafting of ethyl acrylate (Table V).

TABLE V.   Acid Catalyzed Grafting of Ethyl Acrylate to Wool
            Using Styrene Comonomer Technique [a]

| Styrene (%) | Ethyl Acrylate (%) | Graft (%) | S/EA[b] | |
			Found	Calc.
67.5	7.5	8.8	0.116	7.413
62.5	12.5	11.3	0.167	4.457
37.5	37.5	10.3	0.103	1.435
12.5	62.5	9.5	0.085	0.561
7.5	67.5	9.4	0.024	0.366
75	0	35.0		

[a] 0.2N methanolic H_2SO_4, reacted at 43°C for 5 hrs in air;
    liquor to wool ratio 25:1; wool fabric used.

[b] S = styrene, EA = ethyl acrylate. Calculated from classical
    copolymer equation (20).

Additional important information was obtained in this series
since styrene labelled with tritium (17) was used to estimate
accurately the percentage of each of the grafted monomers.   The
data show that even at relatively short conversion times (5 hours)
with grafts of approximately 10%, the more polar ethyl acrylate
is the monomer predominantly grafted, most of the original styrene
remaining unreacted in solution. Further, little homopolymer is
present in the residual grafting solutions from the styrene comonomer experiments after reaction for a number of hours at 44°C.
With methyl methacrylate-styrene and acrylonitrile-styrene in
methanol solutions grafts of up to 4400% were readily achieved.
This corresponded to complete grafting of the monomers present
initially without any homopolymer being formed.
    In addition to reducing homopolymer formation in the grafting
of methyl methacrylate and acrylonitrile, the presence of styrene
in the comonomer mixture increases the magnitude of the graft at
all concentrations of monomer mixtures studied. This percentage
increase in graft is very much higher for both methyl methacrylate
and acrylonitrile at the high monomer mixture concentrations,
particularly above 50% v/v. Inclusion of a second monomer (ethyl
acrylate) retards the rate at which the mixture (ethyl acrylate/

styrene) grafts relative to styrene alone.

Mechanism of Acid Catalyzed Styrene Comonomer Grafting.   An
important feature mechanistically of the present data (Table V),
particularly when ethyl acrylate is used as the second monomer at
concentrations of 75% total monomer solution, is that the percent
graft is virtually independent of the ratio of ethyl acrylate to
styrene. The fact that the observed ratio of styrene/ethyl
acrylate in Table V is significantly less than the value calculated from the copolymerization equation is consistent with the
data of Odian and co-workers for radiation copolymerization to
polyethylene (20), where higher percentages of the more polar
monomer are incorporated than predicted by the copolymerization
equation. This competitive inhibition of the styrene graft
suggests that the monomer other than styrene, *e.g.* ethyl acrylate,
is more strongly adsorbed at the grafting site in the wool trunk
polymer. The presence of polar solvents, through swelling, make
these sites more accessible to grafting monomer. In the presence
of mineral acids, conformations may be altered more drastically
by the breaking of salt bridges and other labile bonds, allowing
rapid swelling with the "mechanical" production (18) of free
radicals which become the actual grafting sites. Again, it
should be noted that swelling alone does not explain these results,
since formic acid is not as effective as nitric acid as a polymerization catalyst (17).

Radiation Grafting of Monomers

A detailed study has been made of the effect of radiation
dose rate and total dose on the grafting of monomers to wool by
the mutual irradiation technique (1,17). No Trommsdorff peak is
evident at lower concentrations of monomer as there is with other
trunk polymers such as cellulose (15,21) and polypropylene (22).
The significant feature of this earlier work is that, at all
styrene concentrations, copolymer formation decreases with increasing dose rate, for the same total dose. Table VI shows that
grafting is more effective from solvents which are small polar
molecules (particularly methanol) than from solvents which are
large and/or non-polar. Thus, even the most effective non-polar
solvent, hexane, gave 14% graft from 60% styrene solution after
10 Mrads of radiation, whilst only 0.2 Mrads was required to graft
28% styrene from 60% styrene solution in methanol. By contrast
with styrene the following monomers achieve the relatively low
graft shown in parentheses after irradiation at 0.1 Mrad/hr to
total doses of 5 Mrads: isoprene (66%), acrolein (23%), ethyl
acrylate (31%) and glycidyl acrylate (0.2%).

Mechanism of Radiation Grafting. If an inhibitor such as
t-butyl catechol is added to either styrene or ethyl acrylate in
methanol, radiation-grafting is reduced (Table VII), confirming

TABLE VI.   Radiation Grafting of Styrene to Wool in
            Various Solvents [a]

Styrene (%)	Graft (%) in Solvent					
	Methanol	Ethanol	Butanol	Dimethyl Formamide	Dimethyl Sulfoxide	Dioxan
20	8	7	3	6	12	3
40	27	6	2	4	13	4
60[b]	28	6	4	3	8	1
80	33	4	3	2	6	4
100	(1)					

[a] γ-Radiation dose 0.2 Mrad at 0.025 Mrad/hr; wool fabric used.
[b] Irradiation of 60% styrene in non-swelling hexane at 0.1 Mrad/hr
to 10 Mrads gave 14% graft.

TABLE VII.   Radiation Grafting of Styrene and Ethyl Acrylate
             in Presence of *t*-Butyl Catechol [a]

t-Butyl Catechol (%)	Graft (%)	
	Styrene	Ethyl Acrylate
0.0	152	22
0.01	109	19
0.1	17	14
0.5	2	4

[a] 60% (v/v) monomer in methanol. Styrene irradiated in air to
0.5 Mrads. Ethyl acrylate irradiated under nitrogen to
0.2 Mrads. Dose rate 0.1 Mrad /hour.

that the predominant mechanism for the grafting is a free-radical
process. However, wool is a relatively polar trunk polymer;
ionic and energy transfer processes are known to occur in ionizing
radiation systems;   thus some contribution from these alternative
processes would be expected in the grafting reaction. Radicals,
i.e. grafting sites, form in wool during exposure to radiation
(6,7,23). Monomers can then copolymerize at these sites via
charge-transfer intermediate formation as proposed earlier for
wool (1) and cellulose (1,15,24). The presence of swelling
solvents is obviously advantageous for the mutual irradiation
technique since swelling of the trunk polymer is necessary to
allow the monomers access to the free radical sites within the
wool structure. Again some mechanism other than swelling by the
solvent must be operative - methanol and ethanol swell wool to the
same extent (25), whilst dimethyl sulfoxide and dimethyl formamide
would be expected to swell wool much more than the alcohols (26) -
yet extent of grafting varies considerably. Different accessibilities to the various histochemical regions of the fibre,

together with different propensities for free radical formation
in these regions, may well be an influencing factor.

Styrene Comonomer Technique in Radiation Grafting.   The
essential problem with radiation grafting of monomers other than
styrene to wool is that generally severe homopolymer formation
accompanies grafting, and virtually precludes use of the technique.
However, if styrene is added to the radiation grafting system
(*e.g.* ethyl acrylate), homopolymer formation is overcome and
finite grafting is achieved (Table VIII).   In addition, even at
high ethyl acrylate/styrene ratios (5:1), the graft predominantly
consists of ethyl acrylate (74%).   These data were obtained using
a novel procedure involving tritium labelled styrene (17).

TABLE VIII.   Radiation Grafting of Ethyl Acrylate in Methanol to
Wool Using Styrene Comonomer Technique [a]

Dose (Mrads)	Styrene (%)	Ethyl Acrylate	Graft (%)	S/EA[b] Found	Calc.
2.7	37.5	37.5	2.7	0.40	1.435
9.5	37.5	37.5	9.5	0.87	1.435
2.1	12.5	62.5	2.1	0.26	0.557

[a] Liquor to wool ratio 25:1.   Wool fabric used.   Radiation
0.1 Mrad/hour.
[b] S = styrene, EA = ethyl acrylate.   Calculated from classical
copolymer equation (20).

Acid Catalyzed Radiation Grafting

In previous preliminary work (17), the presence of acid was
shown to enhance radiation grafting of styrene in methanol to wool
in contrast to the effects for acid alone.   These data showed that
sulfuric and perchloric acids were better catalysts than nitric
acid when combined with the mutual irradiation technique.   Table
IX shows that the effect of solvent on acid-catalyzed radiation
grafting to wool follows a similar trend to that for radiation
without acid (Table VI).   Again, the longer chain alcohols are
less effective than methanol;   with butanol, there appears to be
no enhancement of grafting by the presence of acid.   The most
remarkable result in Table IX is that obtained for dimethyl
sulfoxide, which now becomes the most active solvent of those
studied for this combination of grafting conditions.   Very large
amounts of grafting occur, with a Trommsdorff peak at 352% for the
80% styrene solution, at a total dose of only 0.2 Mrads.
Unfortunately, when radiation was combined with acid catalysis
for the grafting of a range of monomers other than styrene, homopolymerization invariably masked any increases in rate or extent

of copolymer formation. Again this was particularly noticeable
with polyfunctional acrylate monomers.

Mechanism of Acid Enhanced Radiation Grafting. The acid
enhancement, when styrene in polar solvents is radiation grafted
to wool, is broadly analogous to the acid enhancement found when
radiation copolymerizing to other trunk polymers such as cellulose
(27) and the polyolefins (22). However, with wool, the effect is
more complicated because wool is also capable of an extensive
simple acid catalyzed grafting reaction as previously discussed.
The acid catalyzed copolymerization is very much slower than
radiation grafting; however, once the radical sites are formed by
impinging radiation, acid catalyzed grafting can occur at a much
faster rate.

TABLE IX.   Acid-Catalyzed Radiation Grafting of Styrene to Wool
            in Various Solvents a

Styrene (%)	Graft (%) in Solvent$b$				
	Methanol	Ethanol	Butanol	Dimethyl Formamide	Dimethyl Sulfoxide
20	38 (8)	11 (4)	3 (3)	20 (6)	47 (12)
40	58 (27)	14 (7)	3 (2)	24 (4)	103 (13)
60	73 (28)	14 (7)	3 (4)	12 (2)	176 (8)
80	90 (33)	17 (4)	3 (3)	7 (2)	352 (5)
90	–	16 (5)	3 (5)	4 (4)	65 (7)

a Radiation dose 0.2 Mrads at 0.025 Mrad/hour; 0.2N H_2SO_4
    used for acid catalysis.
b Figures in brackets are for radiation grafting without acid.

Alternatively, the acid enhancement in radiation grafting to
wool may be a radiation chemistry phenomenon as proposed for
cellulose (15,27,28) and the polyolefins (22). With the latter
two trunk polymers, the available evidence suggests that radiation
grafting to these materials is associated with, and assisted by,
H atom formation (*i.e.* G(H) yields). In terms of this theory, any
procedure for increasing G(H) in the radiolytic system should also
assist radiation grafting. In the radiation chemistry of solvent
methanol (29-31), addition of mineral acid increases G(H) yields
through secondary electron capture, as in Equation 1. Thus, in a

$$H^+ + e \rightarrow H \qquad (1)$$

radiation grafting system containing styrene/methanol/wool,
addition of acid should increase G(H) yields and also enhance
grafting, as observed. However, at this time it is not possible
to separate the contribution of simple acid catalysis and radiation
to the overall grafting mechanism. In current studies it is hoped
to achieve this aim.

Acid Enhancement of Styrene Comonomer Technique in Radiation
Grafting.   When the styrene conomomer technique is applied to the
preceding system of acid-catalysis combined with radiation
grafting, a large enhancement in copolymerization is achieved for
the same radiation dose (Table X).   Thus with ethyl acrylate/
styrene mixtures at 0.4 Mrads dose of gamma radiation, inclusion

TABLE X.   Acid Enhancement of Radiation Grafting of Ethyl
Acrylate to Wool using the Styrene Comonomer Technique[a]

Styrene (%)	Ethyl Acrylate (%)	Dose (Mrad)	Graft[b] (%)	S/EA Found[c]	S/EA Calc.[d]
37.5	37.5	0	7[e]	-	-
37.5	37.5	0.05	8 (1)	0.11	1.44
37.5	37.5	0.1	13 (2)	0.17	1.44
37.5	37.5	0.2	28 (3)	0.74	1.44
37.5	37.5	0.4	80 (10)	0.87	1.44
50	25	0.2	40 -	1.40	2.25
12.5	62.5	0.2	18 (2)	0.13	0.56

[a] Grafting solutions (75% total monomer) 0.2N methanolic H_2SO_4.
Liquor to wool ratio 25:1. Wool fabric used. Radiation dose
rate 0.1 Mrad/hour.
[b] Values in brackets are for radiation and comonomer technique
without acid.
[c] Estimated by tritium-labelling technique (16).
[d] Calculated from the classical copolymer equation (20).
[e] Acid-catalyzed comonomer technique (no radiation) at 43°C for
4 hours (*i.e.* equivalent to longest radiation time in the Table).

of 0.2N H_2SO_4 leads to an almost tenfold increase in graft with
75% total monomer concentration in methanol. At all ethyl
acrylate/styrene ratios the grafts contain more ethyl acrylate
monomer than is predicted from theory. All grafting yields are
higher than the simple acid catalyzed blank (7%) which was a
reaction carried out for 4 hours at 43°C with acid only, *i.e.* the
same time as for the highest radiation dose sample where the
corresponding graft was 80%.
Methyl methacrylate is one monomer which is difficult to graft
efficiently to wool without the comonomer technique because of
competing homopolymer formation. The data in Table XI show the
grafting of methyl methacrylate using four different radiation
systems, *i.e.* grafting with radiation, radiation with acid,
radiation with styrene comonomer technique, and finally acid-
enhancement of the radiation/styrene comonomer procedure. The
significant advantages of the last technique are apparent,
virtually no homopolymer being detected in any of the runs in the
last MMA column of the table. Analogous data for the acrylo-
nitrile/methanol monomer system are also shown in Table XI.

TABLE XI.   Acid Enhancement in Radiation Grafting of Methyl
             Methacrylate (MMA) to Wool using Styrene (S)
             Comonomer Technique[a]

Monomer (%)	Graft (%)							
	MMA	MMA+H[+]	S/MMA (1/1)	S/MMA+H[+] (1/1)[d]	AC	AC+H[+]	S/AC (1/1)	S/AC + H[+] (1/1)
10	3	7	3	7	3	4	4	10
30	2	6	21	60	0	4	12	94[c]
50	3	51[b]	31	92	2	5	37[b]	182[c]
70	7	78[b]	18	91	4	3	42[b]	214[c]
90	3	20[b]	7[c]	69	3	[b]	24[b]	[e]

[a] Radiation dose 0.2 Mrads at 0.025 Mrads/hour in air. Wool
fabric used with 0.2N HNO$_3$.
[b] Supernatant viscous, indicating significant homopolymerization.
[c] Slightly viscous supernatant.
[d] No viscosity increase in supernatant for any of these samples
[e] Heavy graft, supernatant high viscosity.

Similar conclusions can be drawn from these results, although even
using the styrene comonomer technique with acrylonitrile plus acid
enhancement, some homopolymer was present in the supernatant
liquid. The acid enhanced styrene comonomer radiation grafting
technique has also been applied to the copolymerization of other
monomers (17). In all cases use of the combined techniques was
advantageous for either increasing grafting efficiency and/or
reducing homopolymerization. This is of potential value, e.g.
with polyfunctional monomers such as glycidyl acrylate, which are
usually difficult to graft without accompanying homopolymer
formation.

Mechanism of Acid Enhancement of Styrene Comonomer Radiation
Grafting. The acid enhancement effect of the styrene comonomer
radiation process is consistent with the accelerating effect of
mineral acid in radiation grafting of styrene to wool discussed
earlier in this paper. Monomers other than styrene could only be
grafted to wool in the presence of acid if the styrene comonomer
technique were used, since attempts to graft monomers alone,
without styrene, resulted in predominant homopolymerization or
very little copolymerization.

A number of mechanistic aspects of the radiation comonomer
procedure are similar to the simple acid catalyzed comonomer
technique previously discussed. The data indicate that the
monomer other than styrene (e.g. ethyl acrylate) is strongly
adsorbed to the protein chain at the active grafting site. In the
first technique these sites originate from bond rupture by
ionizing radiation, whereas in the simple acid catalyzed process
it appears that mineral acids alter conformations, probably by
breaking salt bridges and hydrogen bonds and allowing swelling

with the mechanical production of free radicals (18). The added presence of polar solvents then make these sites (whether formed by radiation or simple acid) more accessible by altering the conformation of the protein chain. However, the degree of swelling is not the primary mechanism - some of the acid/solvent systems in this study were not as effective as other systems of lower swelling potential. Presumably differential accessibilities and/or polypeptide chain protonation or side group dissociation also influence the relative rates and extent of copolymerization and homopolymerization.

The explanation of the acid enhancement effect of the radiation comonomer grafting is complicated by the fact that both acid and radiation can initiate copolymerization independently. Although the simple acid catalyzed process has a long induction period at room temperature, the simultaneous use of ionizing radiation reduces this induction time, presumably because additional radicals are formed by radiation. The presence of acid would then expose these additional "radiation-formed" radicals to reaction with monomer due to the mechanical swelling effect of the acid/solvent system.

There is also the purely radiation chemistry explanation for the enhancement of the radiation comonomer grafting with wool. This has previously been discussed in this paper to explain the acid enhancement of the simple radiation grafting reaction to wool. In grafting to wool, it is probable that the radiation chemistry mechanism and the mechanical swelling mechanism both contribute appreciably to the acid enhancement of the radiation copolymerization; with cellulose and the polyolefins, simple acid-catalyzed grafting is insignificant, and the radiation mechanism predominates.

Grafting from Emulsions Using Acid Plus Radiation and Comonomer Techniques

Stannett and co-workers (18) have previously shown that, in an aqueous emulsion system, ethyl acrylate grafts to wool, although a long induction period is involved. In the present work, attempts are made to use discoveries from the preceding sections to eliminate the induction period by including acid and a styrene comonomer procedure. The data (Table XII) show that some grafting of ethyl acrylate occurs from emulsions after simply standing on contact at room temperature, in agreement with Stannett *et al*. (18). In general, higher grafts from emulsions are observed at 50°C than at 18°C.. The presence of acid in the emulsion increases the graft, consistent with the acid enhancement effects already discussed in grafting styrene from methanolic solution. The presence of styrene as a comonomer in the emulsions enhances ethyl acrylate grafting when acid is also present, but not otherwise. Only a small advantage is gained by using mutual irradiation with emulsions, 10% conversion of monomer to graft copolymer being observed.

TABLE XII.   Grafting of Ethyl Acrylate to Wool from Aqueous
             Emulsions with and without Acid, Radiation and
             Styrene Comonomer Techniques

Emulsion^a	Temp. (°)	Graft (%)				
		No Acid^b	0.1N H$_2$SO$_4$^{b}	0.1N HNO$_3$^{b}	No Acid^c	0.1N H$_2$SO$_4$^{c}
50% EA + 4% X200	18	1	8	9	3	5
50% EA + 4% X200	50	3	9	11	-	-
25% EA/25% S + 4% X200	18	1	6	7	3	5
25% EA/25% S + 4% X200	50	2	9	29	-	-

^{a} EA = ethyl acrylate;   S = styrene;   X200 = Triton X200
   emulsifying agent (Rohm & Haas). Emulsions made to 100%
   with water.
^{b} Contact time 18 hours;   liquor to wool ratio 20:1; no radiation.
^{c} With radiation of total dose 0.1 Mrad, dose-rate 0.1 Mrad/hour
   in air. Padded to give liquor/wool ratio of 1:1.

Pre-Irradiation Studies of Grafting.   In this process, gamma
radiation creates free radicals at various sites in the wool.
These sites can then react with monomer from the emulsion or
solvent, if the wool has swollen sufficiently to enable diffusion
of monomer to the radical site. Figure 1 shows the effect of
total pre-irradiation dose on the wool graft when irradiation of
the wool is followed by padding, under nitrogen, of an equal
weight of emulsion containing ethyl acrylate. Copolymerization
increases markedly with total dose. Above 2 Megarads the wool
begins to yellow slightly due to the onset of degradation. Dose-
rates of up to 4.5 Mrads/hour had little effect on percentage
graft.   Extraction was used to terminate further grafting by
removing unreacted monomer, when the required reaction time had
expired. The time required for complete reaction is about 40
minutes (Figure 2). In the first five minutes grafting occurs
very rapidly, but then becomes slower. The temperature of the
sample during the time lag also affects the graft (Figure 3).
Figure 4 shows the effect on the graft of exposing the pre-
irradiated wool to air for various times before padding on of
emulsion, a probable necessity in commercial application of this
process. The reduced grafting with increasing time of exposure
to air reflects the decay of free radical initiating sites in air.
Figure 5 demonstrates the role of long liquor ratios on the
grafting. Increasing the liquor to wool ratio initially increases
the amount of acrylate grafted to pre-irradiated wool until the
liquor to wool ratio is about 4:1. However, the increase in graft
is less than the proportionate increase in monomer present, so
that there is a fall in the percentage conversion of monomer to
graft copolymer. The effect of monomer concentration on the graft
of ethyl acrylate emulsions is described in Figure 6.   The

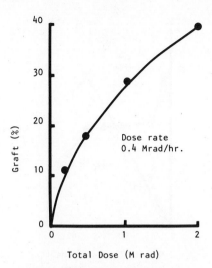

1:1 liquor:wool; contact time 1 hr.;
monomer concentration 50%

Figure 1. Effect of pre-irradiation dose on grafting of ethyl acrylate emulsion to wool

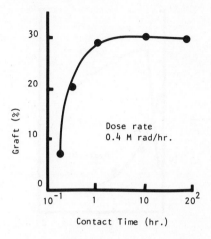

1:1 liquor:wool; 1 Mrad total dose;
monomer concentration 50%

Figure 2. Effect of contact time on grafting of ethyl acrylate to pre-irradiated wool

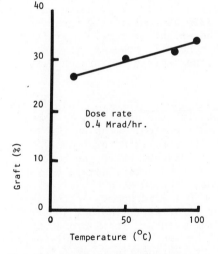

1:1 liquor:wool; 1 Mrad total dose;
monomer concentration 50%

Figure 3. Effect of temperature on grafting of ethyl acrylate to pre-irradiated wool

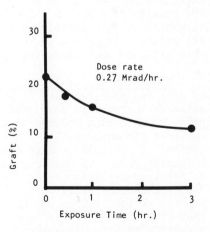

1:1 liquor:wool; 1 Mrad total dose;
monomer concn. 40%; contact time 1 hr.

Figure 4. Effect of exposure to air of pre-irradiated wool on emulsion grafting of ethyl acrylate

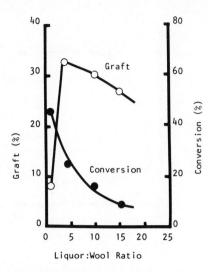 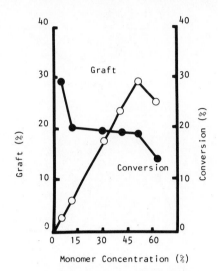

1 M rad total dose at 0.4 Mrad/hr.;
Monomer concn. 20%; contact
time 1 hr.

Figure 5. Effect of liquor ratio on emulsion grafting of ethyl acrylate to pre-irradiated wool

1 Mrad total dose at 0.4 Mrad/hr.;
3:1 liquor:wool; contact time 1 hr.

Figure 6. Effect of monomer concentration on emulsion grafting of ethyl acrylate to pre-irradiated wool

concentration of monomer in the emulsion is limited by emulsion stability and varies with type of emulsifying agent. The concentration limit for which stable emulsions could be prepared was about 55% monomer, using 4% Triton X200 as emulsifying agent. The results in Figure 6 show that the weight of acrylate grafted to wool increases rapidly up to 50% monomer; however, this still represents a reduction in the actual percentage conversion with increasing monomer concentration.

    Mechanism of Pre-Irradiation Emulsion Grafting. The effects of dose and dose-rate are consistent with the model system used, since an increase in dose produces more radical sites on the trunk polymer, whereas a reduced dose-rate (for a fixed total dose) achieves the same result. A limit is reached where the concentration of radicals is high enough for substantial damage to the molecular groups in the wool to occur, as evidenced by yellowing at total doses in excess of 2 Mrad at 0.4 Mrad/hour. Although 70% of the final graft occurs in the first five minutes, about 40 minutes is required to reach a maximum value. It is probable that five minutes is sufficient for the monomer in the emulsion to penetrate to all active sites and that the additional grafting observed over long reaction times represents the lengthening of the chains formed at these active sites. Exposure to air reduces the graft, presumably by deactivation of radical sites in the presence of oxygen (32). The copolymerizations in Figures 1-6 were performed under nitrogen, and pre-irradiation was carried out in vacuum.

An increase in the liquor to wool ratio increases the graft from an emulsion containing 20% monomer, but the increase is less than the relative increase in monomer weight present. This is reflected by the drop in the percentage conversion which is slightly under 50% at 1:1 liquor to wool ratio.

Photosensitized Grafting

Replacement of ionizing radiation with UV (Table XIII) leads to appreciable grafting of styrene from methanol solution in the presence of a range of sensitizers, both organic and inorganic. Without sensitizer, some grafting to wool still occurs, and the presence of a swelling solvent such as methanol assists the process. The photochemical grafting data, obtained without added sensitizer, are consistent with analogous results previously reported by other workers for the effect of swelling solvent in photochemical grafting to wool (14). However, the data in Table

TABLE XIII.   Photosensitized Grafting of Styrene to Wool Fabric[a]

Styrene (%)	Graft (%) with Sensitizer (1% w/v)				
	None	Uranyl Nitrate	Benzophenone	Benzoin Ethyl Ether	Biacetyl
20	2	23	2	–	22
40	29	22	2	54	25
60	55	168	4	114	23
80	53	140	22	169	30
90	73	111	31	407	52
100	5				

[a] Methanol solvent used at liquor:wool ratio of 50:1; samples irradiated with Philips 90W high-pressure UV lamp for 24 hours at 24 cm from source.

XIII show that the efficiency of the UV copolymerization is significantly increased in the presence of sensitizer and such a process is to be preferred for facile copolymer preparation. Of the organic sensitizers, benzoin ethyl ether (BEE) was the most effective in Table XIII, reaching a maximum in grafting at 90% monomer concentration. Biacetyl (BAC) is the next most effective organic sensitizer, with benzophenone the least efficient, in the same Table.

Mechanism of Photosensitized Grafting.   It has been shown that wool keratin molecules can absorb ultraviolet light, leading to excited molecules and/or radicals which are capable of initiating copolymerization reactions with monomers (14,33). The following reaction schemes have been proposed to explain sites in wool generated by UV (Equations 2 through 5):

$$-CH_2-S-S-CH_2- \quad \xrightarrow{h\nu} \quad -CH_2-S^{\bullet} + {}^{\bullet}S-CH_2- \qquad (2)$$

$$-CH_2-S-S-CH_2 \quad \xrightarrow{h\nu} \quad -CH_2-S-S^{\bullet} + {}^{\bullet}CH_2- \qquad (3)$$

$$\begin{matrix} -CO-NH-CH- \\ | \\ R \end{matrix} \quad \xrightarrow{h\nu} \quad \begin{matrix} -CO^{\bullet} + {}^{\bullet}NH-CH- \\ | \\ R \end{matrix} \qquad (4)$$

$$\begin{matrix} -CO-NH-CH- \\ | \\ R \end{matrix} \quad \xrightarrow{h\nu} \quad \begin{matrix} -CONH^{\bullet} + {}^{\bullet}CH- \\ | \\ R \end{matrix} \qquad (5)$$

Additional grafting sites due to "secondary reactions" of wool with UV have also been proposed (14). With the addition of sensitizer, new grafting sites are potentially capable of being formed in the wool trunk polymer in the presence of UV again by energy transfer processes or by hydrogen atom abstraction reactions similar to those proposed in analogous UV grafting to cellulose (15). The specific mechanisms by which inorganic sensitizers such as uranyl nitrate and organic sensitizers like BEE and BAC promote copolymerization have again been discussed in detail for cellulose (15) and analogous reaction paths exist in the sensitized UV grafting to wool. However, UV sensitized grafting to wool is probably more efficient than with cellulose, since the self-sensitization reaction with wool appears to be greater than with cellulose.

Acid Enhanced Photosensitized Grafting. Because of the unique position of wool, in that simple acid catalysis promotes copolymerization of monomers to this trunk polymer, the potential effect of possible UV enhancement of this acid-catalyzed process was investigated. The data in Table XIV show that large increases in sensitized graft are achieved when mineral acid is

TABLE XIV.   Acid-Catalyzed Photosensitized Grafting of Styrene to Wool Fabric^a

Styrene (%)	Graft (%) with Sensitizer (1% w/v)				
	None	Uranyl Nitrate	Benzophenone	Benzoin Ether	Biacetyl Ether
20	8 (2)	160 (23)	32 (2)	80 (-)	103 (22)
40	170 (29)	- (-)	98 (2)	364 (54)	876 (25)
60	246 (55)	1506 (168)	70 (4)	957 (114)	2418 (23)
80	285 (53)	2487 (40)	138 (22)	1463 (169)	3087 (30)

^{a} Methanol solvent containing 0.1N H_2SO_4 used at liquor:wool ratio of 50:1; samples irradiated with Philips 90W high-pressure UV lamp for 24 hours at 24 cm from source. Figures in brackets are graft without acid.

added to all sensitized systems. With BAC, uranyl nitrate and
BEE (in that order), the acid enhancement of the sensitized graft
is particularly large, in the case of BAC the increase was over
one hundred-fold.

Mechanism of Acid Enhanced Photosensitized Grafting. The
fact that the simple acid-catalyzed grafting process to wool (*i.e.*
without addition of sensitizer) is enhanced by UV shows that in
many respects the UV/wool system is analogous to grafting with
ionizing radiation. Since acid alone catalyzes grafting to wool,
the role of UV in enhancing this acid grafting without sensitizer
addition could be simply a radiation effect, involving the photochemical generation of radical sites where acid copolymerization
may occur. Alternatively, the process may be considered as
primarily a UV system enhanced by the presence of acid. The
addition of acid generates more grafting sites in the trunk polymer
by mechanochemical means (discussed earlier); these sites then
lead to increased grafting. Both mechanisms obviously contribute
to the overall process and it is difficult at this time to
unequivocally separate the contribution of each process to the
overall grafting yield.
      Once radical formation has occurred in the trunk polymer, and
monomer has diffused to the site, copolymerization in this UV
system can proceed via a charge-transfer mechanism similar to that
already proposed for grafting in ionizing radiation systems (23,
34). Such a proposal would be consistent with acid catalysis
already observed in general photochemical reactions (35),
especially photo-addition processes involving donor-acceptor pairs
which are intermediates in general charge-transfer theory.
Grafting reactions thus constitute another field in photochemistry
where acid catalysis has been observed.
      With the addition of sensitizer to the acid-enhanced UV
grafting system, the mechanism of the overall reaction becomes
even more complicated. The two complementary processes discussed
above for the unsensitized UV acid-enhanced grafting are operative.
In addition, sensitizer can generate further grafting sites in
the trunk polymer by hydrogen abstraction reactions and also energy
transfer processes. Acid enhancement in UV sensitized grafting may
thus be mechanistically closer to acid catalysis in organic photochemical reactions, especially those processes involving proton
transfer (35) since in sensitized grafting, a donor-acceptor
interaction between sensitizer and trunk polymer prior to H
abstraction is involved as an intermediate in grafting site
formation.

Photo-sensitized Grafting from Aqueous Solution. For a
number of reasons, especially preparative and practical considerations, the ultimate technique for grafting would be a pad-batch,
rapid cure UV system, applied from solvent or (preferably) aqueous
media. In Table XV, aqueous solutions of the listed monomers were
padded on in the presence of sensitizer and exposed for two

three-minute cycles to a six-inch Hanovia lamp (200 W/inch).
Soxhlet extraction of the copolymer revealed that with acrylic
acid, diethylaminoethyl methacrylate and hydroxyethyl acrylate,
virtually 100% conversions were achieved, whilst with methacrylic
acid and hydroxyethyl methacrylate conversions of up to 75% were
observed. One significant feature of the results is that from
calibration experiments (36), if the present runs were carried
out on a commercial 200 W/inch lamp specially focussed for this
work, cure times of a fraction of a second would be expected.

TABLE XV.   Photosensitized Grafting of Some Water-Soluble
             Monomers to Wool Fabric[a]

Monomer Solution	Graft (%)	
	Before Extraction	After Extraction[b]
30% acrylic acid	34	34
20% diethylaminoethyl methacrylate	22	20
30% hydroxyethyl acrylate	41	40
50% methacrylic acid	60	46
40% hydroxyethyl methacrylate	45	27

[a] Aqueous solutions of monomer containing BEE (1% for first
2 runs, 2% for remainder) padded on to 1:1 liquor:wool ratio
and exposed for 2 x 3 min to 6 inch (200 W/inch) Hanovia
high pressure UV lamp.
[b] Soxhlet extraction with water for 8 hours.

Application of Grafted Wools

Ionizing and UV irradiation offer possible alternatives to
the use of chemicals and/or heat for polymerization of monomers
or curing of prepolymers on wool, with the potential bonus of
reduced energy costs and fewer effluent problems. The diversity
of monomer types, plus possibilities for use of comonomer techniques and specific application of monomer or polymer either
internally or externally to the fibre, should allow modification
of many of the end-use properties of wool. Thus Needles *et al.*(3)
and Watt (4) list the following properties as being amenable to
modification by internal deposition (grafting) of polymers -
abrasion resistance, thermal stability, tensile properties,
torsional modulus, elasticity, stiffness, density, swelling
properties, moisture regain and water sorption characteristics,
pilling resistance, shrinkage resistance, oil-, water- and soil-
repellancy, chemical settability, dyeing properties, resistance
to light and microbial attack, and wear properties in garment
and carpet form.

Thus, Batty and Guthrie (11) are using radiation-induced
graft copolymerization of acrylonitrile and vinyl-containing
reactive dyestuffs to increase colourfastness on wool; simple
irradiation of wool containing reactive dyes (37) should increase
the reactivity. Radiation grafting has been studied (6,10) as a
means for stabilizing the improved wrinkle recovery of wool
fabrics conferred by annealing (38). Stannett *et al.* have found
that wool/polyethylacrylate copolymers have increased elasticity
and show increases in rate of drying (39,40). The presence of
polyethylacrylate is also reported to increase abrasion resistance (41,42).

Internal deposition of 4-vinyl pyridine using radiation
procedures (6) has been shown to improve the shrink resistance of
wool fabrics and at the same time modify the dye-binding and
metal-binding capacity (6,17). Simpson *et al.* have used graft
copolymer formation to increase the bulk of carpet yarns (43) and
improve the settability of wool fibres (41). These authors
suggest that the latter process may have applications in wig
making. A combined radiation/chemical curing using N-methylol-
acrylamide has been shown to be a viable means for increasing
crease-retention and improving both the wet and dry-wrinkle
recovery of cotton fabrics (44).

Surface application of polymer finishes can result in
practical improvements in shrink resistance, permanent-press
properties, wrinkle recovery and pigment dyeing of wool (45), and
in this area radiation has potential for curing and adhesion-
promotion of prepolymers to the fibre surface, or in formation of
surface grafts of monomer from the vapour state or from non-
swelling solvents. Needles *et al.* (12,45) have grafted a range
of acrylic monomers onto wool using photo-initiation, while water-,
oil- and soil-repellancy has been conferred on cotton textiles by
UV-grafting of fluoroalkyl acrylates from the vapour state (46).

Current interest involves UV-curing as a replacement for
heat-curing of paints, coatings and inks, using a UV-sensitizer
and polyfunctional acrylate monomer, applied with conventional
prepolymer types such as polyesters, acrylics, alkyls and polyurethanes (47-49). This type of system has been shown to be
applicable to wool fabric (36), as have silicone polymer systems
containing vinyl silicones (36,50). UV and ionizing radiation
have also been used to graft phosphorus containing monomers to
impart flame proofing to wool (6,17), the process particularly
with UV, appearing to be amenable to rapid cure procedures.
Finally, there is the possibility that copolymers of wool prepared
by both UV and ionizing radiation could be utilized advantageously
for the immobilization of enzymes (51) and the heterogenization of
homogeneous metal complexes (52), two fields which at present have
been predominantly confined to the polyolefins (51,52) and poly-
vinyl chloride (53). The results of present work (36,54) suggest
that wool could be of value in this application, particularly in
processes approaching UV rapid cure. These are the types of

systems that are currently being explored for wool uses in the grafting field.

Acknowledgements. We thank the Australian Institute of Nuclear Science and Engineering, the Australian Atomic Energy Commission and the Australian Wool Corporation for continued support. We are also grateful to the following co-workers who at some time were responsible for part of this work: Drs. Davids, Davis, Dilli, Fletcher, Kenyon and Phuoc.

Literature Cited

1. Dilli, S., Garnett, J.L., Kenyon, R.S., Martin, E.C., Phuoc, D.H., Yen, Y., Leeder, J.D., J. Macromol. Sci. Chem. (1972), A6, 719.
2. Delmenico, J., Fleischfresser, B.E., Textile Inst. and Industry (1972), 10, 78.
3. Needles, H.L., Sarsfield, L.J., Dowhaniuk, D.M., Textile Res.J. (1972), 42, 558.
4. Watt, I.C., J. Macromol. Sci. (1970), C5, 175.
5. Gupta, K., Wool and Woollens of India (1968), 5, 43.
6. Garnett, J.L., Guise, B., Leeder, J.D., in preparation.
7. Burke, M., Kenny, P., Nicholls, C.H., J. Textile Inst. (1962), 53, T370.
8. Armstrong, A.A. Jr., Rutherford, H.A., Textile Res. J. (1963), 33, 264.
9. Stannett, V.T., Araki, K., Gervasi, J.A., McLeskey, S.W., J. Polymer Sci. (1961), 3, 3763.
10. D'Arcy, R.L., Watt, I.C., McLaren, K.G., J. Macromol. Sci. Chem. (1972), A6, 689.
11. Batty, N.S., Guthrie, J.T., Abstracts, 5th Int. Wool Text. Res. Conf. Aachen (1975), p.341.
12. Needles, H.L., Alger, K.W., Abstracts, 5th Int. Wool Text. Res. Conf. Aachen (1975), p.316.
13. Needles, H.L., J. Appl. Polymer Sci., (1971), 15, 2559; (1972), 16, 337.
14. Ishibashi, H., Oku, M., 3rd Int. Wool Text. Res. Conf. Paris (1965), Vol. 3, p.385.
15. Garnett, J.L., This Conference, in press.
16. Kenyon, R.S., Garnett, J.L., Polymer Letters (1973), 11, 651.
17. Garnett, J.L., Kenyon, R.S., in press.
18. Williams, J.L., Stannett, V.T., Polymer Letters (1970), 8, 711.
19. Lipson, M., Speakman, J.B., J. Soc. Dyers and Colourists (1949), 65, 390.
20. Odian, G., Rossi, A., Ratchek, E., Acker, T., J. Polymer Sci. (1961), 54, 511.
21. Dilli, S., Garnett, J.L., J. Appl. Polymer Sci. (1967), 11, 839.
22. Garnett, J.L., Yen, N.T., Polymer Letters (1974), 2, 2259.

23. Garnett, J.L., Kenyon, R.S., Leeder, J.D., Murty, G.S., unpublished data.
24. Dilli, S., Garnett, J.L., J. Polymer Sci. (1966), A-1, 4, 2323.
25. Bradbury, J.H., Leeder, J.D., J. Appl. Polymer Sci. (1963), 7, 533.
26. Bradbury, J.H., Chapman, G.V., Textile Res. J. (1963), 8, 666.
27. Dilli, S., Garnett, J.L., Phuoc, D.H., Polymer Letters, (1973), 11, 711.
28. Garnett, J.L., Phuoc, D.H., Airey, P.L., Sangster, D.F., Aust. J. Chem., in press.
29. Ekstrom, A., Garnett, J.L., J. Chem. Soc. A (1968), 2416.
30. Sherman, W.V., J. Phys. Chem. (1967), 71, 4245.
31. Baxendale, J.H., Mellows, F.W., J. Am. Chem. Soc. (1961), 83, 4720.
32. Huglin, M.B., Proc. Royal Aust. Chem. Inst. (1976), 43, 43.
33. Crawshaw, G.H., Speakman, J.B., J. Soc. Dyers Colour (1954), 70, 81
34. Dilli, S., Garnett, J.L., Martin, E.C., Phuoc, D.H., J. Polymer Sci. C (1972), 37, 57.
35. Bryce-Smith, D., Deshpande, R., Gilbert, A., Grzonka, J., Chem. Comm. (1970), 561.
36. Davids, E.K., Garnett, J.L., Fletcher, G., unpublished data.
37. Dorset, B.C.M., Text. Manuf. (1964), 90, 511.
38. Abbott, G.M., Delmenico, J., Leeder, J.D., Taylor, D.S., Appl. Polymer Symp. No. 18 (1971), 963.
39. Williams, J.L., Stannett, V.T., Text. Res. J. (1968), 38, 1065.
40. Williams, J.L., Stannett, V.T., Armstrong, A.A. Jr., J. Appl. Polymer Sci. (1966), 10, 1229.
41. Simpson, W.S., Applied Polymer Symp. No. 18 (1971), 585.
42. Anderson, C.A., Leeder, J.D., Taylor, D.S., Wear (1972), 21, 115.
43. Simpson, W.S., Bratt, R.L., Noonan, K.K., J. Textile Inst. (1973), 64, 449.
44. Stannett, V.T., Proc. 1st Inter. Cotton Text. Res. Conf. Paris, (1969), 625.
45. Seiber, R.P., Needles, H.L., J. Appl. Polymer Sci. (1975), 19, 2187.
46. Hayakawa, K., Kawase, K., Iwasaki, M., Textile Res. J. (1971), 41, 461.
47. Shahidi, I.K. and Powanda, T.M., American Ink Maker (1975), 21.
48. Coppinger, C., Proc. 1st Inter. Meeting Radiation Processing, Puerto Rico (1976), in press.
49. Ang, C.H., Davis, N.P., Garnett, J.L., Yen, N.T., Proc. 1st Inter. Meeting Radiation Processing, Puerto Rico (1976) in press.
50. May, J.M., Am. Text. Reporter (1966), 80, p.54.
51. Garnett, J.L., Kenyon, R.S., Liddy, M.J., J.C.S. Chem. Comm. (1974), 735.

52.   Barker, H., Garnett, J.L., Kenyon, R.S., Levot, R.,
       Liddy, M.S., Long, M.A., Proc. VIth Inter. Cong. Catalysis,
       London (1976), in press.
53.   Barker, H., Garnett, J.L., Levot, R., Proc. 2nd Inter. Symp.
       Polyvinylchloride, Lyon-Villeurbanne (1976), in press.
54.   Garnett, J.L., Levot, R., in preparation.

Pulp and Paper

Technical Needs and Developments in the Paper Industry of the United States

JOHN C. WOLLWAGE and ROY P. WHITNEY

The Institute of Paper Chemistry, Appleton, WI

In recent years, staff members at The Institute of Paper Chemistry have engaged periodically in attempts to assess the future needs of the pulp and paper industry of the United States, in order that our research programs might be better planned and implemented. This exercise has undoubtedly gone forward at essentially every research institution, both in this country and throughout the world, and there has been ample evidence of this in the various papers presented at this meeting. There is no reason to suppose that our approach has been essentially different from those used elsewhere, and certainly many of our conclusions are in good agreement with those which have already been presented.

Our general approach has been to try to identify some of the important external forces and trends which are evident in this country and which must have their effect on the pulp and paper industry. Next, we have tried to assess the impact of these externalities on the industry and particularly on its future development. From these considerations, we have then tried to develop priority areas for research and development to meet the future needs of the industry, as it continues its process of evolution.

Figure 1 lists some of the external forces which we believe will have an important impact upon the future pulp and paper industry of the United States. It seems inevitable that the first entry must be political forces, since they exert such an influence not only on industry but on the daily lives of all of us. Industry must look forward to increased governmental involvement in its affairs, and to greater government regulation.

Social forces can hardly be divorced from those political. Generally, we believe that industry can anticipate higher labor costs, and a decreased rate of rise in the standard of living of the general population of this country. We can also anticipate increasingly stringent requirements with respect to both air and water environmental considerations, and increased pressure for the conservation of natural resources and the reuse of waste materials.

With respect to population trends, the experts tell us that the total population of the United States will continue to increase, but at a decreasing rate, and that the birth rate will continue its present decline.

Inflation will continue to be with us, although hopefully at a more modest rate than that experienced during the past year or two. The present decrease in inflationary trends is certainly encouraging.

The availability of capital for expansion and growth is a force of real concern. Many knowledgeable people have spoken on this point recently, and have projected various shortfalls of capital availability. It appears possible that capital considerations may restrict future industrial growth in this country, unless governmental regulations permit a more attractive return on investment.

The picture with respect to the availability of raw materials is considerably brighter. Fortunately, cellulose is a renewable raw material in quantities which, to some considerable extent, may be controlled. Social forces, however, seek to restrict its harvesting and use.

The availability of energy is a much discussed and highly controversial subject. In our deliberations, we have assumed that adequate energy will be available in the future, although cost will obviously be an important consideration. We have further assumed that the major increases in energy costs have already been experienced, and that further cost increases will be more modest.

These, then, are some of the major external forces which we have identified as exerting an important influence upon the development of the pulp and paper industry.

As noted earlier, the next step in our planning process has been to try to assess the impact of these external forces on the future development of the United States pulp and paper industry. Figure 2 shows some of the categories which have been considered.

There is no doubt that capital costs will be a major factor in the future development of this industry. The pulp and paper industry is highly capital intensive, and the capital cost of new facilities has been increasing at a staggering rate during the past few years. Although costs vary considerably, depending upon the type of facility, the capital cost of constructing a new integrated kraft pulp and paper mill is now in the vicinity of $350,000/daily ton of production. It seems evident that in any research aimed at new processes and new facilities, capital costs must be a major consideration, and complex and intricate processes, however desirable otherwise, may well be ruled out on the basis of cost.

Operating costs must also be a prime consideration in research aimed at new processes and products. In addition to the fixed charges associated with capital, the increasing cost of

Political Forces

Social Forces

Population Trends

Inflation

Availability of Capital

Availability of Raw Materials

Availability of Energy

Figure 1.   External forces acting on
U.S. pulp and paper industry

Capital Costs

Operating Costs

Process Development

Process Control and Automation

Environmental Control

Energy Conservation

Product Shifts

Figure 2.   Impact of external forces on
U.S. pulp and paper industry

raw materials, labor, and energy will play an important role in decision making. Clearly, the researcher must become much more cost conscious than he has been in the past.

It seems evident that the impact of these external forces make it inevitable that increased emphasis must be placed on new process development. It is now trite to say that the pulp and paper industry is saddled with an old and tired technology, but it is nevertheless still true. Our processes were developed at a time when externalities were a minor consideration. They are not good enough for the future.

Process control, and particularly process automation, must play an increasingly important role in our research of today and our processes of tomorrow. Decreases in operating costs, and improvements in product quality, are only two of the reasons why this is so.

Environmental control permeates every phase of the operations of the pulp and paper industry, and certainly its impact will not diminish. It has been estimated that about 30% of the present capital investment of the industry is consumed in environmental control facilities ([1]). This must be an integral part of our thinking and of our research. We accept as axiomatic the viewpoint that no research on new processes or new facilities is viable unless adequate solutions are found to all of the environmental problems which may result.

Energy conservation must also be an integral consideration in all of our research activities. The pulp and paper industry is fortunate in that it generates a considerable fraction of its total energy requirements. Monthly figures compiled by the American Paper Institute ([2]) show that the industry generated almost 44% of its total 1975 energy consumption from bark, hogged fuel, spent pulping liquors, and hydroelectric power. This is an increase from 42% in 1972, and projections are that the industry can generate a considerably higher fraction of its energy requirements, particularly through the use of additional wood waste. Nevertheless, in all of our research, we must strive to keep energy requirements at a minimum.

The last item in Figure 2 is product shifts. The pulp and paper industry has had a continued history of shifts in its product mix, according to market demands. During the past century, it has gone from an industry heavily committed to writing and printing papers to one in which nearly half of its output goes into packaging and paperboard containers. It has continually lost markets to other materials but it has always gained more new markets than it has lost old ones. It is inevitable that it will continue to lose old markets in the future, and therefore that it must continue to gain new outlets for its products. No challenge is more vital to the researcher than the development of new products.

Having attempted to assess the impact of certain external forces on the pulp and paper industry of the future, we turn now to priority areas for research and development. The problems which need to be solved are many, and it is difficult to determine the relative importance of each. We shall choose a few for comments, following the outline of Figure 3, with the stipulation that the earlier discussion regarding the impact of external forces must be applied in each instance.

Wood is the major raw material of the pulp and paper industry. In the years to come, the industry must procure an ever-increasing quantity of wood from an ever-decreasing land base. Thus, the major need is to realize higher yields of wood fiber per acre of land. The forest biologists and foresters have already made considerable progress in achieving this goal.

The development and use of genetically-improved trees shows great promise. Several Populus hybrids have been developed which show twice the growth rate and have longer fiber lengths than our native species of Populus (3). Genetic studies on other species are continuing. Increases in volume growth of 20 to 30% appear possible using selection and seed orchard approaches. Improved forest management is paying dividends. Great interest is presently being shown in more complete utilization of the trees which are harvested. Whole tree chipping is under intense study, and even though serious problems remain, further gains will be made.

The use of wood residues, as from plywood and sawmill operations, has been increasing steadily and will continue to do so. Wood residues now constitute the major supply of wood to pulp mills in the western United States and are becoming more significant in other parts of the country. Research leading to more complete utilization of the harvested tree is certainly a priority area for the future.

After trees, the next most important source of fibrous raw materials comes from waste paper or secondary fiber. Currently, secondary fiber makes up about 22% of the total fibrous materials used by the industry. Its long-term utilization rate is increasing, in spite of the aberration of the past year or so. It is predicted that secondary fiber will make up about 30% of the raw material base within the next decade.

Problems in the use of increased quantities of waste paper are both logistical and technical. Collection and sorting are difficult, and to a considerable extent will probably restrict the major use of secondary fiber to large metropolitan areas. The technical problems are varied, but have to do particularly with the elimination of contaminants which find their way into the waste paper streams. Although the contaminants are many and varied, the ones probably causing the greatest present concern are polychlorinated biphenyls.

Turning now to processes, the pulping of wood is a major priority area for research. Today's commercially-important pulping processes were conceived in the 19th century, although they have been refined and developed considerably in recent decades.

Raw Materials
    Roundwood
    Wood Residues
    Secondary Fiber

Processes
    Pulping
    Bleaching
    Papermaking
    Converting

Products
    Quality
    Specification
    Performance

Figure 3.   Priority areas for research and development

It is probable that the opportunities for further refinement and improvement are limited. The groundwood pulping process remains viable, since it produces a relatively inexpensive pulp ideally suited for newsprint and other low-grade printing papers. Significant improvements are now being made in mechanical pulps, however, probably the most important being in the development of the thermomechanical process. Here, wood chips are mechanically reduced to pulp in a refiner, operated at elevated temperature and pressure. By varying process conditions, the major zones of fracture can be made to occur in the cellulose fibers, thus producing a pulp with relatively large cellulose areas exposed, or can be shifted to the middle lamella area made up largely of lignin. Such fiber bundles, with much of the lignin exposed, show promise of providing a superior material for further chemical treatment. Although much research remains to be accomplished, new mechanical and chemimechanical pulps already show marked improvements over the traditional groundwood pulps, and will inevitably play an important role in the future.

In the chemical pulping area, the kraft process plays an increasingly dominant role. The number of existing kraft mills, and the capital investment which they represent, insure that this will continue for at least the next several decades. In spite of this, the kraft process shows serious shortcomings, perhaps chief among them being a relatively low yield, safety considerations, and a high capital intensity.

Research is underway in many laboratories aimed at the development of improved chemical pulping processes. The goals to be achieved are a significantly increased yield of pulp from wood, freedom from environmental problems, and a marked decrease in capital cost per unit of production.

The research in chemical pulping which appears to show the most promise is the so-called oxygen/alkali process, involving oxygen as the major pulping reagent in an alkaline medium. Although significant progress has been made, serious problems remain. These include excessive carbohydrate degradation and an inadequate increase in yield. Some reduction in capital intensity seems to be possible, and the approach shows considerable promise from the environmental standpoint. Either through the use of oxygen/alkali or other reagents, markedly improved chemical pulping processes are urgently needed for the future.

Most pulp bleaching processes employ chlorine compounds, with chlorine dioxide assuming an increasingly dominant role. Probably the principal deficiency in bleaching is in the environmental area, where large volumes of bleach effluents have been discharged to streams and rivers. It is imperative that the bleach effluent problem be solved, and progress is being made. The use of complete countercurrent washing in the various stages of a bleach plant, previously felt to be impractical, is now coming into commercial use. The oxygen/alkali approach has been shown to be effective in bleaching as well as in pulping, and is

in commercial operation. It seems to be particularly well adapted to the first stage in bleaching, where the major objective is
removal of lignin. Used as a first bleaching stage, the effluent
is essentially chlorine-free and can be combined with the spent
liquors from the pulping operation for chemical recovery.

A major research objective in the bleaching area must be to
close up the bleaching system and to eliminate any aqueous effluent discharge. One interesting approach to this problem has been
proposed, in which the bleaching effluent is combined with the
effluent from the pulping operations, and then sent through the
conventional kraft recovery system. Chlorides are removed from
the system by crystallization-evaporation of the white liquor.
A commercial installation is now under construction (4).

It would appear that a highly desirable long-range objective
is to remove sulfur from the pulping system and chlorine from the
bleaching system. While this can now be accomplished in the laboratory, using such reagents as peracetic acid, any such system
is far removed from an economically feasible commercial operation.
Much research remains to be done.

In the papermaking area, major research objectives center
around product quality, environmental control, and energy reduction. The fourdrinier paper machine, dominant in the manufacture of most paper grades since its invention in 1800, is now
being seriously challenged by the twin-wire formers. Some improvement in sheet quality is possible, but so far the twin-wire
formers have failed to show the great versatility of the fourdrinier. Nevertheless, further improvements will be made, and the
twin-wire formers will undoubtedly find increased application in
the future.

Papermaking in the past has suffered from the environmental
problem of discharging huge volumes of white water containing
fibrous materials, fillers, and other papermaking additives. Although progress has been made in closing up white water systems
and in using the water internally, much still remains to be done.
Progress has also been made on the treatment of paper mill effluents before they are discharged into the waterways. Aeration,
settling, biological treatments, and other approaches have proved
to be highly beneficial, but further work is necessary. For
example, such treatments usually give rise to sludges which de-
water with great difficulty, and the adequate treatment, reuse,
or disposal of such sludges remains a problem which must be solved.

Drying is one of the major consumers of energy in the papermaking process. Although 98-99% of the water used in making paper
is removed mechanically, the energy consumption in removing the
last 1-2% by evaporation is considerable. There has been relatively little progress in paper drying in recent years, and the
problem of energy reduction is one which must be studied more
intensively. Perhaps one of the more promising approaches lies
not in the drier section itself, but in the press section which

precedes it and which governs the water content of the sheet entering the driers. In at least one research institution, a major study of pressing is underway, with the objective of reducing the moisture content of the sheet without damaging its quality.

The operations of converting are highly diversified, and largely mechanical. They have typically represented high labor costs, and relatively low capital costs. Efforts will continue to simplify converting operations, and to develop automation to an extent compatible with the increased capital requirements. To enter into a detailed discussion of the highly varied and diversified operations of converting is beyond the scope of this paper.

Product quality is and must remain a prime concern to the pulp and paper industry. Research studies of the physical and chemical properties of paper and various converted products have been underway for many years and must continue. One area for high priority research lies in the development of means for the on-machine nondestructive measurement of paper properties. While some progress has been made in this regard, particularly as regards moisture content, much remains to be done before the properties related to paper strength and other use characteristics can be measured satisfactorily and continuously on the moving web. Research in this area is still in its early stages, and must be given more attention in the future.

Finally, more must be done to match paper specifications to end use requirements. For example, in this era of great environmental concern, are the ultra-high-brightness sheets now demanded by many consumers really necessary? Are dirt specifications unrealistic? Can greater amounts of secondary fiber, with the attendant deterioration in sheet quality, be tolerated? Can specifications be developed for corrugated containers which bear a more realistic relationship to end use requirements? It seems inevitable that environmental concerns, energy costs, capital and labor costs, and other social concerns will exert a marked effect on many of the future products of the pulp and paper industry.

LITERATURE CITED

1. Amberg, Herman R. "Future Technical Trends and Needs of the Paper Industry; Environmental and Social Factors." Paper presented at the 1976 Annual Meeting, Technical Association of the Pulp and Paper Industry, New York, March 17, 1976.
2. Slinn, Ronald J. "Energy Conservation in the U.S. Pulp, Paper, and Paperboard Industry." Paper presented at the Annual Meeting of the API Pulp, Fiber and Raw Materials Group, New York, March 15, 1976.
3. Einspahr, D. W. Private Communication, March, 1976.
4. Rapson, W. H. "The Closed Cycle Bleached Kraft Pulp Mill." Paper presented at the National Meeting of the American Institute of Chemical Engineers, Boston, Sept., 1975.

14

Interrelation between the Paper and Plastics Industries

VLADIMIR M. WOLPERT

Wolpert & Jones (Studies) Ltd., London, England

The growing symbiosis between the forest-based industry
and the chemical industry is of benefit to both industries, and
this trend is bound to continue at an accelerated rate, as there
are still many not utilized possibilities of extending the co-
operation between these two industries.

Next to co-operation there is also a growing competition
between these two industries, as synthetic polymer products have
been penetrating some markets of the pulp/paper industry, and I
will try to evaluate whether this trend is to continue or whether
it will be reversed.

At present, the chemical industry (of which the plastics
industry is an integral part) is a major supplier of many
products to various sectors of the forest-based industry in
the manufacture of products, the functional properties of which
could not be achieved without these chemicals, including synthetic polymers.

In fact, the pulp/paper industry has gradually developed
from a purely mechanical to a mechanical cum chemical industry.
Increasing tonnages of synthetic polymers are being used before,
during, and after the actual papermaking process.

The forest-based industry (of which the paper industry is
an important integral part) in addition to supplying packaging
materials to the chemical industry, has been supplying the
chemical industry with crude tall oil, turpentine, extractive
products isolated during the kraft pulp process, plus products
from pine trees and stumps, amounting to about 500,000 tpa. in
the United States. In addition, lignosulphonates have been
finding a growing number of applications, like dispersants,
oilwell drilling additives, emulsifiers, etc.

Even if the sulphite pulping process accounts for a com-
paratively small share of the total chemical pulp production
(in the U.S.A. about 10%), the potential of making yeast,
proteins and other high-valued products from effluents is not
to be underestimated.

Reference is made to the production of about 100,000 tpa.
of 'Masonex', a hemicellulose extract, derived from wood and

232

and containing pentose and hexose sugars, which is used for cattle feeding in the United States.

There is room for much larger quantities of crude chemicals to be supplied by the forest-based industry to the chemical industry for further processing. The question, however, is who will carry out the necessary R & D work to achieve this aim. It is significant that the pulp/paper industry spends less than 0.5% of its turnover on R & D, whereas the synthetic polymer industry spends about 4-5% of its overall sales on R & D. It is noteworthy that chemical companies and joint ventures of chemical companies and forest-based companies occupy a prominent position among leading tall oil fractionators.

In 1975, at the Eighth Cellulose Conference in Syracuse, Mr. Benjamin Ward of Westvaco, referring to the U.S. production of crude tall oil which had increased from 190,000 tons in 1948 to about 900,000 tons in 1973 (the rate of the refined tall oil had increased to 90%) said in conclusion that:

> "In 10 to 20 years, it may not be unreasonable to imagine trees being grown strictly as a source of renewable chemicals which play a major role in meeting the needs of the chemical, as well as the consumer, products industries."

These remarks may sound as being of futurological nature to some North Americans, but, in fact, in some regions, specialized trees have been planted for this purpose. In the case of rubber tree plantations in Malaysia and in other countries, the tapped rubber is the main product, and the tree when cut is a by-product used mainly as fuel (the attempts to utilize this wood for pulp production have, on the whole, not met with success). Immediately when one considers the rubber industry, the question of synthetic rubber comes into one's mind. The development of the synthetic rubber industry, partly fostered by the strategic considerations, e.g. during and shortly after the World War II, has no doubt been a strong competitor against the natural rubber industry. However, it has resulted in a more efficient natural rubber production, standardization of its products beneficial to the natural rubber industry, and due to the synthetic rubber industry, the total consumption of rubber has increased considerably (whereby tailor-made synthetic rubbers have augmented this market). It is difficult today to imagine the total requirements of the rubber converting industry, including the tyre industry, being supplied by the natural rubber industry. Without the competition and supplies by the synthetic rubber industry, rubber as such would have never achieved the high tonnage consumption, and in many cases would have priced itself out in many applications.

Co-operation and Competition. The recently published book "The Outlook for Timber in the United States" (U.S. Department of Agriculture, Forest Service, July, 1974) referred to new

products of the paper and board industry with a large market,
including milk cartons, and one has to say that milk cartons
are plastics coated cartons - an example of co-operation between
the pulp/paper and plastics industries.   Multiwall bags with
plastics linings and many other examples of this co-operation
could be listed.

Nearly 50% of the total paper and paperboard production
find application in packaging.   The major shortcomings of
paper and paperboard in packaging are that these products
are not water-resistant, they absorb moisture, and their air,
gas and vapour permeability are very high.   Therefore, in many
packaging applications, a protective coating by plastics is used
to improve the functional properties of paper and board.

These shortcomings of paper and board are among the main
reasons for plastics films penetration of the packaging markets,
replacing paper and paperboard.

Among recent developments, reference is made to 'plastics
paper' (high and medium molecular weight high-density polyethylene film) which has been replacing, at an increasing scale,
glassine, greaseproof paper, vegetable parchment, and even MG
kraft paper in Europe and in Japan.

Shrink film, and lately stretch film, have been registering
a growing penetration of the market.

In technical applications, the replacement of tissue paper
by polypropylene and polyester films in the production of
capacitors is to be mentioned.

In the field of writing and printing papers and of wall-
paper, spunbonded materials (e.g. Tyvek), and plastics film-
based synthetic papers (e.g. Polyart and Yupo FP), have been
competing against conventional papers.

On the other hand, the development of synthetic pulp to be
used as an additive to conventional woodpulp for making paper and
board with improved functional properties (on conventional paper
making machines) is a new chapter of co-operation between the
traditional paper and the synthetic polymer industries. According
to conservative estimates (1), the consumption of synthetic pulp
- on a worldwide basis - during the first half of the '80-ies
will amount to 180,000-250,000 tpa., with a high growth rate in
the second half of that decade.   The addition of synthetic pulp
to the furnish also results in a better drainage rate. Synthetic
pulp has also a good potential market as a binder in nonwovens
production, and in some applications outside the paper industry.

At the present ACS Meeting, references to co-operation and
competition between the pulp/paper and synthetic polymer industries have been made in various presentations.   Prof. Goldstein
(2) stressed the point that combinations of synthetic polymers
and cellulose in the form of blends, composites and coatings,
will become inreasingly important in meeting packaging (3) and
communication needs at low cost/effectiveness ratio. Composites,
such as cellulose or wood fibre reinforced plastics, will also

become more important. (A few years ago, Dr. A.A. Robertson (4),
spoke of encouraging possibilities of the continued development
of products based on combination of synthetic polymers and paper,
and of the growing importance of polymer-paper composites.)
Contrary to the growth of woodpulp consumption for papermaking,
the expensive high-purity dissolving pulp is produced to the
extent of only approximately 2 million tons per annum, and has
been facing declining markets.   This chemical cellulose is the
starting material for rayon and acetate fibres, cellophane,
cellulose ester plastics and cellulose ether gum, and Professor
Goldstein felt that since much of the present cellulose technology is highly energy intensive, the mere availability of
cellulose as a renewable resource will not assure increased
utilization of cellulosic polymers, unless their total cost
becomes favourable.
The significant point is that cellophane film which has been
gradually replaced by plastics films, e.g. oriented polypropylene
film, could somewhat retard its replacement by introduction of
plastics coated cellophane film.
According to a recent ICI study (5), the U.K. energy requirements
(expressed as tonnes of oil equivalent, required as feedstock plus
energy for the manufacturing) in the case of one million square
metres of packaging film compare as follows:

> Polypropylene film   110
> Cellulose film   155

Professor Simionescu (6) referred to investigations aimed at
obtaining a favourable symbiosis between cellulose and synthetic
polymers, the introduction of certain polymers as mass additives
in the paper production, and also referred to the use of certain
chemical fibres in this field.   At the same time, Simionescu
referred to competition, i.e. substitution of traditional papers
by synthetic polymer products.
 Whole-tree utilization for pulp making has been arousing
great interest, and it is to be expected that further developments
in this field will result in - at least partial-utilization of
the high tonnages of stumps, roots, branches and foliage for
making pulp (and, in this way, alleviating the threat of fibre
shortage) and/or for producing crude chemicals, and in this way
improving the financial returns of the forest-based concerns,
particularly as the cost of woodlands has been rising at a very
high rate, influencing the cost of forest-based products (the
index of cost per acre of prime Southern woodland, taking its
cost in 1955 as 100, has increased from 182 in 1965 to 1,367 in
1975). However, studies on the utilization of stump wood in pulp
production by the Institute of Paper Chemistry, Appleton (7),
have shown that stump wood pulp can be expected to be inferior
in most physical properties, other than folding endurance, when
compared with a similar pulp made from conventional pine chips.
The question arises whether it would be economically viable to

improve the properties of kraft paper from stump wood pulp
(tensile breaking length, tearstrength, etc.) by incorporating
into the furnish a small amount of synthetic fibres. Reference
is made to the trials being carried out at present in West
Germany of making kraft paper (with improved properties for
cement sacks) from conventional pulp plus a small proportion of
nylon short-cut fibres.

    General Comments (Feedstock, Energy Consumption, Markets,
Inflation). The crude oil situation is of great importance to
both industries. The pulp/paper industry is a large user of
energy, requiring in the United States about three barrels of oil
for the production of one ton of paper, and the plastics industry
has been using crude oil as feedstock plus for energy to convert
oil into plastics finished products.
Compared with the world production of about 140 million tons of
paper and paperboard per annum, the annual production of plastics
is about 45 million tons, of which roughly 15 million tons find
application in packaging, including bottles, containers and also
films. However, one ton of plastics film - depending on the
polymer involved and the application - replaces between 2 and 3
tons of paper.
The American Petroleum Institute assessed recently that "proved
reserves" of crude oil could be of the order of 98,000 million
tonnes, and the annual world oil consumption was recently estimated at less than 2,800 million tonnes in 1973 and 1974 (BP
Statistical Review).
    The total consumption of the world petrochemical industry
accounts for about 5% of the global oil consumption, and the
bigger share of the petrochemical industry's requirements is
used for the production of fertilizers. Only 2% of the world
oil consumption are used for making plastics materials. As
plastics materials belong to the highest upvalued products
derived from crude oil, it is to be expected that the tonnages
required by this industry will be always available, whereas
technological developments will lead to savings of oil consumption in many other fields due to the growing realisation that
just burning oil is an obsolete practice.
The growing interest of international oil companies in downstream
operations (production of monomers, polymers and even plastics
products) and, at the same time, their involvement in the development of other energy sources, is a noticeable pointer for the
future.
With finding of new oil reserves, including those outside the
Middle East, and their better utilization, together with the
development of other energy sources, which were uneconomic at
the oil price of $ 2 per barrel, but may be viable at present
crude oil prices, the danger of oil prices increasing in future
at a rate above the overall inflation rate is not to be envisaged,
provided that the situation is faced squarely by governments and
industry in an effective manner.

The following factors are to be mentioned in this connection:

The energy consumption in production of plastics together with the oil used as feedstock, is lower than the energy consumption in the production of paper and of many other products. According to the NATO Report (8), the typical energy content of plastics products is 10 megajoules/kg. as against 25 megajoules/kg. in the case of paper products. According to the already mentioned ICI study, the U.K. energy requirements (expressed in tons of oil equivalent, including feedstock and energy) for the manufacture of 1 million fertiliser sacks made from low-density polyethylene film amount to 470, as against 700 when these sacks are made from kraft paper. The difficulty of comparing the energy requirements of various products is partly due to the fact that in some cases only specific sectors of the overall production process are referred to.

The high energy consumption of the pulp and paper industry is well known.   The recent "Fuel Survey" by the American Pulpwood Association, Washington, (published 1975) says that in 1974 pulpwood harvesting required an average of 5.16 gallons of fuel - either gasoline or diesel - to harvest a cord of pulpwood and move it from the stump to a concentration point or mill by truck.   This survey, referring to the continuous trend towards greater mechanisation, says that "it appears doubtful that the average rate of fuel consumption for harvesting pulpwood can be reduced".   It would be an interesting exercise to calculate the additional fuel requirements, including administration of forests prior to the harvesting of pulpwood.

All these energy requirements in the pulp/paper industry (together with those in the actual pulp and papermaking) clearly show that the actual production costs of cellulosic paper reflect directly the changes of the crude oil prices.

A number of studies have been made on the influence of changes of crude oil prices on the production costs of plastics materials and plastics products. The above mentioned ICI study refers to the effect of crude oil increased prices on downstream operations, and illustrates the dilution of the crude oil cost component in the production costs of monomers, polymers, and finished goods. The increase of crude oil price by 300% results in an increase of the price of ethylene by 200%, polyethylene by 100%, and of polyethylene bags by 30%.   In the case of propylene, the increase was even lower, namely 180%, and of polypropylene by only 70%.

The fact is that despite the high increases of crude oil prices since the end of 1973, plastics have not lost (apart from a few exceptional cases) their competitive strength and have continued to penetrate the paper markets.

The present recession has resulted in the lowering of paper prices in various European markets. In West Germany, the biggest papermaking country of Europe, the wholesale prices of some packaging papers in September, 1975, were about 14% lower than in September, 1974.   Some types of paperboard registered an even greater drop

in prices. All indications are that as soon as the market conditions improve, the prices of paper will increase above the
September, 1974, level, reflecting the increased production costs.
It is anticipated that in boom conditions, paper prices will have
to increase at a higher rate than the overall inflation rate, in
order to make papermaking a viable proposition.
Polymer and plastics prices are expected to increase at a rate
lower than the overall inflation rate. Among the reasons for
this are the technological developments taking place in this
industry. A number of examples in the production of polymers
and in the plastics processing industry, which have resulted in
lowering the production costs during the last few years, could
be cited. Whereas a few years ago, a 60 mm. extruder had a
production rate of about 30-35 kg./h. of plastics paper, extruders
of the same size produce today 70-80 kg./h. of plastics paper
of the same thickness.
     The further penetration by plastics of the conventional
paper and board markets is to be expected, and, at the same time,
new products made from cellulosic pulp plus synthetic polymers
will secure considerable markets, representing a growing co-
operation between these two industries.

Literature Cited

     (1) Wolpert, Vladimir M., "Plastics and the Paper Industry",
p. 25, Wolpert & Jones (Studies) Ltd., London, 1975.
     (2) Goldstein, Irving S., "The Place of Cellulose under
Energy Scarcity", presentation at the ACS Centennial Meeting,
New York, 1976.
     (3) Jones, Allen, and Wolpert, Vladimir M., "Composite
Materials for Packaging", 235 pp., Wolpert & Jones (Studies) Ltd.,
London, 1976.
     (4) Robertson, A.A., "Modification of the Mechanical Proper-
ties of Paper by the Addition of Synthetic Polymers", presentation
at the International Symposium "The Fundamental Properties of
Paper Related to its Uses", organized by the British Paper and
Board Makers' Association, Cambridge (England), 1973.
     (5) ICI Ltd., "The Competitiveness of of LD PE, PP and PVC
After the 1973 Oil Crisis: The ICI View", ICI, London, 1974.
     (6) Simionescu, Cristofor I., "The Relation 'Cellulose-
Paper', Options and Developments", pre-print of the ACS Centennial
Meeting, New York, 1976.
     (7) Peckham, John R., and McKee, Robert C., "Pulp & Paper",
(1975), Volume 49, (Number 14), pp. 53-55.
     (8) NATO Report, "Technology of Efficient Energy Utilization",
NATO, Brussels, 1973.

15

The Pulp Mill of the Future—Environmental and Raw Material Considerations

BENGT LEOPOLD

SUNY College of Environmental Science and Forestry, Syracuse, NY

The founding of the American Chemical Society in 1876 co-incides almost exactly with the birth of the modern pulp and pa-per industry. Before the 1870's, most paper was made on a rela-tively small scale from an expensive and increasingly scarce raw material, cotton rags. Then, during a very short time span, the picture changed drastically with the advent of a number of pro-cesses for the production of a new raw material, wood pulp. The first of these was the so-called groundwood process, a mechanical process which was invented in 1844 but introduced to the U.S. in 1867. This development rapidly increased the production of news-print, as indicated by the fact that the price dropped from 14¢ to 2¢/lb in less than 25 years. Nevertheless, it can be argued that the so-called chemical pulping processes had the greatest impetus in making the pulp and paper industry the giant it is today. One of these, the sulfite process, was invented by the American chemist, Tilghman, in 1867 although the first sulfite pulp mill was built in Sweden in 1874. The other important chem-ical process, the kraft process, is of a slightly later date, in-vented in 1884 with the first mill dating from 1891. However, it had its roots in the so-called soda process, which was developed before 1860. So we see that within only a few years, a revolu-tionary change had taken place in the industry (1)

The driving force behind these developments was unquestion-ably the rapidly increasing demand for paper in a society that was fast becoming industrialized. This can be clearly seen in Figure 1, which shows the increase in per capita consumption of paper for the past 100 years or so. Needless to say, the basic assumption behind this vigorous development was that there would always be an unlimited supply of wood, as well as chemicals, water and energy.

Here we are, 100 years later, and we know now that there is no such thing as an unlimited supply of anything, except possibly dire predictions of impending disaster. Because of this, we are again facing drastic changes in the pulp and paper industry, just as we were 100 years ago, but for almost exactly the opposite

239

reasons. We can no longer expect to obtain any of our raw materials as effortlessly as in the past, and this is particularly
true for water and energy. A relatively new factor has also
entered the picture - concern for the environment. Because of
the tremendous efforts in this area, the pulp and paper industry
has been saddled with a number of new constraints, imposed and
otherwise, which has made it even more difficult for the industry
to obtain its raw material economically.

All of these events have increased the consumption of that
most important raw material of all - capital. Capital for new
construction, capital for pollution abatement, capital for mod-
ernization of out-dated equipment - requirements for all of
these have skyrocketed. For example, it now costs $240,000/
daily ton to build a new bleached kraft mill (2); this amounts
to the enormous sum of $240,000,000 for a 1000 ton/day mill, a
typical size. And this at a time when capital is becoming increasingly hard to raise.

It is clear, then, that the changes that will be needed in
the next several decades lie in the direction of better utilization of wood, with less use of chemicals and energy and little
or no discharge of waste products, all at a lower capital cost
than at present. This is a very tall order indeed!

Today, I am not going to indulge in predictions concerning
our relative success in these various endeavors but rather discuss a number of research developments that may offer solutions
to some of these problems in the not-too-distant future. Here,
I shall confine my remarks to a discussion of the pulp mill.

Many innovations that lead to raw material conservation or
pollution abatement are already upon us and do not belong to the
future. One interesting such development is whole-tree pulping,
i.e., pulping all of the tree, including branches, twigs, bark,
and foliage. This is being practiced today to an increasing degree (3-5). Another innovation is the concept of the completely
closed pulp mill, where everything, including bleach effluents,
is recycled and reused. Such a pulp mill, based on the kraft
process, is now being constructed at Thunder Bay, Ontario and is
based on the pioneering work of Rapson and his co-workers (6,7).
This process will, of course, completely eliminate water pollution problems, and it will undoubtedly turn out to be one of the
most important developments of this period.

However, rather than dwell on processes already on the drawing board or in operation, I think it would be more fitting on
an occasion such as this to talk about the future. For the next
30 minutes or so, I intend to let my imagination loose and con-
jure up a picture of the pulp mill of the future, as seen from
the researcher's point of view. This picture will be of the im-
pressionistic variety, with few details, somewhere between dream
and reality. I shall sketch a number of possible schemes, not
only in the light of what we know today but also in terms of
what we have to learn tomorrow if we want to move from dream to

reality.
        My discussion will concentrate on two specific areas that I
think show the greatest promise for the future:

        1) oxygen-alkali pulping, which appears to have the poten-
tial of being one of the major commercial pulping methods in the
relatively short term, and

        2) expansion of the use of mechanical pulps to all grades
of paper and board now requiring chemical pulps, a development
of enormous potential but probably only in the relatively long
term.

                        OXYGEN PULPING

Early Research

        In the oxygen-alkali pulping method, wood is delignified
with oxygen in the presence of alkali. One of the advantages of
this process is that it leads to practically odor-free pulping.
Also, recycling and recovery of effluents is greatly simplified.
In addition, oxygen-alkali pulps are much lighter in color than
conventional kraft pulps and also much easier to bleach, thus
having a potential for simplified bleach plants and less use of
chemicals. Not surprisingly, this process is now the subject of
intensive research efforts in many parts of the world (8-15).
        Unfortunately, the oxygen-alkali pulping process has a num-
ber of very serious drawbacks. Perhaps the most fundamental of
these is its heterogeneity. Since the reaction involves a gas
phase, oxygen, and the latter has a fairly low solubility in the
liquid phase, aqueous alkali, penetration of the wood chip is a
critical problem. In most oxygen pulping schemes to date, this
has been solved by pulping in two or more stages. In the first
stage, the wood is partially delignified in aqueous alkali, with
or without the presence of oxygen. The partially pulped chips
are then fiberized and the pulping completed with oxygen and alkali, typically at 140-150°C and 100-150 psi O_2. A typical
laboratory scheme is shown in Figure 2.
        Using a process of this type, it is possible to produce
pulps with strength properties comparable to those of kraft
pulps, at least from hardwood (Table I). Softwood presents more
of a challenge, and usually there is a problem with tear strength
and folding endurance (Table II).
        On the other hand, it must be said that oxygen pulps are
superior to kraft pulps in some other respects. For instance,
they are always brighter in color than kraft pulps (Table III)
and they beat more easily (Figure 3). I will say more about
this later. The pulps are also much easier to bleach, as we
will see in a moment.

Figure 1.   Per capita consumption of paper and board in the U. S. in lb/yr

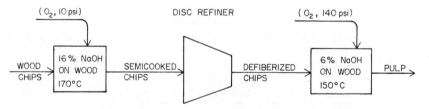

Figure 2.   Two-stage oxygen–alkali pulping scheme

Table I. Comparison of Strength Characteristics of Unbleached White Birch Oxygen and Kraft Pulps

	Unbleached Kraft Pulp Cook No. DJ-17 Elrepho Brightness, 26.5% CED Viscosity, 34.4% cp Kappa No. 18.0 Yield, % - 49	Unbleached Oxygen Pulp 1st Stage Cook No. DJ-16 2nd Stage Cook No. DJ-16C CED Viscosity, 19.9% cp Kappa No. 8.5 Yield, % - 49	% Difference Kraft Pulp Values = 100%
Freeness, CS, ml	495	510	–
Bulk, cc/g	1.24	1.26	–
Burst Factor	91.6	108.0	+17.9
Tear Factor	91	94	+ 3.3
MIT Folding Endurance	1130	1350	+19.5
Breaking Length, m	9930	10,890	+ 9.7
Zero Span Breaking Length, m	16,620	16,570	– 0.3
Energy to Break, cm-Kg	1.82	2.16	+18.7
Bonding Index, %	59.7	65.7	+10.0
Stretch, %	2.3	2.6	–
Scattering Coefficient, sq cm/g	150	164	–
Freeness, CS, ml	295	305	–
Bulk, cc/g	1.18	1.21	–
Burst Factor	100.0	105.5	+ 5.5
Tear Factor	80	81	+ 1.2
MIT Folding Endurance	2160	1640	–24.1
Breaking Length, m	10,130	11,210	+10.6
Zero Span Breaking Length, m	16,090	16,460	+ 2.3
Energy to Break, cm-Kg	1.81	1.96	+ 8.3
Bonding Index, %	62.9	68.1	+ 8.3
Stretch, %	2.2	2.3	–
Scattering Coefficient, sq cm/g	113	138	–

Table II. Comparison of Strength Characteristics of Unbleached Norway Spruce Oxygen and Kraft Pulps

	Unbleached Kraft Pulp Cook No. NS-K2 Elrepho Brightness, 26.2% CED Viscosity, 19.2 cp Kappa No. 25 Yield, % - 45	Unbleached Oxygen Pulp Cook No. NS-14B Elrepho Brightness, 40.1% CED Viscosity, 10.1 cp Kappa No. 12 Yield, % - 44	% Difference Kraft Pulp Values = 100%
Freeness, CS, ml	510	510	-
Bulk, cc/g	1.48	1.44	-
Burst Factor	118	120	+ 1.7
Tear Factor	117	99	- 15.4
MIT Folding Endurance	1,170	990	- 15.4
Breaking Length, m	10,900	10,240	- 6.1
Zero Span Breaking Length, m	19,660	18,650	- 5.1
Bonding Index, %	55.4	54.9	- 0.9
Stretch, %	2.6	2.6	-
Scattering Coefficient, cm^2/g	196	209	-
Freeness, CS, ml	320	330	-
Bulk, cc/g	1.40	1.35	-
Burst Factor	122	120	- 1.6
Tear Factor	107	88	- 17.8
MIT Folding Endurance	1,650	1,240	- 24.8
Breaking Length, m	11,380	10,960	- 3.7
Zero Span Breaking Length, m	20,480	19,290	- 5.8
Bonding Index, %	55.5	56.8	+ 2.3
Stretch, %	2.6	2.5	-
Scattering Coefficient, cm^2/g	188	207	-

Table III

Kappa Number, Brightness, and Bleachability of Spruce Pulps

	Oxygen	Oxygen	Kraft	Oxygen	Kraft	Oxygen	Kraft
Yield, %	45.0	47.3	47.5	48.2	48.1	51.0	50.4
Kappa Number	6.0	11.7	20.7	14.0	26.0	19.8	27.0
Brightness, %							
Unbleached	56.6	46.2	29.2	37.4	20.2	38.1	18.0
Bleached*	83.0	74.5	40.5	-	-	-	-

*3% ClO_2, one-stage

But first I would like to point out that we may be making a mistake by continuing to use kraft pulp properties as our standard. Even though kraft pulps have served us well and will continue to do so for a long time, we do not need their high strength for a large number of our paper grades, while in many cases, it would be a great advantage to get away from hard-to-beat and hard-to-bleach pulps. Maybe we ought to stop considering oxygen pulps as substitutes for kraft and evaluate them for what they are - a new type of product.

Simplification

The capital cost of a pulp mill based on the multistage oxygen pulping process can be expected to be high because it is a very complex and capital intensive process. It consists of two chemical stages of widely different temperature and other reaction conditions, with a defiberizing step in between, obviously a very costly proposition.

What we have to look for now is simplification. After all, relative simplicity is one of the main advantages of the current kraft process. If we could eliminate one of the chemical stages, we would move in the right direction. One way to do this would be to start with defiberized wood (8). This would eliminate most of the penetration problems and would offer the possibility of a uniform reaction.

One intriguing such raw material is so-called thermomechanical pulp (TMP). This is pulp obtained from wood using purely mechanical means. The fiberization occurs at elevated temperatures and pressures so as to soften the intercellular lignin and hemicellulose and make it possible to separate the fibers with a minimum of damage to the cell wall. Currently, TMP is being used to an increasing degree in the manufacture of newsprint and other low-cost grades of paper (16). More about that later.

Table IV shows laboratory results of oxygen pulping of TMP from white oak, a hardwood. The strength properties of the pulp are comparable to those obtained for chips, except for tear strength. We believe this is mostly a question of damage in the fiberization step. Similar conclusions can be drawn from results with Norway spruce, a softwood (Figures 4 and 5). We can conclude, then, that at least for some grades, oxygen pulping can be performed in one chemical stage, which will greatly reduce the complexity and capital cost of the plant. A schematic of such a mill is shown in Figure 6.

Obviously, a further step in the right direction would be to eliminate the fiberizing step and do the pulping in one chemical operation (14), much as today's kraft pulping is carried out. One way of accomplishing this would be by pulping with simultaneous, very vigorous agitation. Preliminary studies in our laboratory have shown that such an approach is feasible. We have, for instance, produced a one-stage hardwood oxygen-alkali pulp

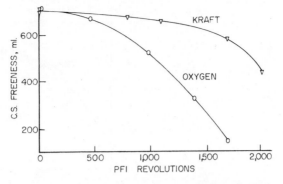

Figure 3. Comparison of oxygen–alkali and Kraft pulp; C.S. freeness vs. PFI mill revolutions

Table IV

Comparison of White Oak Oxygen Pulp: TMP vs. Chips

	Oxygen, TMP	Oxygen, Chips	
		1st Stage	2nd Stage
Pulping Conditions			
NaOH, %	20	20	4
Oxygen Pressure, psi	140	10	140
Temperature, °C	165	165	150
Time, hr	1	2	1
Pulps			
Yield, %	45.7	48.7	
Brightness, %	70.6	54.6	
Refining	PFI	PFI	
CSF, ml	580	550	
Density, g/cm^3	.592	.680	
Burst Factor	59	55	
Breaking Length, m	7140	6900	
Tear Factor	81	117	

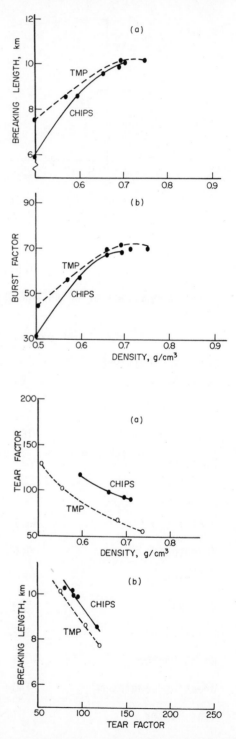

Figure 4. Comparison of oxygen–alkali pulping of chips and TMP from Norway spruce; breaking length (a) and burst factor (b) vs. sheet density

Figure 5. Comparison of oxygen–alkali pulping of chips and TMP from Norway spruce; (a) tear factor vs. sheet density; (b) breaking length vs. tear factor

of acceptable quality (Table V). However a number of very difficult engineering problems would have to be solved.

Table V

Comparison of One-Stage Oxygen-Alkali Pulp with
Kraft Pulp, both from Sugar Maple

	Oxygen-Alkali	Kraft
Yield, %	48.3	49.7
CS Freeness, ml	365	390
Density, g/cm^3	0.680	0.642
Burst Factor	51	62
Breaking Length, m	8,250	8,700
Tear Factor	75	71
Brightness, %	46.1	31.5

Bleaching with Ozone

I mentioned the ease of bleaching oxygen pulps. This is
true for conventional bleaching systems, such as the 5-stage
chlorine-alkali extraction-chlorine dioxide-alkali extraction-
chlorine dioxide (CEDED) sequence commonly used. But even more
interesting might be the discovery that oxygen pulps are particularly suited for ozone bleaching. Ozone has not been used commercially as a bleaching agent yet (17), but it is of great interest because it leaves no chemical residue and as such presents
no water pollution problem. The main difficulty is the cost of
ozone, which is largely tied in with the cost of electricity.
Efforts must now be made to increase the efficiency of ozone generation so as to bring down the power cost. In addition, ozone
is not as selective as one would like, and excessive degradation
and strength loss can result. In the case of oxygen pulps, this
problem appears to be minimized. The results in Table VI show
that a bleached pulp equivalent or superior to kraft bleached
pulp can be obtained from hardwood, such as birch, using the
oxygen-ozone combination. With softwood (Table VII), the results
are not quite as satisfactory.

Application in the Mill

We have now the makings of a very intriguing pulp mill of
the future (Figure 7). This would be a mill where the only chemicals used would be alkali and oxygen. It would be a mill where
excess oxygen from the bleach plant (ozone is carried as 3-4%
mixture with oxygen) is piped back to the pulp mill. It would be
a mill where bleaching would be done at room temperature and

Table VI

Comparison of Conventionally Bleached Kraft with Ozone Bleached Oxygen Pulp, Both from White Birch

	Bleached Kraft Pulp (CEDED) Elrepho Brightness, 85.4% CED Viscosity, 29.8% cp	Bleached Oxygen Pulp (O_3) Elrepho Brightness, 81.5% CED Viscosity, 10.5% cp	% Difference Kraft Pulp Values = 100%
Freeness, CS, ml	520	500	–
Bulk, cc/g	1.27	1.27	–
Burst Factor	85.0	96.5	+13.5
Tear Factor	111	98	–11.7
MIT Folding Endurance	1040	860	–17.3
Breaking Length, m	8800	9890	+12.4
Zero Span Breaking Length, m	15,040	15,600	+ 3.7
Energy to Break, cm-Kg	1.65	1.93	+17.0
Bonding Index, %	58.5	63.4	+ 8.4
Stretch, %	2.5	2.5	–
Scattering Coefficient, cm^2/g	192	196	–
Freeness, CS, ml	320	280	–
Bulk, cc/g	1.21	1.18	–
Burst Factor	90.1	99.8	+10.8
Tear Factor	98	79	–19.4
MIT Folding Endurance	1280	1780	+39.1
Breaking Length, m	9285	10,060	+ 8.4
Zero Span Breaking Length, m	15,960	14,520	– 9.0
Energy to Break, cm-Kg	1.77	1.90	+ 7.3
Bonding Index, %	58.2	69.3	+19.1
Stretch, %	2.5	2.4	–
Scattering Coefficient, cm^2/g	166	152	–

Table VII. Comparison of Conventionally Bleached Kraft with Ozone Bleached Oxygen Pulp, Both from Spruce

	Bleached Kraft Pulp (CEDED) Elrepho Brightness, 81.6% CED Viscosity, 16.0 cp	3-Stage Bleached Oxygen Pulp (O3E03) Elrepho Brightness, 80.0% CED Viscosity, 6.2 cp	% Difference Kraft Pulp Values = 100%
Freeness, CS, ml	500	480	—
Bulk, cc/g	1.40	1.49	—
Burst Factor	119	86.0	-27.7
Tear Factor	115	131	+13.9
MIT Folding Endurance	1,320	950	-28.0
Breaking Length, m	11,130	9,720	-12.7
Zero Span Breaking Length, m	19,830	17,980	-9.3
Bonding Index, %	56.1	54.1	-3.6
Stretch, %	2.9	2.9	—
Scattering Coefficient, cm^2/g	178	292	—
Freeness, CS, ml	300	310	—
Bulk, cc/g	1.33	1.42	—
Burst Factor	114	81.6	-28.4
Tear Factor	114	119	+4.4
MIT Folding Endurance	1,470	930	-36.7
Breaking Length, m	11,380	10,100	-11.2
Zero Span Breaking Length, m	18,020	18,330	+1.7
Bonding Index, %	63.1	55.1	-12.7
Stretch, %	2.7	3.0	—
Scattering Coefficient, cm^2/g	197	285	—

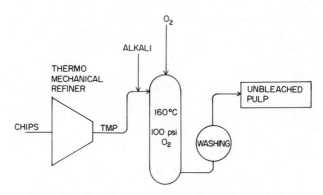

Figure 6.   Flowsheet for oxygen–alkali pulping of TMP

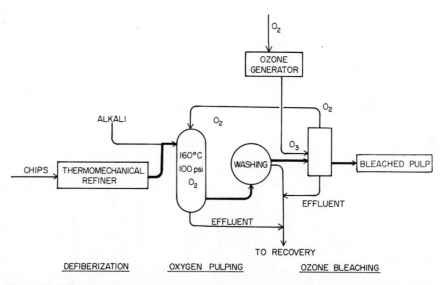

Figure 7.   Flowsheet for manufacture of ozone bleached oxygen–alkali pulp from TMP

atmospheric pressure in a few minutes. It would be a mill where
the various streams from the pulping and bleaching plant would
contain nothing but organic matter and alkali, and thus they
could all go to a recovery furnace to recover the only inorganic
chemical needed - alkali. It would be a mill where consumption
of beating energy would be reduced considerably since oxygen
pulps beat very rapidly. Incidentally, an oxidative treatment
of conventional kraft pulps can have much the same effect, as
shown in Table VIII. As you can see, a light treatment of kraft
pulp with oxygen-alkali leads to a total reduction in beating
energy of 50-70%. Some additional energy, of course, is consumed
in the oxidation treatment, but a rough estimate indicates that
this amounts to no more than 1/3 of the total, so we have a net
savings of 35-50%.

It is clear that this hypothetical mill has many appealing
features. Yet, it is far from practical realization, given today's state of the art. Much research is needed in the next few
years, especially in the engineering aspects of the process.

MECHANICAL PULPING

If the future potential of oxygen pulping is intriguing, the
future potential of mechanical pulping is outright mind-boggling.
Or, as it was billed at last year's TAPPI International Mechanical
Pulping Conference in San Francisco: it is a gold mine, and a
neglected one at that. At that conference, Underhay (18) made an
eloquent plea for greatly increased efforts to utilize mechanical
pulp in all or most paper grades. If this could indeed be accomplished, we would almost double the production from a given
amount of wood, and chemical consumption and water and air pollution would be kept to a minimum.

Is this kind of papermaking revolution really feasible? Before attempting to answer this question, let us first examine
some of the reasons why today's mechanical pulps tend to be un-
satisfactory as raw material for many, if not most, paper products. The deficiencies lie essentially in two areas: appearance
(color) and mechanical performance.

Color

The appearance of the product is marred by its color which is
generally considered to be too dark and too unstable for use in
anything but newsprint and other products designed for a very
short period of use.

Incidentally, this might be a good opportunity to point out
that the determination of what constitutes good quality in terms
of color is at best arbitrary, and there is a growing feeling in
the industry that the escalation in paper brightness that we have
witnessed through the years is not justified in terms of end-use
quality, and is an unnecessary and maybe even harmful development.

Table VIII

Effect of Oxygen-Alkali Treatment of Kraft Pulp on Degree of Beating Required to Reach a Given Strength Value

Original Pulp		Oxygen-Alkali Treated Pulp	Reduction
Kappa No.	No. Revolutions PFI Mill	No. Revolutions PFI Mill	No. Revolutions %
39.7	500	150	70
71.3	1200	350	71
95.2	1700	725	57

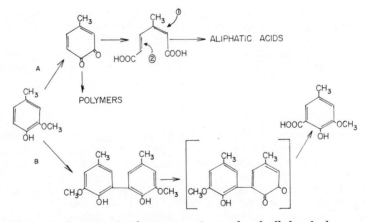

Figure 8.   Sequence for the reaction of creosol wtih alkaline hydrogen peroxide

Interestingly, one of the major manufacturers of equipment for
mechanical pulping has developed a new slogan: THINK YELLOW!
   It is generally agreed that most of the dark color in the
mechanical pulp originates from the lignin (19,20) - the aromatic
polymer acting as a stiff matrix around and in the cellulose fibers in the wood. It has been known for a long time that the dark
color can be partially removed without removal of the lignin by
bleaching with a variety of chemicals (21). The most common of
these is hydrogen peroxide. Through work with lignin model compounds, it has been shown that hydrogen peroxide is capable of
breaking down lignin monomer units containing free phenolic
groups (Figures 8, 9). That such groups are also responsible for
most of the dark color has been shown by spectrographic studies
on lignin model compounds (Figure 10) and lignin itself (Figure
11). Especially interesting is the fact that lignin can be made
practically colorless, and stable, by suitable chemical modification (Figure 12). These results show that it is today possible
to bleach lignin to any brightness without removing it, but the
expense would be totally unacceptable. The challenge now is to
develop a commercially feasible process that can accomplish all
or almost all of this color reduction.

Strength

   Another, equally serious deficiency of mechanical pulp is
its mechanical weakness. Since such pulps are made by mechanical
fiber separation, one of the major difficulties is to achieve
such separation without unacceptable damage to the fiber wall,
which would lead to low strength. Modern technology has come a
long way in this respect, from the original stone groundwood made
on a grindstone as far back as 1844, to today's disc refiners
which produce fibers by rubbing chips between metal discs. One
especially intriguing development is the high-temperature, high-
pressure process I mentioned before, namely, the thermomechanical
process. As I said, TMP fibers are separated relatively intact.
This shows up in the superior strength of TMP (16) compared to
conventional groundwood (Table IX).

Table IX

Strength Values for Stone Groundwood, TMP,
and Kraft Pulp (Norway Spruce)

	Stone Groundwood	TMP	Kraft
CS Freeness, ml	100	90	300
Burst Factor	14	21	122
Breaking Length, m	2500	3200	11,380
Tear Factor	35	63	107

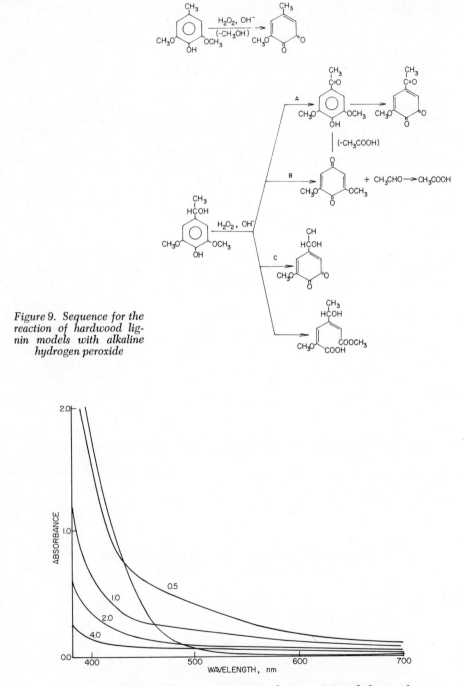

Figure 9. Sequence for the reaction of hardwood lignin models with alkaline hydrogen peroxide

Figure 10. Visible absorption spectra of solutions of 4-methylsyringol treated with varying amounts of hydrogen peroxide

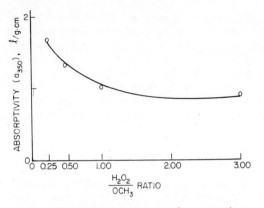

Figure 11. Color remaining (absorptivity) at varying peroxide-to-methoxyl ratios for milled-wood lignin (4-hr reaction time)

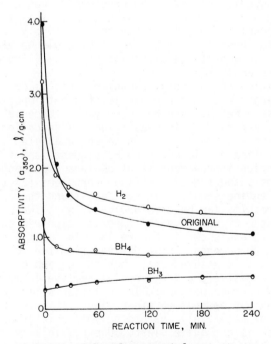

Figure 12. Color (absorptivity) change on treatment of original and modified lignins with H_2O_2 ($H_2O_2/OCH_3 = 1$)

Nevertheless, the strength of TMP is still far inferior to that of kraft. The reason is that the TMP fibers do not bond to one another nearly as well as chemical fibers (Figures 13 and 14), and this, in turn, is ascribed to the presence in the fiber of practically all of the lignin in the wood. So, again lignin is the culprit. It tends to make the fiber stiff and unable to make firm contact with other fibers and thus prevent the formation of hydrogen bonds, the primary force holding fibers together (22,23).

Bonding Agents

Well, can anything be done about this problem? There are two possible basic approaches. One is to use a bonding agent in the papermaking process. Such an agent would tend to "glue" the fibers together and thus increase the strength. Since this type of fiber tends to be stiff, this approach would be of special interest in rigid products, such as paperboard.

There are, of course, a wide variety of polymeric products that could be used as reinforcing agents or "adhesives." Unfortunately very few, if any, products tested to date have shown sufficient promise to be used commercially. The main reason for this is undoubtedly that existing products do not provide sufficient bonding at an economical add-on level. This is at least partially a result of our inability to selectively introduce the additives into those locations where they would be effective, viz., on the surface of the fiber and especially where the fibers cross one another.

The question of how polymers adsorb onto fiber surfaces and how they interact with one another is of great importance to today's papermaker because synthetic polymers, especially polyelectrolytes, are finding increasing use as so-called retention additives. These are additives which enhance retention, in the fiber mat, of fine particles, such as pigments and fiber fragments. Retention improvement is of obvious importance, both for decreasing costs and reducing effluent problems (24-26). In the course of retention studies, it has been found that particularly outstanding results can be obtained by using a two-step, two-component system of additives of opposite electric charge. Some typical results are shown in Figure 15. The most likely explanation for this phenomenon can be derived from the so-called "patch" theory (27). It is assumed that when the cationic polymer is added to the negatively charged cellulose, the former is adsorbed in positively charged patches. These latter will then attach to negatively charged patches on other fibers (Figure 16). Just how the addition of negatively charged polymer reinforces or promotes this mechanism is not quite clear. One possibility is that these polymers, usually of great molecular weight, act as actual physical "bridges" between fibers or particles.

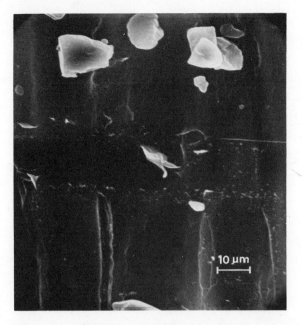

Figure 13.   *Chemical pulp fibers after bond rupture (scanning electron micrograph)*

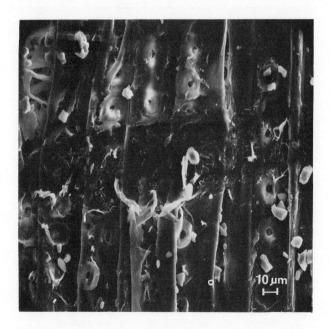

Figure 14.   *TMP fibers after bond rupture (scanning electron micrograph)*

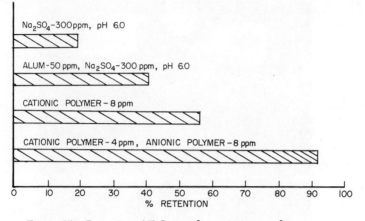

Figure 15. Retention of TiO₂ in a dynamic papermaking system

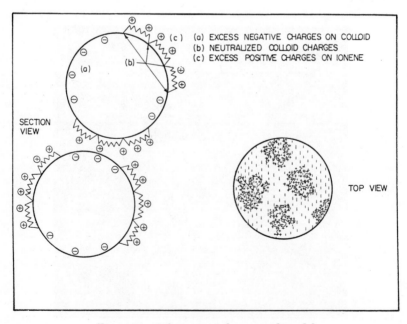

Figure 16. Schematic of charge patch model

Now, returning to the problem of adding polymeric reinforcing agents to the fiber, it appears that the above mechanism
might be of interest. If a suitable cationic polymer were added
and adsorbed, in very low concentration, it would tend to remain
on the fiber surface. Then, if a long-chain anionic polymer were
added, which would form an insoluble salt with the cationic (a
polysalt), this would, of course, be located on the surface and
would tend to concentrate at the fiber crossings by virtue of
the surface tension of the solution. Clearly, research along
these lines could turn out to be well worth the effort.

Chemical Modification

The other approach to bond strengthening is based on chemical modification of the lignin in the fiber (28-31). It so happens that certain chemical treatments modify the lignin in such
a way that the strength of the mechanical pulp increases many-
fold (Table X), presumably because of improved bonding (Figure
17). Unfortunately, these empirical results have been obtained
at entirely uneconomical chemical consumption levels. In my
opinion, our only hope to find a practical modification process
rests on developing a thorough understanding of the mechanism
involved.

The reason for the poor bonding of lignin-rich fibers may
be two-fold: 1) lack of fiber-to-fiber contact as a result of
fiber stiffness and poor conformability, and 2) lignin contains
fewer hydrogen bonding sites than cellulose, and thus its presence reduces the opportunity for bonding. I do not believe that
the second factor is important because the system, even with the
presence of 25-30% lignin, is exceedingly rich in hydroxyl
groups, the principal hydrogen bonding site. One set of experiments that we have performed tends to support this view: We introduced a number of carboxyl groups into the lignin and found
an increase in strength. At first glance, this seems to show
that this is the result of introducing a new and more powerful
bonding site. However, when a hydroxyethyl group was introduced
into the lignin, the same strength increase was observed. It is
unlikely that introduction of a few additional primary hydroxyl
groups into the system should have such a profound effect. It
is much more likely that all these substitutions and chemical
modifications help break up the rigid lignin structure, thus making it more flexible, especially in the presence of water. This
is further supported by the fact that pure substitution tended
to have a limited effect, whereas oxidative treatment showed a
more drastic strength increase. This indicates that the most important effect of the oxidation is a partial depolymerization of
the lignin, allowing greater flexibility of the polymer network.

It appears, then, that we now know what to look for. The
ideal chemical treatment of the fiber would be one that would
partially depolymerize the lignin while at the same time breaking
down all aromatic units containing free phenolic hydroxyl groups.

Table X.　Strength Properties of Treated Pulps (Fiber Fractions)

Treatment	Yield, %	Total Lignin, %	Carboxyl mmol/100 g OD Pulp	Apparent Density, g/cm^3	Burst Factor	Breaking Length, m	Tear Factor
Peracetic Acid							
Control	100.0	25.6	8.1	0.314	8.7	1860	50
30 min	97.9	24.4	16.2	0.350	12.8	2750	54
90 min	94.9	21.5	25.1	0.407	19.6	4370	57
150 min	92.2	19.9	30.8	0.466	26.7	5490	57
Acid Sodium Chlorite							
Control	100.0	25.6	8.1	0.314	8.7	1860	50
30 min	97.6	22.4	31.1	0.356	14.3	2960	54
90 min	96.7	21.0	33.0	0.365	16.5	3200	56
150 min	95.6	20.8	33.3	0.366	16.5	3310	57
Ozone							
Control	100.0	25.6	7.9	0.277	5.0	1350	38
1%	100.7	25.5	9.1	0.290	7.4	1800	42
2%	99.2	25.2	10.9	0.312	9.3	2195	48
3%	99.0	25.0	12.7	0.345	11.9	2780	45

a.

b.

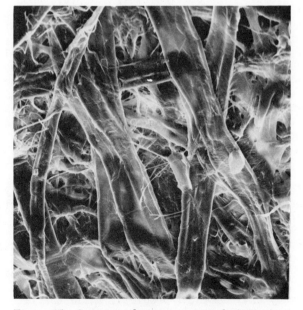

Figure 17.   Scanning electron micrograph (255 ×) of TMP handsheet: (a) untreated; (b) treated with 3% O_3

This would lead to a well-bonded pulp with a stable and reason-
ably high brightness. Since many oxidative treatments can also
be used for bleaching, this is not pure speculation, as shown by
the results in Table XI.

Application in the Mill

Assuming that such a treatment were found, how would it be
applied? In the interest of simplicity and low capital cost,
the ideal place to do it would be right in the refiner. The
thermomechanical refiner is especially suited for this since it
operates at elevated temperature and pressure.

We might climax this little tour into the land of Utopia by
visualizing the ultimate pulp mill. It would consist of a number of refiners, grouped in two or more stages, some or all of
them pressurized, each equipped for a specific chemical treatment or polymer addition. The refiner system would be immediately followed by the paper machine, via a simple centrifugal
cleaning system and the appropriate storage capacity to provide
sufficient flexibility. Such a pulp mill appears to be reduced
to its ultimate essential components, and it is difficult to con-
ceive of additional simplification, except, of course, in the design of the paper machine. But that is another story, as Hans
Christian Andersen would have said.

Like all descriptions of Utopia, this is an oversimplified
story that glosses over difficulties, downplays problems, and
says nothing about the "nuts and bolts" aspects of a pulp mill.
Nevertheless, I think that there is now sufficient information
available to show that radically new pulping schemes are funda-
mentally feasible. Furthermore, success in any or all of the
areas I have sketched here would be of such immense value,
economically and otherwise, that we would be unwise and even
negligent if we did not make a major effort to provide the needed
new knowledge and new technology. It may not be an exaggeration
to say that the future growth and prosperity of the industry depends on it!

SUMMARY

1. The pulp and paper industry will undergo very important
changes during the next few decades, prompted by shortages of
water, energy, chemicals, fiber, and capital, as well as by environmental constraints.

2. Some possible future developments are discussed in the
light of recent research, especially in oxygen-alkali pulping
and the expanded use of mechanical wood pulp, two areas considered as especially promising. The former approach would
alleviate many environmental problems, while the latter would
greatly expand the available raw material supply.

Table XI. Two-Stage Treatment of Spruce Groundwood (35 Mesh) with Peracetic Acid

% Residual Chemical	Control	Stage I 20% Peracetic Acid pH 3.5 Peracetic acid 8.8 H_2O_2 1.8	Stage II pH 7.5 Peracetic acid 3.9 H_2O_2 0.6	Stage I 40% Peracetic Acid pH 3.5 Peracetic acid 16.7 H_2O_2 2.3	Stage II pH 7.5 Peracetic acid 5.1 H_2O_2 2.1
Density, g/cm^3	0.23	0.28	0.29	0.34	0.43
Burst Factor	3.4	6.1	6.6	22.7	24.6
Breaking Length, m	890	1695	1940	4500	4700
Tear Factor	32	41	46	52	55
Brightness, % Elrepho	56	51	64	50	67

3.   Starting out from the current concept of a multistage
oxygen pulping process, a number of possible simplifications are
described. One would involve pulping pre-fiberized wood, the
other pulping of chips in one stage under very vigorous agitation.
4.   A scheme of pulping wood with oxygen-alkali followed by
bleaching with ozone has shown great promise.
5.   Schemes for improving the strength of mechanical pulps
are discussed. One approach involves the use of polymeric additives, the other an oxidative chemical modification of the fiber.
The latter might also be combined with an improvement in pulp
color (bleaching).
6.   The ultimate pulp mill is sketched. It consists solely
of sets of mechanical refiners, some or all equipped for various
chemical treatments.

LITERATURE CITED

1.   Libby, C.E., "Pulp and Paper Science and Technology," Vol. I,
     pp. 10-13, McGraw-Hill Book Co., New York, 1962.

2.   Hannigan, J., Tappi (1976) 59 (1) p. 89.

3.   Young, H.E., Pulp and Paper (1974) 48 (15) p. 46.

4.   Powell, L.N., Shoemaker, J.D., Lazar, R., and Barker, R.G.,
     Tappi (1975) 58 (7) p. 150.

5.   Auchter, R.J., "Whole-Tree Utilization - Fact or Fantasy,"
     TAPPI Alkaline Pulping Conference, Williamsburg, VA, October
     27-29, 1975.

6.   Rapson, W.H. and Reeve, D.W., Tappi (1973) 56 (9) p. 112.

7.   Anonymous, Tappi (1976) 59 (2) p. 26.

8.   Cox, L.A. and Worster, H.E., Tappi (1971) 54 (11) p. 1890.

9.   Palenius, T. and Hiisvirta, L., Pulp and Paper Mag. Can.
     (1970) 72 (21) p. 63.

10. Makkonen, H.P., Sarkanen, K.V., Johanson, L.N., Gratzl, J.S.
     and Ernst, C., "Preliminary Studies of Peroxide and Oxygen
     Pretreatment in Alkaline Pulping," TAPPI Alkaline Pulping
     Conference, Houston, Texas, October 25-28, 1971.

11. Carles, J.E., Choudens, C. de, and Monzie, P., Rev. A.T.I.P.
     (1973) 27 (2) p. 139.

12. Marton, R. and Leopold, B., Appita (1973) 27 (2)   p. 112.

13. Chang, H.-M., McKean, W.T., Gratzl, J.S., and Lin, C.K.,
    Tappi (1973) 56 (9)   p. 116.

14. Minor, J.L. and Sanyer, N., Tappi (1974) 57 (5)   p. 120.

15. Lindström, L.-Å. and Samuelson, O., Tappi (1975) 58 (7)
    p. 146.

16. Mannström, B., Paperi ja Puu (1974) 56 (5)   p. 158.

17. Secrist, R.B. and Singh, R.P., Tappi (1971) 54 (4)   p. 581.

18. Underhay, G.F., Tappi (1975) 58 (7) p. 16A.

19. Van den Akker, J.A., Lewis, H.F., Jones, G.W., and Buchanan,
    M.A., Pulp and Paper Mag. Can. (1949) 50, p. 87.

20. Jones, G.W., Tappi (1950) 33 (3) p. 149.

21. Singh, R.P., Tappi (1966) 49 (7) p. 281.

22. Nissan, A.H. and Sternstein, S.S., Tappi (1964) 47 (1) p. 1.

23. Byrd, V.L., Tappi (1974) 57 (6) p. 87.

24. Britt, K.W., Tappi (1973) 56 (10) p. 46.

25. McKague, J., Etter, D.O., Pilgrim, J.O., and Griggs, W.H.,
    Tappi (1974) 57 (12) p. 101.

26. Frankle, W.E. and Sheridan, J.L., Tappi (1976) 59 (2) p. 84.

27. Gregory, J., J. Coll. and Inter. Sci. (1973) 42, p. 448.

28. Soteland, N. and Kringstad, K., Norsk Skogind. (1968) 22,
    p. 46.

29. Bachorik, T.J., M.S. Dissertation (1969) SUNY College of
    Environmental Science and Forestry, Syracuse, New York.

30. Liebergott, N., Pulp and Paper Mag. Can. (1972) 73, p. T214.

31. Becher, J.J., Hoffman, G.R., and Swanson, J.W., Tappi (1976)
    59 (1) p. 104.

Contribution No. 104 from the Empire State Paper Research Institute, SUNY College of Environmental Science and Forestry, Syracuse, New York 13210.

Energy and Environment

Responsible Husbandry

ROBERT W. SINGLETON

Man-Made Fibers Producers Assoc., 1150 17th St., N.W., Washington, D.C. 20036

I wish to express my thanks to the program committee for inviting me here today to lead-off this most interesting symposium. This afternoon and tomorrow you will hear very specific examples of a general topic which I now have the privilege to introduce. All of our speakers collectively will attempt to communicate to you the basic message that the man-made fiber producers of this country as well as all related activities in the conversion of fibers to finished consumer products run a "tight ship" in terms of efficiency, fuel conservation, and minimal adverse impact on our earth's environment -- that our industry in fact practices good husbandry.

Many dire predictions have been heard concerning the impact of the energy shortage on the availability and price of man-made fibers. Part of this is due to the fact that oil and natural gas play a two-fold role in our industry. These energy sources are intrinsic raw materials as well as sources of energy to operate the fiber forming process.

However, our industry has been known from its inception for its efficiency and boasts of its 95% conversion efficiency of chemical intermediates to finished fiber. In order to place the man-made fiber industry's use of petroleum into perspective, it should be pointed out that raw materials plus the energy to convert these into finished fibers utilizes only 1% of the nation's entire petroleum demand. This fact along with legislation ensuring priority allocation to our industry, makes long term shortages of man-made fibers unlikely.

In spite of this our industry has voluntarily
subscribed to a 15% reduction in energy consumption
for the period of 1972 to 1980. Let's see how we are
doing. The Textile Economics Bureau, Inc. has just
completed estimating the energy to convert intermediates to fibers on a per pound of production basis for
the years 1971, 1973, and 1974 for all of the fibers
made by our industry. Table I lists these figures.
Using these numbers it is evident that the goal of
energy conservation has already been reached well
ahead of schedule.

TABLE I

Energy Consumption in Fiber Production
(BTU per pound of Fiber X 10^3)

Year	BTU/lb. Fiber	% Conservation[1]
1971	35.2	
1973	25.9	26
1974	28.0	20

[1]Using 1971 as a base.

The lower level of conservation in 1974 compared with
1973 reflects a reduction in production with our member companies operating significantly below optimum
production capacity. Whenever this occurs, it is expected that energy consumption will be less than optimum in efficiency.

The next subject to be considered in the attempt
to further increase process efficiency is that of better utilization of by-products. Let me give you several examples of how member companies are extracting
useful products from their waste streams. One large
fiber producer has been shipping by-products of its
adipic acid plant to a chemical company in Houston.
This company reprocesses these by-products into five
types of dibasic esters (DBE) to be sold as raw materials for other processes.

Carbon dioxide, a leftover from ammonia manufacture, is being made into liquid CO_2 and used in the
manufacture of methanol or as an aid in oil recovery.
CO_2 is injected into old oil wells to help bring more
oil to the surface.

These examples of conservation suggest a significant level of chemical intermediate supply from products normally discarded when conservation was not such
a prime consideration.

Good husbandry is not only optimum conservation.
It must include maintaining a clean house. Our industry has an obligation to maintain clean water and air
in districts of our country where we practice our
efficient manufacturing.

The Federal Water Pollution Control Act Amendments
of 1972 require the installation of "best practical
treatment" by 1977 and "best available treatment" by
1983. A majority of the chemical industry, including
fiber producers, is on schedule to meet this requirement. Industry has installed waste water treatments
using the best practical treatment and in some cases
even has gone beyond this to meet specific local regulations. In fact, one member company returns effluent water to the Tennessee River much cleaner than
that which they take out.

The capital costs for water purification are
staggering and, therefore, we are requesting that the
Federal Government reconsider the 1983 goal by first
studying the overall impact of the 1977 goal in terms
of water quality before it mandates the 1983 requirement. The investment required to make this marginal
change from the 1977 requirement to the 1983 statute
will be disproportionally high and should not be required unless absolutely necessary.

Let me digress here to suggest that it is not
wishful thinking to assume the Federal Government will
be receptive to a lessening of water pollution restrictions are overburdensome in terms of cost with no added assurance of public protection. Recently the Council on Wage and Price Stability (CWPS) cautioned regulatory agencies to resist issuing proposed rules that
would potentially prohibit even a minimal, non-inju-
rious presence of a given substance believed to be a
health hazard at a high level of concentration. CWPS
points out that the additional cost to insure zero concentration of a substance rather than a non-hazardous
level can be extensive with no benefit whatsoever to
the consumer. In this particular case in point, industry had responded to the problem and their process
changes reduced the level of contaminant to a safe
level. This opinion of CWPS taken as a general preced-
ent gives man-made fiber producers confidence that a
more realistic yardstick can and will be applied by the

Government in all areas of regulation.

Next let us consider air borne pollutants. Again industry has been responsive to the Federal requirements and expects to meet all local and natural goals. Let us consider the level of effort required for both air and water pollutant control. In 1974, one of our member companies spent $120 million to operate and maintain pollution abatement facilities and conduct environmental research and development programs. By the end of 1975, this company will have committed to expending a total of $550 million for pollution control equipment in the U. S. facilities alone. Granted this is for their entire operation of which fibers is only a portion, but a significant one. Considering the number of fiber producers in the U. S., I would estimate a total expenditure of close to $1 billion spent to date in pollution abatement by the man-made fiber producers since the enactment of environmental control legislation. Now, we feel that it is only fair to inform the consumer that they must share in this expense in terms of higher retail costs. These are inevitable to maintain a satisfactory profit margin.

When we consider air pollutants, we must consider the toxicological effects of these materials both to the citizens in the surrounding community and, perhaps even more critically, to those who come into direct contact with chemicals in our plants. So little is known about the adverse effects of chemicals through long term exposure. The whole subject is receiving intense attention by Government regulatory agencies and by our own member companies. Even before the intense Government interest was expressed, our member companies established programs to investigate the effects of commonly used chemicals on our employees' health. More recently, several of our members, working through their parent organizations, have banded together to support the Chemical Industry Institute of Toxicology (CIIT).

This organization, funded by the chemical industry, grants contracts to laboratories to perform research into the safety of exposure to chemicals. Hopefully, as the Institute grows it will develop its facilities. Among the Institute's goals are:

1. Provide a sound, forceful, scientific industry presence in the complex area of chemical safety evaluation.

2. Generate and interpret data on chemicals from the viewpoints of toxicology, epidemiology, biology, and other relevant fields.

3. Develop new test methods bearing relation to the potentially deleterious effects of chemicals on human health.

4. Disseminate information on potential hazards of chemicals and encourage use of such knowledge to minimize human risks.

5. Promote the professional development and training of toxicologists, epidemiologists, and other scientists in related fields.

To date, 18 companies have joined in support of the Chemical Industry Institute of Toxicology committing a total budget of $14 million to be dispersed in research grants. The Institute opened its offices in the Research Triangle Park in Raleigh, North Carolina, this February (1976) and has begun its study of the possible toxicology effects of several commodity chemicals.

In summary then: The man-made fiber industry has improved upon its high level of efficiency in terms of energy conservation and maximum utilization of by-products. In addition, we have been responsive to the need of preserving clean air, water and the health of our workers. While we support many of the voluntary and Government mandated targets, we ask for a continued assessment of these targets to insure appropriate environmental protection at acceptable cost. While it is technologically feasible to meet the present targets, the capital expenditure will be substantial. This cost must be passed on to the consumer resulting in significant price increases. There is some indication that the Federal Government in the form of the Council on Wage and Price Stability is responsive to this point and we look forward to a cooperative effort to attain an optimum level of husbandry, i.e., optimum effectiveness at an acceptable cost.

17

Energy Conservation in Caprolactam Recovery

G. KIOPEKLY

Central Engineering, American Enka Co., Enka, NC 28728

The increase in the cost of energy in recent years has made it necessary to consider the recovery or utilization of thermal energy at relatively low temperatures. In virtually all chemical plant operations, significant quantities of process heat energy are removed and rejected, in water-cooled heat exchangers, either to once-through river water or to water in circulating cooling tower systems.

In the manufacture of nylon-6 fibers, caprolactam is polymerized to form the basic polymer which is eventually spun into fibers. Because of the usual kinetic and equilibrium relationships, the polymer from the polymerization process contains unreacted monomer and some higher molecular weight oligomers which must be essentially removed before the polymer is spun into a fiber. One method of effecting the removal of unreacted monomer and oligomers is by extraction with hot water. The extract is fairly dilute containing 5 - 10 wt. % organics. For obvious economic reasons and for pollution control considerations, the organics are recovered for recycle to the polymerization process. Since caprolactam is relatively non-volatile, with a normal boiling point of $270^{o}C$, separation from water is fairly easy. However, the quantity of energy required is substantial when the separation is accomplished by the evaporation of water. In addition, water contaminated with caprolactam at various low concentrations from the plant areas is collected for recovery and for pollution abatement.

In 1972, the American Enka Company initiated a program to reduce the cost of caprolactam recovery. At that time, the price of purchased caprolactam was relatively low, ca. $0.20/lb., and although the economics of recovery were not particularly attractive, pollution considerations mandated operation of a recovery system. More recently the price of caprolactam has increased to $0.35 - $0.40/lb., providing an additional economic incentive for more efficient recovery. Since cooling towers were already in use at American Enka Plants, the possibility of using their evaporative capacity in the recovery operation was explored.

Initial tests were made with an existing three-cell cooling
tower. A schematic flow diagram of this system is shown in
Figure 1. The cooling tower was of standard construction with
redwood fill, transite sheathing, galvanized steel fittings and
induced draft. The feed to the system shown consisted of contaminated water from a number of sources, e.g., pump leaks, equipment or line cleanouts and condensate from the spinning and other
plant areas.

For a year-round average of $20^\circ F$ temperature differential
across the cooling tower and a total water circulating rate of
2,700 gallons per minute to the three-cell tower, a water evaporation rate of 26,000 lbs./hr. was realized. The value of this
evaporation, in terms of direct steam required to accomplish the
same evaporation, is about \$500,000/yr. at today's cost of \$4.50 -
\$5.00 per ton of steam.

The initial tests were not without problems. As might be
anticipated, the drift (entrainment) from the cooling tower
resulted in the loss of organic materials which was environment-
ally unacceptable as a routine operation. The drift was essentially eliminated by the installation of a two-inch layer of Enkamat, a nonwoven mesh of relatively coarse nylon-6 filaments.
After nine months in operation, the fan gear box and superstructure above the Enkamat were completely clean. Cells in which
Enkamat had not been installed had crusty deposits on the fan
gear boxes and on the superstructure. The cost of the Enkamat was
10 percent of a comparable stainless steel mesh.

During a period of operation when the concentration of caprolactam in the cooling tower water was fairly low, ca. 2 wt. %,
the growth and accumulation of algae proceeded to a sufficient
degree that the wood-fill in one of the cells collapsed from the
weight of the algae. Caprolactam at concentrations of 6 - 7 wt. %
acts as an algicide or at least as a strong inhibitor to the
growth of algae; at concentrations of about 2 wt. % or lower,
caprolactam is apparently a nutrient for algae.

The use of caprolactam-containing water as the cooling medium
in heat exchangers has not resulted in any serious fouling
problems. Periodic cleanouts of approximately once a year are
sufficient.

Based on the experience with the existing cooling tower, a
project for the installation of such a system was approved. In
the proposed installation, the cooling tower will be constructed
of stainless steel Type 304. For the same performance requirements, the installed cost of a stainless steel cooling tower is
essentially the same as for the more conventional wood-fill
cooling tower. The reasons for this cost equivalence are:

1. The stainless steel tower has an integral basin; wood-
   fill cooling towers usually require a separate concrete
   basin.

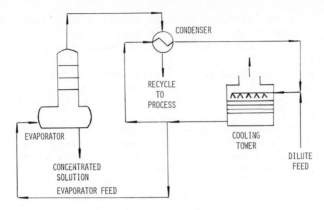

Figure 1. Process schematic

TABLE I

SUMMARY OF TEST & PROPOSED COOLING TOWERS DATA

DESIGN PERFORMANCE

	WOOD	STAINLESS [1]
Water Flow per Cell, gpm	900	500 (975)
Initial Water Temperature, °F	120	132
Final Water Temperature, °F	85	85 (56)
Air Wet Bulb Temperature, °F	75	78
Air Flow per Cell, cfm	175,000	70,000

PHYSICAL DATA

	WOOD	STAINLESS
Number of Cells	3	2
Width (per cell), ft.	7	4.5
Length (per cell), ft.	16	12
Height of Fan Deck, ft.	14	Grade
Fan Motor Horsepower per Cell	25	30
Shipping Weight, lbs.	67,800	16,500

(1) Numbers in parentheses are alternate performance
     specifications.

2. The stainless steel tower is inherently fireproof; a wood-fill tower requires a sprinkler system.

3. The stainless steel tower requires less plan area, less height and weighs about half of an equivalent wood-fill tower.

Additional advantages of a stainless steel cooling tower are:

1. Resistance to corrosion and weathering.

2. Virtually no maintenance.

3. Stainless steel is claimed to be algae-proof.

4. Periodic replacement of the fill is not required.

5. Operation at higher temperatures, i.e., above the 130°F maximum for wood-fill towers.

The proposed stainless steel cooling tower is being installed as part of an evaporation system which includes a single-effect evaporator. The single-effect evaporator is rated to evaporate 15,000 lbs./hr. of water; the associated cooling tower has a similar evaporative capacity. Thus, the cooling tower acts as a second evaporator effect. Since the installed cost of the single-effect evaporator is estimated to cost $650,000 and that of the cooling tower, $100,000, the combined system has a substantial capital cost advantage.

A summary of the design performance and physical data for the test and proposed cooling towers is shown in Table I.

A similar application of cooling towers has recently been reported (1) (2). In both cases, the cooling tower is used as a "finishing" step of an evaporation process, utilizing the sensible heat of the solution from prior high temperature evaporation steps.

Acknowledgment to D. M. Rock and F. J. Fisher, of the American Enka Company, who conceived and carried out the program described in this paper.

References

1. Horton, N. H. and Kunel, K. L., "System Evaporates 27,000 Lb./Hr. With High Pressure Steam," Chemical Processing, Vol. 38, No. 11, p. 17, 1975.
2. Farin, W. G., "Low-Cost Evaporation Method Saves Energy By Reusing Heat," Chemical Engineering, Vol. 83, No. 6, p. 101, 1976.

18

Improved Polyester Radial Tire Yarn for Material, Pollution, and Energy Savings

MICHAEL J. COLLINS

Celanese Fibers Marketing Co., Charlotte, NC

A new polyester tire yarn which significantly reduces energy, pollution, and dip costs during fabric treating has been developed for carcass reinforcement of passenger radial tires. This product, designated T-865, is adhesive activated and dimensionally stabilized. It is designed to give good adhesion to rubber with conventional RFL dipping at temperatures as low as 420°F. Standard, non-adhesive activated polyester typically requires either an isocyanate pre-dip or RFL dip additives to achieve acceptable adhesion. These adhesion promoters are expensive, require high treating temperatures and, in most cases, produce polluting by-products. The combination of adhesive activation and dimensional stability offers the potential for significant energy savings by allowing the use of lower treating temperatures and fewer zones. The dimensional stability of this product allows standard modulus-shrinkage properties to be achieved at these lower treating temperatures. One zone treatments at temperatures of 420°F are feasible, resulting in energy savings of well over 50%. This product can also be utilized to obtain improved radial tire uniformity, using standard treating temperatures.

Review of Standard Polyester Tire Cord Treating

General Description. High tenacity polyester fiber is sold to the tire industry in yarn form. This yarn is single and ply twisted into specific cord constructions and woven into fabric. The fabric is adhesive dipped and heat treated under controlled conditions of temperature, time, and tension. The specific treating conditions used are determined by the adhesive system and the final fabric physical properties which are required. Normally, polyester requires treating temperatures in the range of 465 - 480°F to achieve desired adhesion levels and shrinkage/elongation (heat set) properties.

Standard, non-adhesive activated polyester requires special dip systems to obtain satisfactory adhesion. Rayon and nylon fibers have traditionally used resorcinol - formaldehyde latex dip

systems (RFL) for adhesion to rubber. The resorcinol formaldehyde (RF) forms a resin network which provides adhesion between
the fiber surface and the latex. The latex rubber adhesion is
then formed during the actual curing of the tire. Because polyester has a much less reactive surface and fewer sites available
for hydrogen bonding than rayon or nylon, standard RFL dips do
not give good adhesion with non-adhesive activated polyester.
Special dip systems were developed for polyester to overcome this
problem. These systems involved either an isocyanate pre-dip or
RFL dip additives used to achieve acceptable adhesion. The most
commonly used dip systems are described in more detail.

D-417/RFL Dip System. The D-417/RFL (1) dip system is a two
dip system developed specifically for polyester by DuPont. The
pre-dip, designated D-417, contains an epoxy and a phenol blocked
isocyanate, Hylene MP, (Figure 1), which is dispersed in water.
Dip solids typically range from 4 to 6% with a total dip pick-up
of 1 to 2.5%. After the fabric is dipped in the D-417 bath, it
is cured at high temperature to unblock and activate the isocyanate. Curing temperatures of 460°F are normally required to
achieve acceptable adhesion. During curing, phenol is liberated
as a by-product. Phenol represents 43% of the total weight of
Hylene MP. At a dip pick-up level of 2.0%, this means that approximately .8 lbs of phenol is liberated per 100 lbs of treated
fabric. Obviously, this phenol represents a significant pollutant which must be managed in using this system.

The D-417/RFL was one of the original systems developed for
polyester and has been used for many years. It gives excellent
initial adhesion; but it is expensive, pollutant, and very sensitive to treating conditions.

RFL Dip + Additives. Two RFL dip additives which are most
commonly used with polyester are chemicals designated N3 (2) and
H7 (3). These substances, again, were designed specifically for
polyester adhesive treating. Both additives are designed to improve the adhesion between the RF resin and the fiber surface to
achieve good overall adhesion. Fairly high levels of these additives (20 - 30%) and high treating temperatures (465 - 480°F) are
required to obtain satisfactory results.

Other additives used with RFL dips for polyester include certain isocyanates (4). In all cases, these additives are very expensive compared to the RFL dip and add significantly to the overall dip cost. Also, each of these additives generate pollutant
by-products during fabric heat treatment which, in some cases,
present major pollution control problems.

Treating Conditions. As indicated earlier, after the fabric
is adhesive dipped, it is heat treated under conditions of controlled temperature, time, and tension. These conditions are
designed to achieve specific adhesion levels and fabric physical
properties. Typical treating conditions required for polyester
are shown as follow:

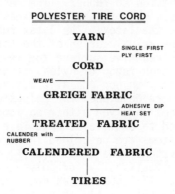

POLYESTER TIRE CORD

YARN

SINGLE FIRST
PLY FIRST

CORD

WEAVE

GREIGE FABRIC

ADHESIVE DIP
HEAT SET

TREATED FABRIC

CALENDER with
RUBBER

CALENDERED FABRIC

TIRES

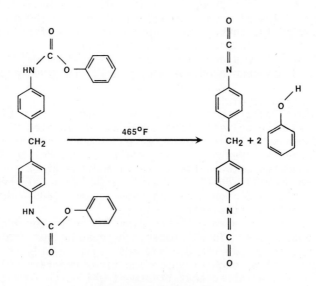

465°F

GENERAL DESCRIPTION

1. System Developed By DuPont
2. D-417 Predip-Isocyanate (Hylene MP) & Epoxy
3. Hylene MP Activates (Unblocks) at 465°F
4. Hylene MP Liberates 43% Phenol When Activated

Figure 1.   D-417 RFL dip system.   Hylene MP.

	Zone 1	Zone 2	Zone 3
Temperature (°F)	300	465	465
Time (Seconds)	50	50	50
Stretch (%)	+2	0	-2

The fabric goes from the first dip tank into Zone 1 where it must be dried. Zones 2 and 3 at the higher temperatures are used to heat set the fabric to reduce shrinkage and obtain the desired dimensional stability. The stretch - relax conditions or tensions are adjusted to achieve specific modulus/shrinkage properties at given treating temperatures. The relationship between treating temperature and shrinkage for standard polyester is shown in Figure 2. The modulus/shrinkage relationship at a given treating temperature is shown in Figure 3. Generally, treated cord shrinkage must be in the range of 7 - 8% @ 350°F, thus requiring minimum treating temperatures of 460°F for standard polyester.

Most treating units presently use natural gas as the primary energy source. Recently, some of these units have been modified to use either fuel oil or natural gas due to the concern about availability of natural gas. Also, due to concerns about energy availability and cost, most of these companies have initiated major efforts aimed at energy conservation in their fabric treating processes. Obviously, total energy required for fabric treating is a function of treating temperatures and dwell times. With standard polyester and existing adhesive systems, there is very little flexibility in terms of energy conservation.

T-865 Polyester Tire Cord

General Description. A new polyester tire yarn which significantly reduces energy, pollution, and dip costs during fabric treating has been developed for carcass reinforcement of passenger radial tires. This product, designated T-865, is adhesive activated and dimensionally stabilized. It is a surface activated product designed to give good adhesion to rubber with conventional RFL dipping at temperatures as low as 420°F. The combination of adhesive activation and dimensional stability offers the potential for significant energy savings by allowing the use of lower treating temperatures and fewer treating zones. The dimensional stability of this product allows standard modulus/shrinkage properties to be achieved at these lower treating temperatures (5). One (1) zone treatments at temperatures of 420°F are feasible resulting in energy savings of well over 50%. T-865 treating is described in more detail below.

"RFL Only" Dip System. T-865 polyester is surface activated to eliminate the need for the adhesion promoters which are required with standard polyester. The recommended RFL dip formulation is shown in Table I (6). As indicated, it is basically a standard RFL dip similar to those used with rayon and nylon.

TYPICAL POLYESTER TIRE CORD TREATING SYSTEMS

SYSTEM NUMBER	1	2
DIP (1)	D-417	RFL + ADDITIVES
ZONE 1		
TEMP. (°F)	465	300
TIME (SEC.)	50	50
STRETCH (%)	+1	+1
DIP (2)	RFL	---
ZONE 2		
TEMP. (°F)	300	470
TIME (SEC.)	50	50
STRETCH (%)	0	0
ZONE 3		
TEMP. (°F)	440	470
TIME (SEC.)	50	50
STRETCH (%)	-1	-1

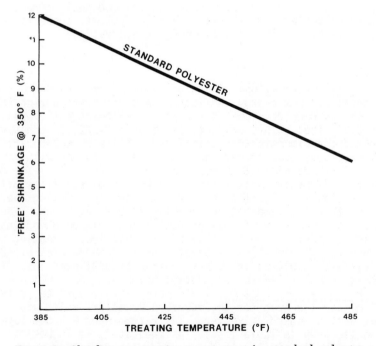

Figure 2. Shrinkage vs. treating temperature for standard polyester

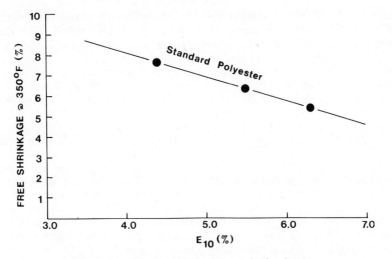

Figure 3. E_{10} vs. shrinkage for standard polyester

<u>TABLE I</u>
<u>RECOMMENDED RFL DIP FORMULATION</u>

<u>CEL-1</u>

<u>RESIN SOLUTION</u>

WATER	365.0
NaOH (50%)	2.6
RESORCINOL	16.6
FORMALIN (37%)	<u>14.7</u>
TOTAL	398.9

AGE FOR 1 3/4 HR. @ 75°F

<u>LATEX</u>

VINYL PYRIDENE TYPE (GENTAC 41%)	215.0
SBR TYPE (PLIOLITE 2000 41%)	53.8

<u>AGE DIP 24 HRS. BEFORE USING</u>

<u>DESCRIPTION</u>

DIP SOLIDS	-	20%
F/R RATIO	-	1.2:1
RESIN/LATEX	-	.20
VP LATEX/SBR LATEX	-	80/20
DIP SHELF LIFE	-	TWO (2) WEEKS

Generally, the RFL formulation is not critical although lower F/R ratio (1.2:1) and non-ammoniated dips are recommended. In some cases, it may be necessary to optimize the dip formulation for the particular rubber compound being used to obtain good results. The relationship between dip pick-up and adhesion is shown in Figure 4. Based on trade experience, a dip pick-up level of 5 to 6% is recommended to achieve the optimum combination of adhesion and fatigue properties. Obviously, higher pick up levels can be used if higher adhesion is required.

Treating Conditions. The sensitivity of adhesion to treating temperature for T-865 using an "RFL only" dip is shown in Figure 5. As indicated, adhesion is very insensitive to treating temperature in the range 420 to 480°F. This means that good adhesion can be achieved with T-865 at treating temperatures as low as 420°F as compared to standard polyester treating which normally requires much higher temperatures (465 - 480°F) to obtain good adhesion. Figure 6 shows a comparison of shrinkage (at constant modulus) versus treating temperature for T-865 and standard polyester. This comparison shows that, due to the improved dimensional stability of T-865, standard shrinkage levels can be achieved at much lower treating temperatures (410°F) than are normally required for non-stabilized polyester. Thus, the combination of adhesion activation and improved dimensional stability allow T-865 to be treated at temperatures as low as 420°F while still achieving adhesion and physical properties (shrinkage/modulus) which are equivalent to standard polyester treated at higher temperatures (465 - 480°F). Also, since T-865 requires much less heat to achieve standard properties, the number of treating zones can be reduced. At treating temperatures as low as 420°F, it actually becomes feasible to eliminate the drying zone and use a one (1) zone treatment. Comparative treating systems for T-865 and standard polyester are shown in Table II.

Advantages of T-865 Treating. There are three major advantages of T-865 treating versus standard polyester. These advantages are savings in energy, pollution, and material costs, each of which are discussed in more detail below.

Material Savings. T-865 tire cord treating offers significant dip cost savings by eliminating the need for the adhesion promoters normally required with polyester. These adhesion promoters are very expensive relative to standard RFL dip and thus significant savings can be realized by eliminating their use. A dip cost comparison of "RFL only" system versus the most commonly used systems with standard polyester is shown in Table III. As indicated, dip cost savings of 3¢/lb. of treated fabric are available with T-865.

Pollution Savings. T-865 significantly reduces the pollution problems of treating, again, by eliminating the need for adhesion promoters with their associated pollutant by-products and by allowing the use of lower treating temperatures which reduces the amount of material volatilized. As discussed earlier,

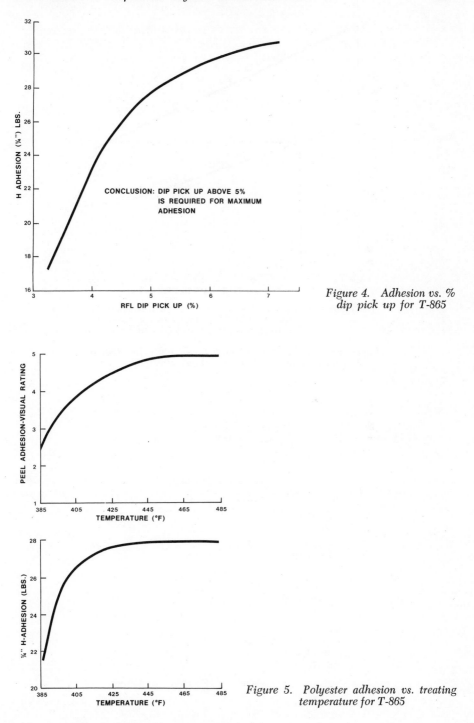

Figure 4. Adhesion vs. % dip pick up for T-865

Figure 5. Polyester adhesion vs. treating temperature for T-865

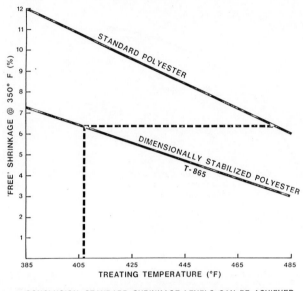

CONCLUSION: STANDARD SHRINKAGE LEVELS CAN BE ACHIEVED
WITH DIMENSIONALLY STABILIZED POLYESTER AT
TREATING TEMPERATURES AS LOW AS 405°F.

Figure 6.   Shrinkage vs. treating temperature for dimensionally stabilized T-865 and standard polyester

TABLE II
COMPARATIVE TREATING SYSTEMS FOR
T-865 AND STANDARD POLYESTER

SYSTEM NUMBER	1	2	3
FIBER	STANDARD	T-865	T-865
DIP	RFL/H7	RFL	RFL
ZONE 1			
TEMP. (°F)	300	300	420
TIME (SEC.)	50	50	50
STRETCH (%)	+2	+2	-1
ZONE 2			
TEMP. (°F)	465	465	---
TIME (SEC.)	50	50	---
STRETCH (%)	0	-2	---
ZONE 3			
TEMP. (°F)	465	---	---
TIME (SEC.)	50	---	---
STRETCH (%)	-2	---	---
PROPERTIES	STANDARD	DIMENSIONALLY STABILIZED	STANDARD
ADVANTAGES	---	RADIAL UNIFORMITY	ENERGY SAVINGS

Table III

DIP COST SUMMARY

System	% Dip Pick Up	Additive (%) Of Dip Pick Up	Additive Cost ($/Lb. Of Solids)	Additional Cost Over RFL Alone (¢/Lb. Of Fabric)
D-417/RFL (Double)	4.5	20	3.25	2.9
N3/RFL (Single)	4.5	30	2.25	3.1
H7/RFL (Single)	4.5	16	2.65	1.9

CONCLUSION: ADHESIVE ACTIVATED POLYESTER USING CONVENTIONAL RFL DIPPING CAN RESULT IN DIP COST SAVINGS UP TO 3.1¢/Lb. OF TREATED FABRIC.

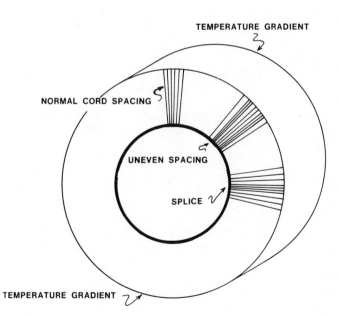

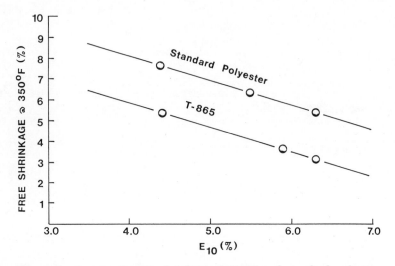

Figure 7.   Comparative E_{10}-shrinkage of T-865 and standard polyester

TABLE IV

COMPARATIVE TREATED CORD PROPERTIES
OF T-865 AND STANDARD POLYESTER

	STANDARD POLYESTER			T-865		
RUN	1	2	3	1	2	3
BREAKING STRENGTH, LBS.	33.1	32.2	31.9	31.5	30.4	30.2
E_B (%)	17.2	19.8	21.3	16.0	18.6	20.4
E_{10} (%)	4.4	5.5	6.3	4.4	5.9	6.3
SHRINKAGE (350°F)						
'FREE' %	7.4	6.4	5.3	5.3	3.6	3.1
"0.05 G/D" %	3.1	2.0	1.7	2.0	1.3	1.0
TENSION, GRS.	780	540	460	700	400	370

TREATING CONDITIONS:
    455°F
    50 SECONDS
    TENSION

the D-417/RFL system produces phenol as a by-product (.8 lb. phenol/100 lbs. of treated fabric) which presents a major pollution problem. T-865 treating eliminates the phenol problem by eliminating the need for this pre-dip. The H7 and N3 RFL dip additives also generate by-products which can cause pollution problems. The high treating temperatures (465 - 480°F) required by all of these dip systems cause volitilization of fiber finish and polymer components and dip components which result in pollution associated with stack emissions. In many cases, pollution control equipment such as scrubbers, catalytic converters or electro-static precipitators will be required to meet Federal and State environmental standards. Lower temperature treating using T-865 may eliminate the need for some of this equipment.

Energy Savings. Energy savings result from the lower treating temperatures (420°F versus 470°F) and the possibility of using fewer treating zones. Using a one (1) zone treatment with T-865 could result in energy savings of well over 50%. This energy savings is particularly significant because natural gas is presently the main source of energy for these treating units.

Improved Radial Tire Uniformity

As discussed earlier, T-865 is a dimensionally stabilized polyester which results in lower shrinkage/higher modulus properties at standard treating temperatures. A comparison of modulus (E10) and shrinkage of T-865 versus standard polyester is shown in Figure 7 and Table IV. It is generally believed in the tire industry that improved dimensional stability of the polyester will translate into improved radial tire uniformity. If this is true, T-865 treated at standard temperatures should result in improved radial tire uniformity. Large-scale trials are now underway to see if this advantage does exist.

As shown earlier, Figure 5, dimensional stability is directly related to treating temperature. Thus, T-865 offers the flexibility of optimizing tire uniformity versus energy savings. As treating temperature is increased, tire uniformity should increase at the expense of increased energy usage. The relative economics of tire uniformity versus energy cost and availability will determine the optimum treating temperature. This flexibility in treating temperature is unique to T-865 polyester because it is adhesive activated and dimensionally stabilized.

Conclusions

A new polyester tire yarn, designated T-865, which is adhesive activated and dimensionally stabilized can be used to achieve significant material, pollution, and energy savings during fabric treating. This fiber can also be treated at higher temperatures to achieve improved dimensional stability which should translate into improved radial tire uniformity.

INDEX

INDEX

FRI DEC 08 1989

DATE DUE

SCARBOR

scarborough public library